£8.95

D1134197

The Migrant Presence

Australian Responses 1947–1977

Studies in Society

A series edited by Colin Bell, series adviser Jean I. Martin, which sets out to cover the major topics in Australasian sociology. The books will not be 'readers', but original works—some will cover new ground and present original research, some will provide an overview and synthesis of source materials and existing research, all will be important reading for students of sociology.

Titles include:
  Cities Unlimited Kilmartin and Thorns
  The Migrant Presence Martin
  Social Stratification in Australia Wild
  The Nature of Sociology Bell
Forthcoming:
  Sex Roles in Australian Society Cass
  Race, Class and Rebellion in the South Pacific Mamak and Ali

Studies in Society: 2
Series editor: Colin Bell   Series adviser: Jean I. Martin

The Migrant Presence

Australian Responses 1947–1977

Research Report for the National
Population Inquiry

JEAN I. MARTIN
*Research School of Social Sciences, Australian National University,
Canberra*

Sydney
George Allen & Unwin
London Boston

First published in 1978 by
George Allen & Unwin Australia Pty Ltd
Cnr Bridge Road and Jersey Street
Hornsby NSW 2077

National Library of Australia
Cataloguing-in-Publication entry:

Martin, Jean Isobel.
    The migrant presence.

    (Studies in society; 2)
    Index.
    Bibliography.
    ISBN 0 86861 280 4 Paperback.
    ISBN 0 86861 272 3

    1. Social institutions—Australia. 2. Australia—Foreign
    population. I. Title. (Series)
301.451'0994

Library of Congress Catalog Card Number 78–57602

Set in 10 on 11 point Times and printed in Australia by
Academy Press, Brisbane

Foreword

A major objective of the National Population Inquiry from its inception has been the preparation and publication of a series of Research Reports. These were intended both to provide material appropriate for inclusion in the Inquiry's main Report and to stand as monographs in their own right as expert studies upon different facets of population issues that were felt to have significant policy implications. Some of these Research Reports were published as a companion series to the First and Supplementary Reports of the Inquiry published in 1975 and 1978.

In other cases the initial material made available to the Inquiry was part of a wider research study being prepared by the author for later publication through other channels. The present study falls into this latter category, and the Inquiry is pleased to accept some responsibility for initiating a project that has now developed into a substantial research publication.

As Chairman of the National Population Inquiry, I feel that this important study sheds much new light upon the difficult and complex issues of the interactions of immigrants and non-immigrants in building and sustaining Australian society.

W.D. Borrie,
Chairman, National Population Inquiry
Canberra
May 1978

Contents

Tables

Figures

Preface

In the six years that have passed since Professor Borrie asked me to write a short paper for the National Population Inquiry a number of things have happened to change the scope of the enterprise and my approach to it. The original intention was that I should attempt an overview of the response of Australian institutions to changes in the population brought about by the immigration programme pursued since the end of the Second World War.

Although I had been studying migration and the settlement of migrants since my postgraduate work on Displaced Persons in 1951–54, I had been more interested in the migrants' experience than in the experience of the 'established' Australian community in incorporating the large number of settlers of non-Anglo-Saxon origin whom the immigration programme, initiated in 1946, had brought to Australia. A survey, begun in Adelaide in 1967, of group organisation among eastern European (formerly Displaced Person) migrants had made me aware of what I called denial and non-confrontation on the part of Australian community groups and churches, but it was not until I began a wider enquiry in Victoria in about 1970 that I realised in concrete terms what non-confrontation meant across the whole spectrum of established institutions. When I embarked on the National Population Inquiry paper I expected to find—in the literature of economics, political science, law, contemporary history, education, medicine and welfare—material that I could pull together to test and develop this notion of non-confrontation, scattered and elusive though I knew this material must be. I soon discovered, however, that there was little to work on: like myself, the few social scientists and practising professionals who had taken an interest in immigration had been concerned with the migrants' perspective or situation. Clearly the task I had undertaken needed re-appraisal: my intention to present a general interpretation of the responses in education, health, welfare, medicine, the church, industry, law, trade unions and political parties would have to be abandoned in favour of something closer to a primary research effort in selected areas.

9

The first area—education—selected itself: in 1974 the Academy of the Social Sciences in Australia, in conjunction with the Commonwealth Department of Immigration, asked me to take responsibility for one of several projects on migrant education. The Commonwealth provided funds for Mr H.F. Willcock to prepare a bibliography on the history of child migrant education 1947–75, and on the basis of this material I wrote an historical essay which covered in some detail the response of education to the migrant presence over this period. That essay has been revised, shortened and brought up to date to form Chapters 3 and 4 in this book.

Commensurate resources were not available for work in any of the other areas that I had planned to cover. It was therefore necessary to be very selective, and I chose to concentrate on health services and trade unions. The results are contained in Chapters 5 and 6 and in Chapter 7, respectively.

The choice of these last two areas was dictated partly by my own interest and partly by the fact that, along with education, they provided examples of different kinds of data base: education, a comparatively large number of commentaries, until the last few years scattered through parochial journals but now including some substantial national inquiries; health, a smaller number of papers, nearly all written by doctors and published in the national professional journal, the *Medical Journal of Australia*, with only one Australia-wide study and that arising out of the Poverty Inquiry; trade unions, with minimal documentation of any kind.

Another reason for concentrating on education, health and trade unions was that the work of other researchers was beginning to fill in the picture in some of the areas I had originally in mind. In his study of the response of the Catholic Church to migration, Frank Lewins had dealt in detail with one of the obviously relevant areas, and in their research report for the Poverty Inquiry Andrew Jakubowicz and Berenice Buckley had scrutinised the response of the law. In addition, the work on migrants in industry and the professions, sponsored by the Academy of the Social Sciences, is expanding, both directly and indirectly, knowledge of the response of economic institutions.

As the scope of the study narrowed and I found myself more involved than I had expected to be in collecting basic data, my own approach also took a different turn. Or, more correctly, I realised that here was an opportunity to pursue a long-standing interest in what I once called the 'sociology of social data' (1972c: 12) and the processes by which public 'definitions of the situation' are evolved, disseminated and used. I came to see the enterprise as a case study in the soicology of knowleddge, in a sense an affirmation of the view that the further development of this area of sociology—at present suffering some degree of obfuscation and marking time as past wisdom is repeatedly rediscovered—depends on empirical investigation of how meaning is socially constructed in specific situations and how the distribution of knowledge is related to the distribution of resources and power, and the experience of groups differently located in the social structure.

It is important to emphasise that this is a book about public, institutionally relevant knowledge. Although in the chapters on education I have drawn on internal documents of government departments and other bodies to clarify how and by whom public knowledge has been generated, my focus is not on the behind-the-scenes story of negotiation, dialogue and dispute out of which public definitions of migrants, migrant characteristics, experiences and problems have emerged. It is rather on the structure of that knowledge and its relation to institutional policies, organisation and services. One outcome of this specialised focus is that readers anticipating a general history of Australian responses to migrants since the Second World War will be frustrated to find that significant aspects, even of the areas I have claimed to cover in detail, are not touched upon. (An obvious example is the reaction of trade unions, teachers and the health professions to the recognition of migrants' overseas qualifications.) I hope that fellow-researchers who experience this frustration will find they can use the public definitions and structural changes that I have outlined as a scaffolding to assist them in further work. It is basic to my understanding of what cumulative enquiry means in sociology that one scholar's abode can serve as another's framework for building a very different kind of habitat.

Public interest in immigration and migrant settlement has increased enormously during the seventies. Much of this book is devoted to examining how and why this dramatic change has occurred. At the same time, the very recent proliferation of relevant documents—now flowing from a great variety of sources—has presented me with two intractable problems: keeping up with the literature (much of it in fairly inaccessible form as, for example, conference papers or submissions to government inquiries) and avoiding an undue engagement with the current and in some cases ephemeral issues which, in quantitative terms, dominate the total volume of material produced over the thirty-year period covered in this book.

To present a picture that is up to date with changes in government policy and services without becoming blurred by excessive detail has also proved difficult, because in recent years every few months have yielded some new initiative on the part of the Commonwealth or States and many of these initiatives would have been landmarks had they occurred as unique events some time earlier. Indeed, the day after this Preface was originally typed the Prime Minister tabled in Parliament the report of the Review of Post-arrival Programs and Services for Migrants (chaired by Frank Galbally) which, apart from other claims it may have to count as an historic document, has the distinction of being the first report commissioned by the Commonwealth to be tabled in a language other than English: the ten copies Mr Fraser presented were in ten languages. As in the case of other developments that have occurred, or materials that have come to hand, since the manuscript of this book went to press, I have added an endnote about the Galbally Review in Chapter 2. The implementation of the Review's recommendations will carry into a new stage the history of a number of institutional responses dealt with in this book and leave others little affected. It will almost certainly reinforce the differentation in response—as between States and institutions and as it affects different migrant groups—that emerges as a main theme of change in the seventies.

It is not possible to acknowledge in detail the help I have received from an immensely wide range of individuals and organisations in carrying out a study that touches on such a large segment of our institutional life. I am grateful to them all for their interest and patience, and for taking seriously what must have often seemed to them pedantic or irrelevant questions.

A number of government departments have provided indispensable help: in particular the State and Commonwealth Departments of Education, and the Commonwealth Departments of Immigration and Ethnic Affairs (and formerly Immigration and Labor and Immigration) and Social Security, the Public Service Board and the Australian Bureau of Statistics.

When I began work on the original project I was at La Trobe University where Margaret Purvis, at that time Research Assistant in the Department of Sociology, began the collection of data. Since coming to the Australian National University I have also had the assistance at various times of Judy Dillon, Wendy Edgar, Elaine Kruger and Marijka Saltet, while Michele Robertson has worked on one aspect or another of the project more or less continually and has been responsible for the computer analysis. I am glad to acknowledge my diverse debts to these six women for their competence, flexibility and good humour. I am grateful to Val Lyon, of the Geography Department of the School of General Studies at the Australian National University, for the interest and care she took in drawing the figures.

As on many previous occasions I have reason to thank Betty Gamble not only for her speedy and immaculate typing of the manuscript, but also for her acute sense for style and consistency. I also appreciate the skilful editing provided by Christine Astley-Boden.

The child migrant education project already referred to was a joint study with Frank Willcock, the excellent bibliography that he prepared forms the basis of Chapters 3 and 4, and the analysis and interpretation offered there owes much to his mastery of the subject.

While I alone am of course responsible for what now appears in the following pages, several people have given me the benefit of their reactions to reading all or part of the manuscript. I am grateful to Charles Price for commenting on Chapter 2, R.B. Scotton on Chapters 5 and 6, and Ross Martin on Chapter 7. Frank L. Jones kindly read the whole manuscript; his probing questions and comments sharpened my thinking and expression on a number of matters.

Allan Martin also read the manuscript in full and in various drafts; Bill gave the final draft his own Reading and David subjected it to yet another kind of scrutiny. I am grateful to all three as much for their exacting criticism as for their sensible advice and familial encouragement.

Finally, I wish to express my thanks to Professor Borrie for giving me the incentive to embark on the project in the first place, for his good counsel as I went along, and for waiting so patiently—and without once conveying a doubt that something would come of it in the end—while the short paper he originally proposed was transformed into this book.

Jean I. Martin, Canberra
June 1978

1 Definitions

The modern states that emerged following European expansion into the new world all passed through phases when established social arrangements were stretched, strained, changed, overturned or replaced in the face of new situations created by high rates of immigration of people of diverse cultural origins. Although Australia was never in fact a truly homogeneous society in terms of the ethnic and cultural origins of its people, the institutional arrangements that had been consolidated by the time the population reached seven million in the middle of this century were based on assumptions of an essential and continuing homegeneity—and, when the Commonwealth Government sponsored a large-scale immigration programme at the end of the Second World War, the Labor Minister for Immigration, A.A. Calwell, reaffirmed the Government's commitment to the principle 'that our population shall remain predominantly British'. 'It is my hope', he said, 'that for every foreign migrant there will be ten people from the United Kingdom' (Aus., House of Reps., *Parl. Debates*, Vol. 189, 1946: 508). Like the Liberal ministers who followed him, however, Calwell authorised immigration agreements that raised the 'foreign' element well above the level of 'safety' which political rhetoric advocated.

Now, thirty years later, the total population has doubled, and, of the four million who are first- or second-generation immigrants, over half are of non-British origin. This book is about some institutional changes that have occurred, been considered, attempted or resisted in response to the presence of these non-British elements in the Australian population. While there is no implication that change goes in one direction only—that is, from increased population differentiation to structural change—my focus here is on the analytically distinct situation that arises when the population of an established society becomes rapidly more differentiated in a short span of time. There may then develop new structural arrangements which stimulate further differentiation, as, for example, when a community forged from newly arrived immigrants influences the government in

15

favour of further migration from their home country. But ensuing developments of this kind are outside the scope of this study.

Migrants and ethnics

I am not concerned with the non-British migrants who have come from English-speaking countries such as New Zealand, Canada and the United States, so the population elements to which the discussion refers are better described as of 'non-Anglo-Saxon' or 'non-English-speaking' origin than as of 'non-British' origin. While a good case can be made for saying that all of us—Aborigines and whites, old and new—are ethnics (as ultimately we are all of migrant origin), I find it more useful to reserve the term 'ethnic' for groups and cultures of non-Anglo-Saxon background. By coupling 'ethnic' with 'minority', I try to convey the social and cultural distance between the majority, culturally dominant groups of Anglo-Saxon origin and the other groups. Aborigines are clearly an ethnic minority in these terms, but I trust that the context will ensure that 'ethnic minorities' are here understood to include only people of recent migrant origin (that is, immigrants and their Australian-born children).

Like 'ethnic', the term 'migrant' is used in countless different ways, and why it has different connotations in different contexts is an important sociological question in present-day Australia. But in one form or another—'migrant' or 'immigrant'—it has a legal status that 'ethnic' lacks.[1] The relevant Commonwealth powers derive from Section 51(xxvii) of the Constitution, which provides that the Parliament has power to enact laws with respect to 'Immigration and emigration'. Enid Campbell and Harry Whitmore note that 'A considerable body of law, much of it conflicting' has developed over the extent of the immigration power (1966: 105). The issues with which the courts have been concerned are extremely complex (see Campbell and Whitmore, 1966; Bartholomew, 1966; Lane, 1972; Lumb and Ryan, 1974; Jakubowicz and Buckley, 1975; Coper, 1976). For our purposes they may be subsumed under four headings: whether the immigration power extends only to the act of entry or covers persons 'who *have been* immigrants' (Justice Higgins, 1923, quoted by Bartholomew, 1966: 173); whether the power extends only to persons who arrive with the intention of settling or to visitors also; whether an Australian-born person or British subject seeking to enter the country can come within the Commonwealth immigration power; whether there is a point in time at which an immigrant becomes a settler and so moves beyond the Commonwealth power of deportation. On this last and most fundamental question, two opposing answers have been put to the courts and the question remains open. The wide view was first expressed by Justice Isaacs in 1923 in the aphorism, 'once an immigrant always an immigrant' (Lane, 1972: 130 n.61). The narrow view is that the Commonwealth's power over immigrants ends when they have become 'absorbed into the community' or have established their 'real home' in Australia. Although there are no accepted criteria for what constitutes absorption or residence, the narrow view appears to be the favoured one (Lane, 1972: 131; Coper, 1976: 351).

From an examination of the diverse routes by which the judges reached a common decision in a 1975 High Court case, M. Coper concludes that 'the case does little to resolve the controversy about the width of the immigration power' (1976: 358). In this case a more complex conception of the wide view appeared: although Justice Jacobs accepted that absorption into the community places a person beyond reach of the Commonwealth's immigration power so far as deportation is concerned, that position does 'not preclude the making of laws relating to the special needs or special characteristics of immigrants which would apply even after an immigrant had become absorbed into the community' (quoted by Coper, 1976: 354). The implication of this view is that 'once an immigrant always an immigrant' applies indefinitely so long as it is in a person's interests to claim immigrant status, but that immigrant status cannot be imposed to his disadvantage once he has become a settler.

The legislation covering the migration power is contained in the *Migration Act 1958–1973*. Separate legislation, the *Australian Citizenship Act 1948–1973*, derives from the Commonwealth's power under Section xix of the Constitution to make laws with respect to 'Naturalization and aliens'. The two Acts are not precisely complementary and, in Geoffrey Bartholomew's words,

> The High Court . . . keep distinct the test of immigrant status from that of citizenship but without resolving the ambiguity . . . as to what constitutes the criterion of immigrant status, although subsequent cases . . . have tended to accept the 'absorption into the community' test . . . (1966: 177)

The courts, says Bartholomew, 'have shown no disposition to assimilate the tests for citizenship with those of immigrant status'. Indeed, the High Court has 'expressly asserted that possession of Australian citizenship did not prevent a person from being an immigrant and therefore liable to deportation' (1966: 176).

The Migration Act legislates in terms of aliens, immigrants who have been in Australia less than five years and immigrants who have been in the country five years or more. Even though immigrants can acquire Australian citizenship within three years of arrival, they remain subject to deportation under the terms of the *Migration Act* for a further two years. Aliens (persons who are not British subjects, Irish citizens or protected persons) may be deported at any time and it is in respect of aliens that the question, 'when is an immigrant no longer an immigrant?', remains particularly significant. Andrew Jakubowicz and Berenice Buckley argue that the *Migration and Citizenship Acts* as they stand give excessive power to the Minister, through his absolute discretion over whether an application for naturalisation is approved and through his right to deport aliens no matter how long they have been resident in Australia (1975: 62–3). Both Acts allow so much ministerial discretion that variations in the criteria used to distinguish 'immigrants' from 'members of the Australian community' in fact arise in large measure from administrative decisions, rather than from legislation or decisions of the courts.

Although persons who have gained citizenship by naturalisation acquire substantially the same legal status as Australian-born people once the five-year period of residence is up, they may still have to face special administrative requirements to provide proof of citizenship when, for example, they apply for government employment or re-enter Australia from overseas. Whether naturalised or not, immigrants are peculiarly subject to control by the state in that their freedom to establish a family unit is limited by the state's power to decide what other family members may join them as settlers in Australia.

Taking the legal status of 'immigrant' as a starting point, I shall use the term—mostly in the shorter version 'migrant'—to refer to residents who, by virtue of their not being Australian citizens by either birth or descent, belong to a category of persons whom the state can control, direct or provide for (to their advantage or disadvantage) in some specific way.

Since ethnic minorities in Australia are overwhelmingly of recent (that is, post-Second World War) migrant origin, I shall often use the terms 'ethnic' and 'migrant' (of 'non-Anglo-Saxon origin') interchangeably, but it will become clear that sometimes the ethnic or culturally distinct aspect, and at other times the migrant aspect, is salient.

A document

The most immediate way to convey how I have approached the writing of this book is to give an example of the mode of analysis that has formed my main research procedure. The example is a passage from a document of a kind very different from those that have provided most of my material, but there are good reasons why I have chosen it. The passage occurs in Dorothy Rabinowitz's remarkable book,

New Lives: Survivors of the Holocaust Living in America (1977). It describes a New York court room where hearings are being conducted in connection with the proposed deportation of a woman previously, in Austria, convicted as a war criminal, and now facing additional charges brought by the United States Immigration Service. The witness had been an inmate of the Maidanek concentration camp where the woman, Hermine Braunsteiner, was a Vice-Kommandant. He is describing an incident in which Hermine Braunsteiner, he says, whipped two women to death.

Could the witness tell how long Hermine Braunsteiner beat the two women, and how many blows of the bullwhip she gave them? Maybe twenty minutes, maybe less; he had not counted the number of blows. The camp inmates did not need too many blows to be killed.

'Did the other women between the wires come to help the two women?' Mr Barry asks.

'How will they come to help?'

Several times more Mr Barry asks the question: 'And others, they never came over to help the other two?'

'What are you talking about, help? She would kill all of them. I don't understand you.'

'They never came over to help?'

'How could they help?'

'But they didn't?'

Twice more Mr Barry asks whether the other prisoners had come forward to aid the women who were being beaten.

The witness peers into the very mouth of his examiner during the course of these inquiries, as if seeking, by intense concentration on their source, to fathom them. Not that he does not recognize the intent of the questions, which suggests that Maidanek was a place like any other in the world: that it housed a society like any other, composed of people who might choose between one form of behavior and another, and who could, if they but would, intervene when they saw their fellows victimized.

'You just watched also? And the others never came over to help?'

For a long moment he says nothing, until, in the struggle between fury and propriety that the questions have produced in him, propriety wins; the place to which he has come to be a witness this day is a court, after all, with a judge and lawyers, where questions put to witnesses must be answered. Subdued by the consciousness of this fact, the witness sits back in his chair and answers the questions, the last of them in a monotone that bespeaks resignation, if of a very temporary sort.

'You just watched also?'

'Yes.'

'And the other forty or so men, they just watched?'

'Yes . . . ' (1977: 11–12)

Overtly there is nothing in common between this document and the substance of my own work. But it testifies to almost every theme I wish to take up: from their different mental worlds, the different webs of meaning that hold them in place, Mr Barry and the witness seek to attach totally incongruent interpretations to the *same* act, or failure to act; the repressive coercion of the camp is contrasted with other situations of voluntary compliance where people 'might choose between one form of behavior and another', but at the same time the court and the politico-legal institutions on which it stands exert their own formidable control in determining what is relevant information, what words mean and how the participants will interact—even to the point of requiring that questions '*must* be answered'; the witness eventually gives in and in doing so confirms the attorney's pre-eminent position —yes, the question is answerable, as the attorney insists it is; and what the witness contributes to the picture that finally emerges is not his understanding of the experience of the participants in that terrible scene but a muffled distortion, for the benefit of Mr Barry's uncompromising view of the world.

Webs of meaning

The response that I am concerned with, when I speak of response to the presence of non-Anglo-Saxon elements in the Australian population, is the response of the aware actor. Awareness involves attaching meaning to the data of experience. That meaning-giving should be at the heart of the enquiry undertaken here follows from a concept of man, culture and sociological analysis, which are nicely conveyed by Clifford Geertz:

> Believing, with Max Weber, that man is an animal suspended in webs of significance he himself has spun, I take culture to be those webs, and the analysis of it to be therefore not an experimental science in search of law but an interpretive one in search of meaning. (1973: 5)

The web of meaning attaches to objects (people, action, social relations, invisible structures, ideas, material phenomena and so on) in the form of values, norms, attitudes, aspirations and beliefs or knowledge. Part of this knowledge is shared group knowledge about the nature of objects. For the sake of convenience I shall call this social knowledge, as compared with private knowledge (while recognising that all knowledge is social in the sense that it exists in the form of language and accrues to the individual by virtue of his social position). A major component in the construction of knowledge is the determination of what knowledge is (a question I shall not pursue further) and what its parameters are, that is, what are the relevant, desirable or necessary objects of knowledge. In courts of law or in the determination of a committee's brief, the business of establishing parameters may be the subject of rigorous and refined debate, but

these are exceptional circumstances. For the most part, parameters
are defined unobtrusively—by default, as it were—the relevant and
appropriate being taken for granted, the irrelevant and inappropriate
being scarcely given a nod. Weber's account of the nature of
bureaucracy is a classic statement of this process. The specific nature
of bureaucracy, Weber says,

> develops the more perfectly the more the bureaucracy is 'dehumanized',
> the more completely it succeeds in eliminating from official business love,
> hatred, and all purely personal, irrational, and emotional elements which
> escape calculation. (Gerth and Mills, 1947: 215–6)

The parameters of any particular body of knowledge are thus
embedded within larger constructs, which automatically negate or
neutralise alternative definitions of what legitimately belongs to that
body of knowledge. The predominance of assimilationist constructs in
Australia up to the mid-sixties, for example, meant that questions
about how Australian institutions had responded to an influx of people
of non-Anglo-Saxon origin simply did not come to the surface. There
was no 'decision' to rule such questions out of order. They did not
arise; they were not 'confronted' (see Martin, 1971).

The content of social knowledge also consists largely of taken-for-
granted elements which, most of the time, no one is aware of
constructing: they are simply there. But for its survival such taken-
for-granted knowledge must be continually confirmed, and this process
of confirmation shades over into the business of constructing new
knowledge or moving knowledge from one domain where it is
established to another where it is new. In societies like our own with
a complex structure and technology (including a complex communication system), the affirming-constructing process goes on as a self-
conscious part of managing the society's affairs and is often highly
institutionalised. This book is a study of the way in which knowledge
about migrants and their place in Australian society has been affirmed
and constructed, denied and destroyed, over the past thirty years. The
knowledge I am concerned with is that part of social knowledge
relevant to decision and action on the part of the government and
other publicly responsible institutions. Sometimes I shall call this
public knowledge, but when I use the term social knowledge it is also
in this restricted sense.

The extent to which public knowledge is elaborated is a function
not only of complexity, but also of the source of sanctions for social
participation. The more that participation depends on intelligent or
responsible compliance, the more occasion there is for public knowledge to provide information, explanation and justification for the
action and the position of the actors. The limiting case occurs where
the fact of coercion itself constitutes all that is required by way of

public knowledge. But even the grimmest coercive situations are likely to be couched in terms that give submission the cloak of compliance. The witness at the Hermine Braunsteiner deportation hearings described the former Vice-Kommandant telling an assembly of women that they had to part with their children:

> And she said to them they have to give the children to the people on the wagon; they are going to a summer camp and they will get milk in the morning and at night. (Rabinowitz, 1977: 10)

Knowledge and power

The construction of knowledge takes place within a structure of relations among groups: the ordered processes of constructing knowledge, bodies of social knowledge and group relations (particularly relations of dominance and subordination) provide a three-sided framework of analysis for the present study. Although the intellectual and political enterprise with which Michel Foucault is concerned goes far beyond the task I have attempted, his formulation of the concepts of 'truth' (process of constructing knowledge), 'statements' (knowledge) and 'power' encapsulates the relationship I am seeking to unravel:

> By 'truth' is meant a system of ordered procedures for the production, regulation, distribution and circulation of statements.
> 'Truth' is linked by a circular relation to systems of power which produce it and sustain it, and to effects of power which it induces and which redirect it. (1977: 14)

For my purposes there are three important dimensions along which the process of constructing knowledge (that for brevity from now on subsumes communicating and affirming it, unless indicated otherwise) within a structure of group relations can be analysed. They are: the extent to which the process articulates, develops or legitimates group/sectional as compared with inter-group, societal or universal interests and identities; the extent to which the groups/sections which the knowledge is about contribute to the process; and the extent to which the knowledge produced has been validated or is valid in the terms that are claimed for it, or on the contrary is spurious, not validated as claimed, directly or by implication, or incapable of validation.

In the kind of situations that I am concerned with—where the participation of parties in social relations is secured by compliance rather than coercion—the dominance of some parties implies their capacity to define interests and identities, to monopolise access to knowledge and its construction and to assert that certain knowledge is valid, irrespective of whether it has been validated in the way claimed, or not. To the extent that certain parties dominate the construction of knowledge to the exclusion of others, the knowledge so produced is ideological. But it is important to remember that such ideological effects can be identified only where an object has been admitted as an object of knowledge. The most fundamentally powerful 'effect' is the effect of ruling out certain objects as objects of public knowledge. In their conception of how the political system works, P. Bachrach and M.S. Baratz call this nondecision-making. Political systems, they say, develop

> a set of predominant values, beliefs, rituals, and institutional procedures ('rules of the game') that operate systematically and consistently to the benefit of certain persons and groups at the expense of others . . . A nondecision . . . is a decision that results in suppression or thwarting of a latent or manifest challenge to the values or interests of the decision-maker. (1970: 43–4)

The construction of knowledge is not a mental process separate from 'real life'. Rather, as Burkart Holzner says of what he calls reality constructs, they are 'formed in the interpretation and re-interpretation of experience' (1968: 15), and the nature of experience is defined in terms of existing constructs. Each new experience (of action or of reflection-without-action) affects existing knowledge. This effect may take the form of confirming that knowledge or questioning, reordering or overturning it. Part of the capacity to dominate the construction of public knowledge is the capacity to decide what will happen to new private knowledge or new social knowledge that arises in a limited domain—whether it will be permitted to become public knowledge, and in what context, or whether it will be ignored or suppressed.

Interests and identity

The dynamic forces that produce 'the fundamental forms of "knowledge/power" ' (Foucault, quoted by Gordon, 1976: 31) are, as I understand them, interests and identities—both concepts being conceived in terms of social relations.

Individuals and groups construct social knowledge in pursuit of interests and in fulfilment of identity, but interests and identity are also objects of knowledge. I shall try to avoid the ever-present danger of reifying interests and identities by keeping close to the social processes by which they enter into public knowledge.

An interest involves 'participation in some property or benefit or advantage, that is, in some value whether tangible or otherwise . . . An interest . . . is a share and it carries with it the suggestion of other sharers' (Krabbe, 1922: LVII–LVIII). An interest has, as Geertz puts it, a psychological as well as a sociological aspect: 'referring both to a felt advantage of an individual or group of individuals and to the objective structure of opportunity within which an individual or group moves' (1973: 203).

Identity I take to mean the set of self-images held by an individual or group. It 'is formed by social processes. Once crystallized, it is maintained, modified, or even reshaped by social relations' (Berger and Luckmann, 1971: 194). Despite the risk of reification, the division which A.F.C. Wallace and R.D. Fogelson make into real, ideal, claimed and feared identity is useful for our present purposes because it provides a conceptualisation of the dynamic force of identity in social relations. The individual, say Wallace and Fogelson,

> *works* to achieve a real identity that is positive in affective value and to avoid the experience of negative affect in connection with his real identity. . . To the extent that real, ideal, and feared identities are internalization[s] of the implicit or explicit commentaries and values of others, they are built upon, and require, repeated validation in social communication. But the individual also privately monitors and evaluates his own behavior and thus both refines his concept of ideal identity by the requirements of experience and also estimates for himself any discrepancy between real and ideal and between real and feared identity. Identity formation thus is dependent upon both self-evaluation and interpersonal communication. (1965: 382; my italics)

In pursuit of a real or claimed identity, an individual or group tries to secure particular social positions, and complementary positions for others, and to establish certain self-definitions, and complementary definitions of others, as social knowledge. What Wallace and Fogelson call the 'identity struggle, in a social sense' is

> a form of negotiation between parties (whether individuals or groups) whose interests and characteristics are mutually perceived as being in certain respects presently antithetical but potentially complementary. It has the form of conflict, but its proper outcome is an agreement or contract on mutual rights and duties (with their necessary identity concomitants) such that the two parties can interact to mutual satisfaction in an equivalence structure. (1965: 386)

Because constructing knowledge is not an arbitrary activity, but takes place in the service of interests and identities, the constructs have to work (see Holzner, 1968, ch.3). That is, the predictions or implications they point to have to stand up to retrospective checking or be borne out in the event if they are to sustain their claim to validity. But an important part of the definers' power consists in their determination of what *is* a proper test and in their control over the clarity or ambiguity of a body of knowledge: some degree of ambiguity means that there is room for different interpretations of what is 'retrospectively confirmed' or 'borne out in the event' and implies that the constructs cannot readily be invalidated. The contingent nature of knowledge testing is nicely illustrated in Oliver Goldsmith's judgement on doctors:

> If the patient lives, then has he one more to add to the surviving lists; if he dies, then it may be justly said of the patient's disorder, 'that as it was not cured, the disorder was incurable.' (Goldsmith, n.d.: 203)

Institutional response

To the extent that webs of meaning cluster densely around particular functions or purposes, they give rise to what I have called institutions. The patterned social relations to which meaning within a certain institutional context attaches are social structures, and formally constituted and bounded structures are organisations or associations. These structures are not directly observable but are themselves conceptual maps or models of and for action (Geertz, 1973: 93). They may represent the models used by the participants in the action, or different models, which the participants might not even recognise or might reject, developed by an observer (that is, an outsider not involved in that set of relations). For the meaning of action is not exhausted by the perceptions of the participants. On the contrary, any action at any time can be incorporated into a non-participant's domain of meaning. Whether, as field-workers, sociologists participate in the social relations they are examining or whether they do not, they are always, *qua* sociologists, involved in weaving a reversible cloth: the same fabric shows the participants' domain of meaning on the one side, the sociologists' on the other. Or, as Geertz puts it in his description of what he calls interpretive anthropology:

> Our double task is to uncover the conceptual structures that inform our subjects' acts . . . and to construct a system of analysis in whose terms what is generic to those structures, what belongs to them because they are what they are, will stand out against the other determinants of human behavior. (1973: 27)

While action is always meaningful, meanings are not necessarily manifested in action: the symbolic world that men make and inhabit is immensely larger and more fertile than the world they act in. Experience is action from ego's idiosyncratic position in the structure of social relations. In the chapters that follow I shall examine the response of a number of established institutions to the migrant presence, and to ethnic diversification, in terms of the constructs that have been attached to migrants and their relation to those institutions and in terms of the changes in social structures and action that have taken place in acknowledgement of that presence. To explicate these processes I shall make the analytic distinction between definers of public knowledge and actors or participants in structures. The questions to be asked about the construction of knowledge are: who have been the definers, and what have they propounded about the parameters of knowledge (the objects the knowledge is about), the facts of the case and the explanation of those facts? What have they predicted about change or—to put the same question in different form —what solutions have they proposed for perceived problems of public import? I shall be aware of, but shall not probe into, the enduring frames of reference— the beliefs about relevance, the nature of man and knowledge itself, about causality and values—that stand in the shadows behind these more readily discernible products and organising principles of social experience.

Chapter 2 will trace the response of several institutions to the migrant presence over the past thirty years in very broad terms. Then in Chapters 3–4 and 5–6 respectively, I shall deal in some detail with the institutions of education and health and certain important structures—schools, hospitals, the Australian Medical Association, for example—which pattern action relevant to those institutions. The discussion of trade unions in Chapter 7 does not exactly parallel the education and health care chapters, because here I am concerned only with one structure and do not go into the institution of industrial relations within which trade unions operate. To have done so would have expanded the research beyond reasonable compass. Partly because the sources of public knowledge are different for each of the three areas of inquiry, and partly because I worked on the material in each area at different times and in different circumstances, the mode of analysis is different in each case.

NOTES

1. Some of the questions raised by the migrant-ethnic distinction in the Australian context are dealt with in Taft (1972) and in McKay and Lewins (1977). Two Melbourne journals, *Migration Action* (Ecumenical Migration Centre, Richmond) and *Ethnic Studies* (Centre for Migrant Studies, Monash University), between them canvas the spectrum of current thinking in Australia on the uses and abuses of the terms. Little attention has been paid in this country to the possibility that ethnicity might become a legal concept applicable to migrant minorities. However, in an interview in 1977, V. Menart, barrister and Vice-chairman of the Ethnic Communities Council of New South Wales, foreshadowed the importance that may come to be attached to such a development when he said: 'Australia's present legal system does not allow for a multicultural society . . . There is no reason why ethnic minorities could not be protected by special legislation' (Lukas, 1977).

2 Overview

The most comprehensive attempt that has ever been made to survey post-1945 migrant settlement in Australia appeared in 1966, when public consensus on the 'success' of the migration programme was on the verge of breaking down and the period of assimilationist approaches to the migrant presence was coming to an end. James Jupp's informative and prescient *Arrivals and Departures* crystallises the state of knowledge at that point of transition and so forms a bench mark against which subsequent changes can be assessed. Jupp—a British migrant who had then been in Australia nine years and was a political scientist on the staff of the University of Melbourne—was prompted to examine 'post-war immigration and its social effects' by what he saw as an anomalous lack of interest in the subject beyond the specialist work of a few academics. He found migrants in general inarticulate and politically impotent, their views neither known nor heeded. Migrant communities were not integrated into the decision-making process. There was a high rate of economic achievement, but also much invisible frustration and suffering which, he claimed, could readily be attenuated by more vigorous, humane and imaginative action on the part of government and other bodies such as trade unions. Indifference rather than prejudice blocked such responses. In sum, 'For all the apparent influence of Australia's 2,000,000 migrants they might just as well not exist' (1966: 122).

They did, however, exist and the economic development to which the country was committed in the fifties and sixties required that the intake of migrants be accepted as a normal element in population growth. If only to be fixed into position and then ignored, they had to be defined. The definition forcefully promoted by the Commonwealth Government became confirmed as public knowledge: migrants were lucky to have found a home in Australia, away from the tensions and economic desolation of post-war Europe; they were essential to economic growth and they were assimilable. From the beginning of the immigration programme in 1947, Commonwealth authorities put a great deal of effort into convincing the Australian community that migrants of non-British origin—now for the first time systematically assisted and encouraged—could be as readily assimilated as the British: that is, they were capable of being absorbed without strain and of learning 'that the things Australians believed in were practical, British things that they, too, could embrace and cherish' (McKell, 1952: 8). The notion that the 'minds of the Australian people . . . must be "conditioned" to accept these people whole-heartedly into the community' was behind the Commonwealth's establishment of the Good Neighbour movement in 1950 (Commonwealth Immigration Advisory Council, 1949, quoted by Kelly, 1974: 133). In addition to Australian goodwill, what was required for migrants to realise their capacity for assimilation was that they should have work and learn English, and the main thrust of the Commonwealth response lay in the organisation of English classes for adults and the expansion of the Commonwealth Employment Service.

To define migrants as assimilable was to predict how they would settle and much of the rhetoric of the period took the form of ebullient anticipations of future success and felicity for migrants and future benefit for Australians. A series of eighteen Australian Citizenship Conventions (ACCs)—sponsored by the Department of Immigration between 1950 and 1970 to bring together members of community groups involved in Good Neighbour work—provided the occasion for government and citizens alike to perpetuate these predictions and affirm the conviction that they were being fulfilled. As the printed papers given at the Conventions and the published *Digests* of proceedings show, consensus was ensured both by what was excluded from the deliberations (matters that the Commonwealth was concerned to preserve as areas of nondecision-making) and by the bland, self-congratulatory treatment of the subjects that were covered. Jupp described the Conventions as 'carefully organised to avoid controversy' (1966: 54).

The claim that migrants were assimilable was the easier to sustain because communication between migrants and Australians was limited and superficial in the extreme, and sources of knowledge about migrants were few and fragmented. The employment officers of the Commonwealth Employment Service rarely knew any language other than English. The Department of Immigration—oriented overwhelmingly towards migrant recruitment rather than settlement—was not well-informed about migrant experiences in Australia. It employed a very few multilinguals (except for local staff recruited to overseas posts) and had little research capacity; the inquiries it did conduct were limited in scope and rarely made public. State Governments and non-government bodies claimed that the responsibility for obtaining information about migrants or responding to their special needs lay with the Commonwealth Government which had brought them to the country. There was, in any case, the Good Neighbour movement, with its branches in each State, to prove that they were doing their bit for the human side of the migration programme. The Good Neighbour movement might in fact have been expected to provide a channel of communication between migrants, on the one hand, and the churches and voluntary bodies, as well as the Government, on the other. But it concentrated on British migrants, did not accept 'national'—that is, non-British, ethnic—groups as members until the sixties, and employed almost entirely English-speaking staff. From a survey of migrant attitudes to government policy, Jupp concluded: 'The clearest finding was that the "assimilation" work of the Good Neighbour Council is largely confined to those that need it least' (1966: 139).[1]

Organised interpreting and translating services were almost non-existent. Anglo-Australians had no access to the foreign-language press (as it was unselfconsciously called), with its abundance of information about migrant experiences, beliefs and attitudes, until the publication of an academic study in 1967 (Gilson and Zubrzycki, 1967). Although stereotypes of particular ethnic groups came into use—the fighting Yugoslavs or the hard-working Dutch, for example—there was little occasion to distinguish one group from another and no knowledge on which to base such distinctions. To acknowledge inter-group differences would in any case have run counter to the assertion that these differences were irrelevant, if not dangerous, in the Australian context. Newcomers from an immense variety of backgrounds were therefore lumped together under a series of common definitions—first as Balts, then as New Australians and later simply as migrants—which the people themselves deeply resented as a denial of their separate national identities (Martin, 1965: 51).

The title of Jupp's book signified the ambivalence that, by 1966, was undermining public confidence in the immigration programme and consensus about migrants and their place in Australian society. Despite vigorous and costly recruiting campaigns in northern and western Europe, migrant arrivals from those areas declined rapidly in the sixties. A new spurt in migration from Britain after 1961 brought the average annual net gain from migration during 1961–1966 to only 0.8 per cent of the total population, a figure well below the target of 1 per cent that had guided intake policy since 1947. Even the southern Europeans, who had been ready enough to come—at their own expense for the most part, and under discriminatory conditions that strictly limited family reunions—were no longer arriving in sufficient numbers and the Government found it necessary to make concessions which, as C.A. Price says, tossed overboard 'the old notion that southern Europeans were less desirable settlers, and deserved less favourable treatment, than Britons and northern Europeans' (1971: A14). The Department of Immigration also began actively seeking migrants in the Middle East and in 1967 made an agreement to extend the assisted passage scheme to Turks; by a subtle but decisive act of re-definition, Turkey was now 'for all intents and purposes . . . an entirely European country' (Price ed., 1971: A14). The relaxation of entry restrictions three years earlier had already increased the intake of Lebanese and persons of mixed European and non-European descent. The new thinking was getting to the point where no people were too alien in race, culture or religion to be assimilable in a modern Australia, provided the economic system could absorb them. Symbolically—and as a pointer to future population implications of Australia's involvement in Asia—the most significant expression of this new thinking was the decision in 1966 to allow highly skilled non-Europeans to settle in Australia, and to permit those already here to change their status from temporary to permanent. This decision was publicly acknowledged as the end of the White Australia policy.

If the rate of arrivals had become a problem, so had the rate of departures. Complaints and expressions of disillusionment by British migrants in the fifties, though well-publicised, were easily turned aside as the outpourings of a disgruntled and ungrateful minority. In this period, according to A.J. Davies, Ministers for Immigration and migration officers perpetuated a 'six per cent dogma': that is, they repeatedly asserted 'that of British immigrants only 6 per cent returned and, of these half returned [to Australia], giving a net loss of three per cent'. Davies goes on to suggest that it was 'outside researchers and investigators such as R.T. Appleyard in 1961 and the Vernon Committee in 1965' who forced the Government to acknowledge that the rate of departures was higher than it had admitted and called for 'policy and administrative changes' (1971: 257).

But already in 1957 the historian and demographer C.A. Price had suggested that official estimates of the net gain from British migration in the post-war period were much too high, and studies published in 1962 by Price and also by Appleyard, his colleague in the Demography Department at the Australian National University, confirmed these doubts (Appleyard, 1962; Price, 1957, 1962a). In a general overview of 'Overseas Migration to and from Australia 1947–1961', also published in 1962, Price estimated that for this period the return rate of intending settlers from Britain was between 6 per cent and 14 per cent 'and about half that for most other peoples' (1962b: 168).

It was becoming inescapably clear that a substantial departure rate formed an intrinsic element of the immigration programme and that 'immigrant' did not necessarily equal 'settler'. By 1966 the issue loomed large enough for the Commonwealth Immigration Advisory Council's Committee on Social Patterns to initiate an inquiry into the subject. Price and Appleyard were appointed consultants to the Committee, and Price estimated that for the period 1959–1965 total settler loss was over 16 per cent of settler arrivals. The Committee, however, refrained from fully associating itself with Price's estimate, which it described as 'considerably higher than the official figures', and concluded cautiously that the departure rate lay somewhere between 9 per cent and 16 per cent of settler arrivals for the six-year period (Aus., Immigration Advisory Council, 1966: 9; 1967: 3).

Subsequent research showed that departure rates were even higher than the Committee's top figure and that, just when the Committee was doing its best to damp down concern about settler loss, departures were in fact increasing. Detailed figures published by Price in 1971 revealed that German, Dutch and Italian return rates rose sharply in the early sixties. By 1966, over a fifth of all post-war German settlers had departed, about 18 per cent of Dutch (the same figure as for the British) and 13 per cent of Italians (Price ed., 1971: A9–10). Departure rates of this order could not readily be reconciled with an unalloyed faith in migrant assimilability. Though not excessive by international standards, they took on a serious aspect to a government now threatened with a shortage of migration sources.

When a newly constituted Committee on Social Patterns, chaired by the sociologist J. Zubrzycki (a former member of the Department of Demography at the Australian National University), made a further inquiry into departure rates in 1972–1973, it adopted a method of calculation more like that which had given the figure of 16 per cent for 1959–1965 than that which had produced 9 per cent. In an Appendix to the Committee's progress report, published in 1972, Price —again consultant to the Committee—showed that, no matter what method of calculation was adopted, settler loss increased substantially during the sixties; furthermore, the method that gave the most favourable figure of 9 per cent for the 1959–1965 period also yielded the greatest *increase* in settler loss during the decade of the sixties. Price's figures are given in Table 2.1.

Had the Government of the day heeded some of its critics, or even some of its advisers like the Vernon Committee of Economic Enquiry, it would have lowered the migrant target. Concern to create a favourable climate of opinion towards Australia in Britain and other source countries might not then have emerged as strongly as it did in the late sixties. However, instigated by employers—and strongly committed to the idea that neither its own recruitment machinery nor

Table 2.1   *Estimate of settler loss, 1959–1971*

	Annual averages of settler loss per calendar year		
	1959–1965 %	1966–1969 %	1970–1971 %
Method A (which yielded 9 per cent in the 1966 inquiry)	8	15	17
Method B	19	21	27
Method C (which yielded 16 per cent in the 1966 inquiry)	17	23	25

Source: Aus., Immigration Advisory Council, 1972, Appendix B:10.[2]

the delicate and time-consuming process of reaching agreements with source countries could stand the migration tap being turned on and off—the Government rejected warnings and cautions and steadily raised intake targets each year during the final years of the sixties. The 1968 target of 160 000 was the highest since 1950. Migrants were to be wooed to come and kept once they were here; greater attention to their well-being after arrival would serve both interests.

A report from the Immigration Planning Council to the Minister for Immigration, B.M. Snedden, in 1968 captured the changing trend of official thinking at that time. The report, on *Australia's Immigration Programme for the Period 1968 to 1973*, showed that the net gain from immigration had fallen short of the annual target of 1 per cent of population in every year since 1956–1957 and examined the 'internal' and 'external' considerations that had led to this undesirable result. Convinced of 'Australia's tremendous capacity for growth and development', the Council reaffirmed the need for continuing high rates of immigration—high enough to compensate for settler departures—but concluded that in order to reach the target of 1 per cent,

> there should be sustained and expanded effort in the field of recruitment, increased flexibility of methods, and special measures implemented of an economic and social character to attract migrants and to hold them once they arrived in Australia. (Aus., Immigration Planning Council, 1968: 81)

There was no doubt about the importance that the Council attached to 'social factors' nor about the reasoning behind this thinking:

> The Committee considered that there was a distinct co-relation between the success of migration programmes and such major social factors as housing requirements and social service benefits, which migrants now took into consideration when making immigration decisions. This was

particularly true today, as Australia had lost much of its former attractiveness in terms of the employment, wage levels, and the standard of living it could offer compared with those of migrants' home countries, or of Australia's competitors . . .

Action was necessary to improve Australia's attractiveness through the taking of measures that might appear, prima facie, as special privileges to new settlers, but in reality did nothing more than off-set the disadvantages at which re-settlement placed migrants vis-à-vis indigenous Australians. *Continuation of these disadvantages placed severe limits on Australia's ability to attract and hold migrants.* (Aus., Immigration Planning Council, 1968: 83–4; my italics)

In the meantime, other and largely independent influences were forcing migrant welfare on the attention of a wider section of the Australian community and calling increasingly into question past definitions of migrant assimilability. The potency of these influences lay in their undermining effect on the work of established institutions. Up to this time, schools, hospitals, welfare services and government bureaucracies of all kinds had been able to continue in their established practices without disruption or change due to the migrant presence. To say that this became more difficult in the mid-sixties means two things: first, that experience was showing that predictions about migrant assimilability were often not borne out in reality; second, that the staff of a number of organisations were finding non-English-speakers a disturbing obstacle to the adequate performance of their jobs (often exacerbating other distinct problems such as overcrowding in schools).

It is not possible to say whether there was a point at which sheer pressure of numbers forced the needs and situations of non-English-speaking migrants onto the attention of the established institutions, but there is no doubt that the increases in absolute numbers during the sixties made the migrant population more visible than it had been before. The data presented in Figures 2.1 and 2.2 give some indication of why pressures built up in hospitals and schools, but there is little evidence that the increase in the number of working migrant wives ruffled the complacency of employers or trade unions. Until the results of R.F. Henderson's 1966 Poverty Inquiry were published in 1969, migrants were not publicly defined as economically disadvantaged or vulnerable. (Indeed, they were more likely to be held up as examples of the success to be won through hard work and thrift or an obsession with money.) But Henderson's finding that certain groups of non-Anglo-Saxon origin had exceptionally high rates of poverty appeared exactly at a time when a number of workers in the welfare field were becoming critical of the lack of help given by established services to non-English-speakers (Henderson, 1969; Henderson *et al.*, 1970; J.I. Martin, 1975*a*).

Southern European migrants became particularly visible during the sixties because, with their increased numbers, they began to develop concentrations of population, complete with social centres, churches, shops and eating places, in the inner-city areas of Sydney and Melbourne. In Melbourne a number of teachers and other school personnel—with immediate experience of the educational problems of migrant children, and of the schools that were failing to meet their needs—generated the first serious public debate over institutional response to the migrant presence. But inner-city concentrations also rekindled the community apprehension about the formation of 'national groups', which the authorities had been at such pains to allay at the beginning of the immigration programme.

Towards the end of the sixties, migrant issues also became caught up in the Labor Opposition's accelerated attack on the Liberal Government that had held office in the Commonwealth since 1949. At the 1969 elections, where Labor increased its numbers in the House of Representatives by 18, winning a total of 59 out of 125 seats, migrants—along with other 'disadvantaged' groups such as the poor, women and Aborigines—were prominent in Labor's welfare platform.

Figure 2.1 *Population born in a non-English-speaking (NES) country: births, deaths, working women, children 5–14 years: numbers 1947–1975*

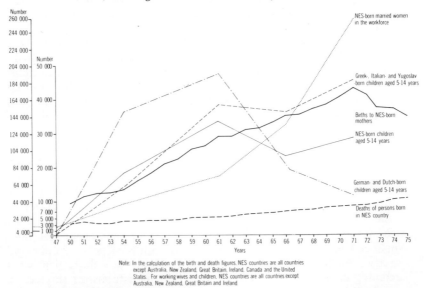

Note: In the calculation of the birth and death figures, NES countries are all countries except Australia, New Zealand, Great Britain, Ireland, Canada and the United States. For working wives and children, NES countries are all countries except Australia, New Zealand, Great Britain and Ireland.

Source: Australian Bureau of Statistics, *Censuses, Demography Bulletins* and unpublished data. Richmond (1973).

The definition of migrants as victims of economic exploitation, and of official and community neglect, gained support from the situation in other countries, particularly the intransigence of black poverty and the emergence of black militancy in the United States.

Figure 2.2 *Population born in a non-English-speaking (NES) country: births, deaths, working women, children 5–14 years: percentages 1947–1975*

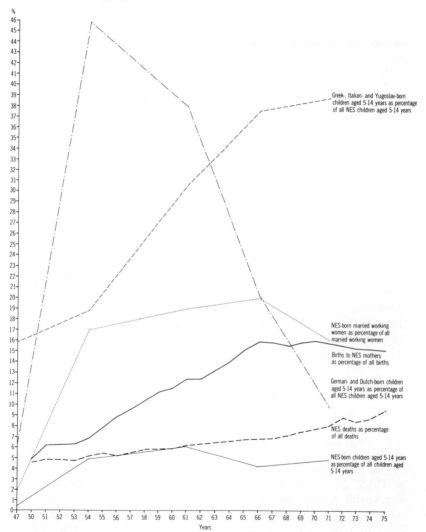

Figure 2.3 gives an indication of how an increase in publications on migrant health and child migrant education conformed to the general upward trend, from about 1964, in the production of books in general and in the social, medical and physical sciences and in education in particular.

As the result of these various influences, there gradually consolidated a definition of migrants as a social problem. Previously isolated and faint voices that had been trying to make this point for a long time were now joined or overtaken by new and vocal allies. A few individuals of non-Anglo-Saxon origin contributed to the change, but rarely came forward as migrant spokesmen, and ethnic communities as such played almost no part in moving public thinking in this direction. When, later, ethnic groups did become vocal in the English-speaking community, it was to confirm the picture of themselves as deprived minorities. It is only very recently that some groups have made a special effort to dissociate themselves from the 'problem' image. Jupp foreshadowed their reaction in a passing comment:

> The whole 'organisational' approach to assimilation . . . may . . . overlook the resentment which is sometimes generated by treating migrants as though they were problem children who need to be sorted out. An irate editorial in *Il Globo* (21.9.65) condemns 'so-called social experts, ministers of religion, matrons of benevolent associations and other civic leaders and political personalities who are excessively concerned with "poor migrant youth" '. (1966: 151)

At the end of the sixties, then, those who developed the concept of migrants as a disadvantaged group were Australians located within established organisations, but they were often in some way or other in marginal positions, like social workers in the Victorian Education Department or Protestant clergy with views about social responsibility that ran counter to their church's traditional priorities. Academics studying the social aspects of migration also began to contribute to the public debate (see Price ed., 1966, 1971; Zubrzycki, 1968; Wilkes ed., 1971).

The role of the Commonwealth Department of Immigration in governing certain institutional responses to migration and establishing the climate in which other responses occurred merits detailed examination on its own account.[3] Unfortunately no such study is in existence and it was beyond the scope of this present work to fill the gap. I shall therefore be brief, relying on some newly available information on the staffing of the Department and on the information contained in Table 2.2 to convey the scope and timing of changes in Commonwealth policy and practice.

It is of course extremely difficult to assess the significance of individual ministers and departmental secretaries in mediating the

Figure 2.3 *Publications in Australia 1957–1977: all titles (books and pamphlets), social sciences, pure sciences, medical sciences, and education; child migrant education and migrant health*

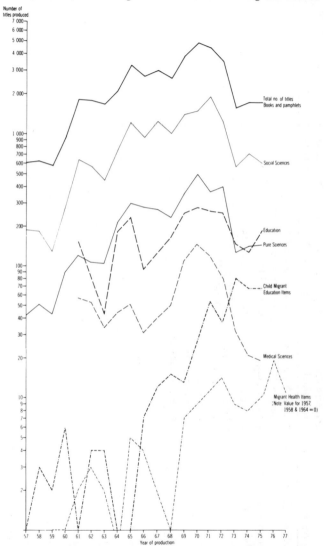

Source: All titles (books and pamphlets), social sciences, pure sciences, education and medical sciences, UNESCO, *Statistical Yearbooks,* and Australian National Library, *Statistics on Book Production* and *Australian National Bibliography;* Child Migrant Education Items, Willcock (1976); Migrant Health Items, survey reported in Chapter 5.

Table 2.2 *Table of events: selected Commonwealth Government activities relevant to migrant settlement, 1950–1977*

Settlers arriving*	Legislation	Bureaucracy: new developments	Programmes and services established	Standing committees, councils established	Special committees of inquiry established	Publications of Government inquiries
1950 or before	Nationality and Citizenship Acts 1948, 1950	Department of Immigration (established 1945)	†Good Neighbour Councils (GNC's) †Citizenship Conventions †Adult Migrant English Service (responsibility of Commonwealth Office of Education 1947–1951)	†Commonwealth Immigration Advisory Council (IAC) †Commonwealth Immigration Planning Council (IPC)		
1951						
1952	Nationality and Citizenship Act 1952	Commonwealth Hostels Ltd				
1953	Nationality and Citizenship Act 1953					
1954						
1955	Nationality and Citizenship Act 1955	Publicity Section in Department of Immigration				

Year	Number	Legislation	Units/Sections	Other	IAC Reports
1956					
1957					IAC, *Third Report of the Committee Established to Investigate Conduct of Migrants*
1958		Migration Act 1958 Nationality and Citizenship Act 1958			
1959		Nationality and Citizenship Act 1959			IAC, *Progress and Assimilation of Migrant Children* IAC, *The Incidence of Mental Illness among Migrants*
1960	105 887	Nationality and Citizenship Act 1960	Translations Unit in Department of Immigration		
1961	108 291				
1962	85 808		Survey Unit in Department of Immigration	†Immigration Publicity Council	
1963	101 888		Training Section in Department of Immigration		

Table 2.2 *Continued*

	Settlers arriving*	Legislation	Bureaucracy: new developments	Programmes and services established	Standing committees, councils established	Special committees of inquiry established	Publications of Government inquiries
1964	122 318	Migration Act 1964	Assimilation Section of Department of Immigration changed to Integration Section				
1965	140 152		Language Training Programme for Migration Officers in, or selected for, overseas service with Department of Immigration				
1966	144 055	Migration Act 1966 Nationality and Citizenship Act 1966					
1967	138 676	Nationality and Citizenship Act 1967				†Grant from Department of Immigration to the Social Science Research Council for migrant research	IAC, *Departure of Settlers*

Year	Number	Legislation	Programmes / Services	Commissions / Committees	Reports / Inquiries
1968	137 525		†Grants to Community Agencies		IPC, *Australia's Immigration Programme for the Period 1968 to 1973*; IAC, *Immigration and the Balance of the Sexes*
1969	175 657	Citizenship Act 1969	Migrant Services Division and National Groups Unit in Department of Immigration	†Committee on Overseas Professional Qualifications (COPQ)	
1970	185 099		†Child Migrant Education Programme (CMEP)		
1971	170 011	Immigration (Education) Act 1971	†Migrant television project, providing English instruction and community education	†National Population Inquiry (NPI) (W.D. Borrie)	
1972	132 719			Commission of Inquiry into Poverty (Commissioner R.F. Henderson)	
1973	107 401	Migration Act 1973; Immigration (Education) Amendment Act 1973; Australian Citizenship Act 1973	Structured Selection Assessment System (for selection of migrants); †Telephone Interpreter Service (TIS); †Establishment of bi-lingual welfare officer positions	Schools Commission; †Migrant Task Forces in each State; Commission of Inquiry into Poverty (Commissioners R.T. Fitzgerald, R.C. Gates, G.S. Martin, R. Sackville); †Committee on Community Relations (W.M. Lippmann)	Migrant Task Force reports from each State; Department of Immigration, *Survey of Interpreting and Translating Needs*; IAC, *Inquiry into the Departure of Settlers*

Table 2.2 *Continued*

Settlers arriving*	Legislation	Bureaucracy: new developments	Programmes and services established	Standing committees, councils established	Special committees of inquiry established	Publications of Government inquiries
1974 112 712		Department of Immigration amalgamated with Department of Labour Migrant Services transferred to Department of Security		†(IAC abolished)	Royal Commission on Australian Government Administration (H.C. Coombs) Royal Commission on Human Relationships (E. Evatt) Committee on the Teaching of Migrant Languages in Schools (J.W. Mather) Committee to Advise on Policies for Manufacturing Industry (R.G. Jackson)	COPQ, *The Language Barrier* Department of Education, *The Multi-Cultural Society* Department of Immigration, *Survey of Views of Local Government Authorities relating to Immigration Settlement and Integration*

| 1975 | 89 147 | Racial Discrimination Act 1975 | Adult Migrant Education Service and CMEP transferred to Department of Education Information Branch to Department of the Media | †Ethnic radio Access radio | †Australian Population and Immigration Council (APIC) | NPI, *Population and Australia* Commission of Inquiry into Poverty, *Poverty in Australia, Law and Poverty in Australia* Committee on Community Relations *Final Report* Committee to Advise on Policies for Manufacturing Industry, *Policies for Development of Manufacturing Industry: A Green Paper* Department of Education, *Report of the Inquiry into Schools of High Migrant Density* Department of Social Security, *Directory of National Group Organisations* |

Table 2.2 *Continued*

	Settlers arriving*	Legislation	Bureaucracy: new developments	Programmes and services established	Standing committees, councils established	Special committees of inquiry established	Publications of Government inquiries
1976	52 748	States Grants (Schools) Act 1976 States Grants (Schools) Amendment Act 1976	Department of Immigration re-established as Immigration and Ethnic Affairs Child Migrant and multicultural education transferred to Schools Commission	(CMEP terminated) †*From the Ethnic Press*		Review of the Commonwealth Employment Service (J.D. Norgard) Task Force on Co-ordination in Welfare and Health (P.H. Bailey) Interdepartmental Working Party on Interpreters and Translators	APIC, *A Decade of Migrant Settlement* Commission of Inquiry into Poverty, *Social/Medical Aspects of Poverty in Australia* Department of Education, *Report of the Committee on the Teaching of Migrant Languages* Parliament, Joint Committee on Foreign Affairs and Defence, *The Lebanon Crisis* Royal Commission on Australian Government Administration, *Report* Senate Standing Committee, *Australia and the Refugee Problem*

| 1977 | 70 916 | States Grants (Schools Assistance) Act 1977 Broadcasting and Television Amendment Act 1977 | Interdepartmental Working Group on Women's Affairs, Task Force on Migrant Women Information Branch returned to Department of Immigration and Ethnic Affairs | †Australian Ethnic Affairs Council (AEAC) †National Accreditation Authority for Translators and Interpreters (NAATI) National Ethnic Broadcasting Advisory Council (NEBAC) | Review of Post-arrival Programmes and Services to Migrants (F. Galbally) | Task Force on Co-ordination in Welfare and Health, *Proposals for Change* AEAC, *Australia as a Multicultural Society* APIC, *Immigration Policies and Australia's Population: A Green Paper* Interdepartmental Working Party on Interpreters and Translaters, *Report* Review of the CES, *Report* Royal Commission on Human Relationships, *Final Report* |

*Figures for settler arrivals are not available before 1959–62. Figures are shown against the year corresponding to the second half of the financial year to which they apply.

†The responsibility of the Department of Immigration, Labour and Immigration, or Immigration and Ethnic Affairs.

social influences described above, on the one hand, or in expressing more personal, idiosyncratic interests and values, on the other; the history of child migrant education in Chapters 3 and 4 attempts such an assessment to a modest and partial degree, and illustrates the complexities involved. In his study of the origins of the Department of Immigration and changes in its organisation and functions up to 1970, A.J. Davies sees the role of the first Minister, Arthur Calwell (1945–1949), as decisive. Davies considers the transition from the long incumbency of the first Secretary, Tasman Heyes (1946–1961), to that of the second, Peter R. Heydon (1961–1971), as coincident with important changes in the Department's role and structure. Heyes, regarded as an 'excellent administrator', consolidated the planning operations of the Department in terms of publicity, recruitment of migrants and processing—and secured for the Department a respected position within the Commonwealth bureaucracy. 'By the time he retired immigration was accepted as a "good thing" and its permanence, and that of the department, seemed assured.' While Heyes 'was believed to have no regard for "intellectuals" ', his successor was an academic of some distinction, favourably inclined towards research and the 'scientific handling', as he himself put it, of social problems (Davies, 1971: 257, 274).

Important though the differences in orientation between Heyes and Heydon may have been, it was not in fact until Heydon had been Secretary for about six years that the Department began to develop new structures and practices that indicated a more generous concept of its responsibilities towards migrant settlement. In 1966 Jupp found the Department doing 'a good job' in fulfilling its attraction and regulation functions, but 'falling down' in its absorption function. The Department's efforts in this direction were well-intentioned, but totally inadequate and of low priority compared with its other activities (1966: 164).

How far the Department moved in the direction of a more active 'absorption' role towards the end of the sixties is indicated by the initiatives listed in Table 2.2. Information on staffing also provides one crude index. It could be expected that an increased commitment to migrant settlement and welfare activities would be associated with an increase in the numbers of overseas-born staff, of graduates in the social sciences and of staff employed as professionals. As Table 2.3 shows, between 1966 and 1971 the numbers and proportion of staff with post-school educational qualifications did increase, but by 1971 only 192, or 13 per cent of the permanent staff, had university degrees or diplomas; most of the increase between 1966 and 1971 was accounted for by an increase in pass Arts graduates. Overseas-born staff and professionals also increased substantially more than the increase in total staff, but the numbers in both categories remained extremely small. Of the professionals, social workers were the only group to increase significantly in number, from 9 to 23. However, the 1971 figure could scarcely be regarded as a dramatic re-ordering of Departmental priorities, particularly in view of the fact that the intake of settlers born in countries other than the United Kingdom increased from 63 000 in 1966–1967 to 105 000 in 1970–1971 and the total settler arrivals (including the British-born) averaged 160 000 a year during the 1966–1971 period (Aus., Department of Immigration, 1973*a*: Table 24; Price and Martin eds, 1976*a*: Table 3).

The migrant problem that attracted by far the most attention towards the end of the sixties was the education of migrant children. The community's growing awareness of migrants focussed around this issue, particularly in Victoria, where it became a topic of vigorous political debate. What led the Commonwealth to move into the area in about 1967 and to go on to establish the Child Migrant Education Program in 1970 is dealt with in the following chapters.

By the beginning of the seventies a number of independent changes had accumulated in the practices and structures of various institutions. Most of these were minor changes aimed at providing some service or facility for migrants without disturbing the status quo. Indeed— as the Child Migrant Education Program patently illustrates—most took the form of concessions or adaptations that would allow migrants to be dealt with as marginal, special or exceptional problems and so would protect established practices from pressures for radical restructuring. Designed to contain change, these modifications, in fact, entailed several unintended consequences. Important among these were the opportunities thus created for communication between people with views on the experience of migrants. At the beginning, the main yield from this communication was agreement that there existed migrant problems for which the established institutions had some responsibility. Subsequently in the mid-seventies, this perception splintered as new practices gave more people more varied experience and as previously invisible groups made their presence felt for the first time.

The end of political and community consensus on immigration and settlement policies was signified in the sharp debate among industrialists, bureaucrats, politicians, journalists and academics that occurred at a Summer School on 'How Many Australians? Immigration and Growth', organised by the Australian Institute of Political Science (AIPS) in February 1971. C.R. Kelly, a Liberal MP, summed up the changing mood:

> Way back in 1947 we designed an immigration machine and really we ought to be proud of the way it has functioned . . . It has solved a great number of personal problems with surprising humanity and . . . it receives the general approbation of political parties . . .

We have a debate on some immigration issue and they trundle the machine into the House and put it on the table. The Minister for Immigration sits on one side of it and the spokesman for the Labor Party, Fred Daly, sits on the other; and they polish it and themselves . . . We all come in; the good and the great admire the machine and pat on it from a great height, and the rest of us polish it with our tongues. We trundle it across King's Hall and take it into the Senate where they do the same things only with longer words. Then they wheel it out and take it down to the Immigration Council where they tighten up a few bolts, ask for more oil in the form of money, more grease in the form of flattery, and away it goes again—off round and round the paddock. And some of us are getting concerned . . . we know it's a good machine . . . but we don't know what the hell it is doing. So we trot alongside it and ask anxiously: 'What are you doing it *for*?' And there are fellows inside it, working—dedicated chaps they are—and they say: 'Can't answer—too busy!' (Wilkes ed., 1971: 187)

Table 2.3 *Characteristics of staff of Commonwealth Department of Immigration, 1966, 1971 and 1976*

Characteristic	Year		
	1966	1971	1976
Category of employment of full-time staff employed under the Public Service Act			
Permanent	993	1510	1309
Temporary	257	224	104
Exempt	486	388	2
Total	1736	2122	1415
Age and place of birth of permanent staff			
Under 40, Australian-born	518	852	928
Under 40, overseas-born	103	224	
40 and over, Australian-born	366	390	381
40 and over, overseas-born	6	44	
Total	993	1510	1309
Designation of permanent non-clerical/ administration staff			
Medical officer	1	4	2
Psychologist	5	7	0
Social worker	9	23	0
Librarian	0	1	0
Other	0	1	5
Total	15	36	7

As in 1969, the Commonwealth elections of 1972 stimulated a lively interest in welfare, education, and social planning and policy in general. This time Labor won and embarked on a brave, if often breathless and sometimes ill-considered, programme of social inquiry, restructuring government bodies and social expenditure. It immediately reduced the immigration target for 1971–1972 from 140 000 (a figure already cut by the Liberals from the original 180 000) to 110 000 and initiated a period of overhaul, dismantling and re-assembly of the 'immigration machine' which continues to the present day.

Table 2.3 *Continued*

Characteristic	Year		
	1966	**1971**	**1976**
Level of educational qualifications of permanent staff			
Graduates			
Higher degree	2	5	1
Honours degree	9	32	16
Pass degree	42	124	83
Level unknown	2	5	2
Total	55	166	102
Diploma	15	26	17
Other	923	1318	1190
Total	993	1510	1309
Type of educational qualifications of permanent staff with degree or diploma			
Accounting	2	3	2
Administration/Management	5	9	11
Agriculture	2	3	0
Arts	41	136	68
Economics/Commerce	15	23	19
Education	1	4	1
Law	2	7	4
Medicine	1	4	3
Science	1	3	11
Total	70	192	119

Source: Aus., Public Service Board, unpublished information provided 1977.

Differentiation in the seventies

Although the proliferation since 1972 of discussions, conferences and committees of inquiry related to migrant and ethnic issues has far outstripped changes in structure and activities, changes of the latter kind have certainly occurred. The overview that follows is illustrated from institutional areas not covered in detail in later chapters, particularly welfare.

The most general way of characterising the past five years is that it has been a period of increasing differentiation among definers and in constructs and action. Of all the relevant structures developed since 1972 (some, like the Telephone Interpreter Service, were foreshadowed by the Liberal Government, but most were the work of its Labor successor), the one that had the most potential for change in relation to migrant questions was probably the Australian Assistance Plan (AAP), which aimed to develop an integrated network of welfare services 'at a regional level within a nationally co-ordinated framework' (Aus., Social Welfare Commission, 1973: 3). This potential was not acknowledged in the AAP itself, which largely ignored migrants, but came from the operation of the Regional Councils for Social Development through which the AAP was to be implemented. Some Regional Councils in areas of migrant concentration established ethnic committees of various kinds. Project officers employed under the AAP in these areas also became conversant with the practicalities of migrant welfare. Their experience had an unprecedented import because they were part of a national authority and plugged into a system with the capacity for nation-wide communication, and because they had the concrete task of developing ways of dealing with migrant welfare problems and engaging migrants in community development. The tensions and insecurity associated with such new roles, and the way these led to the formulation of new interests and identities, are illustrated in a statement prepared by Mauro Di Nicola, Migrant Liaison Officer of the Inner City Regional Council, Sydney, in June 1975, at the time of the formation of a Migrant Resources Committee:

> We are people from a number of government departments and organisations mindful of what Mr Grassby has termed the 'conspiracy of silence' in Australian institutions with regard to ethnic communities. We have met first of all to meet each other; the migrant field has exploded within the past 12 months and it is difficult, if not impossible to obtain an overview of what is happening. We meet to discover perspectives to pool our resources, to solve common problems . . .
>
> Some of us are very new at our jobs and some of the jobs themselves are very new. For this reason, up to now we have been able to talk to each other as individuals rather than as representatives of organisations. Inevitably and regretably, individuals within this committee will come

under pressure from their respective employers to remind others of roles, boundaries, jurisdictions, traditions and politics. It will remain to be seen whether the common interests and concerns which unite us are stronger than the institutional boundaries which divide us. (Di Nicola, 1975)

At the time of his resignation from the position as Migrant Liaison Officer, shortly after the formation of the Migrant Resources Committee, Di Nicola described his job in these words:

> I was thus employed at a time of rapidly expanding activity and confusion, by an organisation which was still working out its fundamental philosophy, whose structure was suspect as far as 'sectional' interest groups were concerned and within a Regional Council still in the process of seeking a direction and an identity. (1976: 46)

The AAP also brought to light issues concerning the role of ethnic communities that did not arise in earlier years, when lack of opportunities for ethnic groups to be involved in welfare matters allowed rhetoric about the merits of such participation to go unquestioned. The philosophy underlying the AAP was that welfare needs could be met only by organisation at the local level, that is, by active community participation. Two opposing implications for ethnic involvement could have been drawn from this philosophy: ethnics should participate as residents of their locality, on the one hand, or as members of local ethnic communities, on the other. '[H]ysteria surrounding the non-participation of migrants' in the AAP, as Margaret Roberts, a Project Officer with the Inner City Regional Council, put it (Roberts, 1976: 30), brought these two alternatives into the open. In either case, it seemed, 'agitators'—project officers or others—were needed to get migrants involved, but how far they should be directing their efforts to ethnic-group organisation was clearly a matter for debate. Some Regional Council representatives at a Sydney seminar, reported in *Migrants and the AAP*, described effective ethnic committees. Others said that ethnics who had participated in the Councils did not wish 'to be seen as "migrants" participating but simply as people who were contributing what they could' (AAP, 1976: 5). Even if it were agreed that ethnic group participation was desirable, difficult questions of strategy remained. Margaret Roberts echoed a question that has also been asked in relation to the Grants to Community Agencies scheme for the employment of social workers:

> The availability of capitation money to be sliced up and handed out to deserving groups was seen [by the seminar participants] as being a neat way of getting round the real problem of organizing the unorganized and making them vocal, and had created a great deal of confusion and guilt among people working with or for the Regional Councils. Instead of denying migrant groups money because they were not properly 'organized' the same money should perhaps have been spent in seriously helping them to get organized. (AAP, 1976: 7)

Migrant participation in the AAP was connected with a 'basic question' raised by the Royal Commission on Australian Government Administration (the Coombs Commission, after its chairman H.C. Coombs). This question, yet to be resolved, was: 'to what extent government programs in health and welfare are more efficient and effective when directed at the family or other social group rather than at individuals' (1976, *Report*: 326). In a recent analysis of Commonwealth welfare policies, Adam Graycar describes the welfare policy of the 1972–1975 Labor Government, and specifically the AAP, as embodying 'a respecification of target groups': instead of the targets of government aid being conceived as unorganised categories of beneficiaries, as they had been in the past, they came to be thought of as communities, organised to be active participants in the definition of welfare needs and the allocation of welfare resources (1977: 154). Had the AAP survived, either in its original regional form or in modified form to accommodate the objections of local government that the Regional Councils were 'a threat to the "hierarchy" of tiers of government' or 'a development of a "fourth tier" ' (Aus., Royal Commission on Australian Government Administration, 1976, *Report:* 140), it would very likely have stimulated the organisation of ethnic communities as target groups. However, the scheme was dismantled by the Liberal Government in 1976, before the structural anomaly pointed out by Di Nicola—that while the AAP was regionally organised, ethnic communities were not (1976: 50)—could become an issue.

Although the AAP did not last long enough for its implications regarding ethnic communities to emerge in any clear way, it had an important indirect role in New South Wales as the catalyst for the first significant attempt on the part of ethnic groups to combine, in order to represent common ethnic interests in public affairs. This attempt took the form of the establishment of an Ethnic Communities Council (ECC). The first bodies of this kind were formed in Victoria and South Australia in 1974. The impetus to the foundation of the ECC of New South Wales came (in 1975) from the Ethnic Communities' Group within the Inner Western Regional Council for Social Development; a major factor 'was the feeling that the AAP could not adequately deal with the whole range of ethnic issues' (Di Nicola, 1976: 54). The aims of the ECC of New South Wales are spelled out in a document produced for the inaugural meeting, which reads, in part:

> The proposed Ethnic Communities Council would need to be an independent organization expressing the viewpoints and interests, and reflecting the aspirations of ethnic and migrant minorities in New South Wales. Wide representation based on effective participation is essential,

if the proposed Council is to speak on behalf of all, to promote their rights, and to achieve a voice in decision making, and the use of funds affecting their welfare and interests. Further, the Council would need to be a co-ordinating body and not an ethnic government, nor to become involved in party politics. (ECC of NSW, Organizing Committee, 1975: 2)

The ECCs are indeed consolidating their position and becoming agents for the crystallisation, and on occasion the manufacture, of a viewpoint on what Vlado Menart, Senior Vice-chairman of the ECC of New South Wales, has called 'ethnical involvement, aspirations and needs' (1977: 2). But internally the ECCs face the same problems of differentiation among member groups and distance from the immediate experience of the non-participating majority as those that occur between ethnics and Anglo-Australians in the wider society. The chairman of the ECC of New South Wales, W. Jegorow, recently acknowledged the problem of differentiation when he referred to the need to ensure 'that minorities within ethnic communities themselves, based on religious, regional, political or other reasons, be also given representation on the Executive' (1977: 2). Already in 1976 Margaret Roberts had described the ECC of New South Wales as a powerful lobby group; its ' "key" people' she saw as 'very articulate, accomplished', but the possibility of grass-roots participation 'seemed very unlikely and perhaps, given the aims the organization had set itself, not really necessary' (1976: 30).

Outside the ECCs, individual ethnic groups are also establishing themselves as definers of ethnicity in Australian society. With the Department of Immigration's initiation in 1976 of a service for providing translations of extracts from the ethnic press into English, ethnic communities have for the first time a direct, regular line of communication to the English-speaking community, or at least to those government departments, non-government bodies and interested individuals to whom *From the Ethnic Press* is distributed.

The more active certain groups become, however, the more apparent are the differences between one group and another. Some, particularly the more recent arrivals with few educated English-speakers among them, are never heard. Others are highly vocal and—whether they claim to represent ethnics in general or not—are often taken as spokesmen for the ethnic viewpoint. The Melbourne Greeks probably make the most systematic contribution to public thinking: partly through organising or actively participating in conferences and meetings; partly through the English-language *Greek Action Bulletin*, the official organ of the Australian Greek Welfare Society, published regularly since 1972; and partly through the submissions that they now make to all relevant government enquiries.

Finally, voluntary welfare groups have also bred a new body of definers with close experience of the complexities of migrant welfare. The Italian welfare agencies, CO.AS.IT., in Sydney and Melbourne, the Ecumenical Migration Centre at Richmond, Melbourne, with its associated documentation service, Chomi Das, and the Centre for Urban Research and Action (CURA) at Fitzroy, Melbourne, have made major contributions. In a paper for the Poverty Inquiry, David Cox, a former director of the Richmond Centre, has presented the most detailed and coherent account available of the capacity of ethnic populations to operate as organised groups in the articulation of needs and the delivery of welfare services (Cox, 1975).

As the process of differentiation of the defining group occurred, in varying degrees in several major institutions, migrant questions came to be seen as more complex and less amenable to penetration by the conventional tools of goodwill and common sense. Attention continued to focus on problems, but ethnic issues emerged as distinct from migrant issues, and ethnicity came to be defined as embracing far more than the settlement problems of new arrivals.

The conception of migrant problems itself diversified. New areas came under scrutiny, particularly industry, the law and the media. Some observers still found the source of migrant problems in migrants themselves, as individuals, but new voices claimed that the attitudes and values of Australians and the structures of Australian society had been decisive in creating those problems. A comparison of a statement made in 1966 by Elsie Needham, of the Australian Council of Churches, with two statements that appeared ten years later nicely illustrates this distinction. At a Refugee and Migrant Service Conference, Needham described the conclusion she had reached from a recent visit overseas to study refugee and migrant resettlement:

> I was interested to see the same difficulties arising again and again.
>   Many of the basic and recurring problems do not appear to be the fault of the host country, but in the main, are problems deep within the resettler, himself. (1966: 100)

Andrew Jakubowicz and Berenice Buckley, in their report on *Migrants and the Legal System* for the Poverty Inquiry, saw things very differently:

> In the body of this report we are dealing with serious problems. They have often been labelled as 'migrant problems', but this they are not. They are problems which are generated by Australian society and its consistent refusal to accept responsibility for certain results of an immigration program that was the basis of Australia's post-war affluence. (1975: 7)

In 1976, Di Nicola echoed the same theme in relation to migrant welfare:

Migrant problems do not 'belong' to migrants alone, their resolution impinges on the larger society and on the adaptability/sensitivity of its institutions. (1976: 48)

As a complement to this changing conception of the source of migrant problems, a new notion of ethnic communities also filtered and then rushed noisily into public thinking. Where ethnic communities had previously been seen, at best, as marginal, transient and the repositories of safe and (from the larger society's standpoint) irrelevant traditions, and, at worst, as a threat to national unity, they now presented themselves as legitimate interest groups, integral to the social structure as a whole. They may not quite have come to occupy the 'high moral ground' that, according to Nathan Glazer, ethnic minorities in the United States have captured from the trade unions (1977), but they certainly have acquired an aura that associates their claim to exist and be heard with the universally sensitive issue of the right of ethnic minorities to survival in the modern world. The search for a formula or definition that will reconcile this claim with continuing apprehension about the divisiveness of ethnicity—a concern greatly exacerbated by the drama and horror of ethnic confrontations in other countries—has produced some support for the concept of cultural pluralism.

The definition that has come to be attached to cultural pluralism in Australia was foreshadowed in a paper given by J. Zubrzycki to the Australian Citizenship Convention of 1968. While making the assumption that structural assimilation was the ultimate goal, Zubrzycki put forward a case for a modest commitment to cultural diversity through the maintenance of immigrant languages and the development of studies in European culture. One reason for encouraging foreign languages was to promote group and individual interests 'that are not in conflict with national interests' (1968: 27).

In 1973 in a statement called *A Multi-cultural Society for the Future*, A.J. Grassby produced a manifesto for the plural society which, as Minister for Immigration in the new Labor Government, he was to acknowledge and promote. It is a comprehensive document, presenting a position on a range of relevant questions—from child migrant education to ethnic group organisation. Despite its title, it went a long way towards accepting that cultural pluralism entails social pluralism and even touched on ethnic political participation, 'the only acceptable means by which disadvantaged groups may seek to reverse the forces militating against them' (1973: 14). Although, in education in particular, the Commonwealth has given serious attention to working through the implications of Grassby's concept of 'a multi-cultural society', no subsequent official statement has gone on to develop the position that he sketched out. The only government document that comes close to this, it seems to me, is the submission made by the Australian Ethnic Affairs Council (AEAC) to the Australian Population and Immigration Council, *Australia as a Multicultural Society* (Aus., AEAC, 1977).

Several official and committee documents, however, give expression to diverse conceptions of cultural pluralism with varying degrees of concreteness and penetration. One of the most eloquent, the final report of the Commonwealth Committee on Community Relations, chaired by Walter Lippmann (1975), reveals the edginess and ambivalence usually evoked by any sustained examination of what a culturally plural Australia is or would be like. It is difficult to do justice to the Committee's discussion in a few sentences, but the relevant themes can be brought out by quoting directly from the report. The Committee strongly supports the 'pluralistic concept of integration' and

> recommends that community relations in Australia should be restructured in terms of a concept of pluralism which denotes the willingness of the dominant groups . . . to promote or even to encourage some degree of cultural and social variations within an overall context of national unity. . . Pluralism, as defined here, implies first and foremost mutual tolerance and respect for cultural differences by all the members and institutions of Australian society. . . It is in striking a balance between the pressures and requirements of a wide range of ethnic groups and the host society that a fine line divides cultural pluralism from structural pluralism. . . Separatism and segregation become characteristic of [such] a situation which allows a society to develop 'plural structural units' and enshrines the potentiality of conflict and tension between these units. Institutional differences will inevitably prevent common sharing and participation in a universalistic value system and sharing in key social institutions. . . However, the viewpoint of 'cultural pluralism', as advocated by the Committee does enable ethnic groups, if they so desire, to establish their own structures and institutions usually of a cultural and social nature, for example, the media, clubs and restaurants, shops, and community organisations. . . While recognizing the utility and value of ethnic structures in achieving the ends of pluralistic integration, it has to be borne in mind that an excessive emphasis on self-interest programs may prove harmful both to ethnic groups and the host society. These inherent dangers—really the dangers of structural pluralism—can be avoided if the exchange and interaction between all groups is sustained at all levels and in particular through their common participation in the shared and 'universalistic' structures of the wider society. (Aus., Committee on Community Relations, 1975: 48–50)

While cultural pluralism appears to some people an undeveloped concept whose relevance to social policy has yet to be demonstrated (in education, as we shall see in Chapter 4, it often has this connotation), to others it still has an innovative, radical aura, and to others again it seems more like a sedative that inhibits the effort of coming to grips with what I have called elsewhere a 'robust pluralism' (Martin, 1976).

Some ethnics and Australian spokesmen for ethnic interests see the promotion of cultural pluralism as no more than a means of diverting attention from the crucial question of ethnic rights. Aggressive expressions of ethnic rights have come from migrant trade unionists, whose activities will be described in Chapter 7, but the most sustained efforts to promote ethnic rights have been made by the Australian Greek Welfare Society of Melbourne. Like this group, two other Melbourne bodies that have taken a strong position on ethnic rights—the Ecumenical Migration Centre at Richmond, and CURA at Fitzroy—see ethnic rights as attainable only through ethnic group organisation. Writing in 1974 in support of an ethnic rights programme, Alan Matheson of the Ecumenical Migration Centre clearly saw welfare rights workers as operating through ethnic groups:

> Some ethnic groups could receive immediately direct funding and recruit and support their worker; others already have such a person operating in his spare time and it therefore requires appropriate financial resources to be made available to enable more effective work. On the other hand some of the newly arrived groups can best use the resources of a welfare rights worker if he is attached to an already existing community development program. Arrangements like the latter suggestion must always be seen as interim measures, for *the fundamental principle underlying rights programs is that disadvantaged groups themselves have program responsibility.* (1974: 13–14; my italics)

Although the term ethnic *rights* tends to be associated with this position, we have already seen that in the case of the AAP there was no consensus that migrants' rights to welfare could be secured only —or always most appropriately—through ethnic group organisation. On the contrary, some contributors to *Migrants and the AAP* saw the AAP itself as providing an alternative and more viable structure for meeting ethnic welfare needs. Similarly the measures recommended by Jakubowicz and Buckley to facilitate migrants' access to the law involve above all new structures and changes in established arrangements and services (the police courts and the Commonwealth Employment Service, for example), rather than the building up of ethnic groups as vehicles for education and access. Writing on 'citizens' rights' in general, Ken Buckley, President of the Council of Civil Liberties in New South Wales, treats the discrimination experienced by migrants in law as an aspect of the denial of rights to individual members of minorities of all kinds. Citizens' rights are to be protected by public education and vigilance, supported by an Australian Bill of Rights; the work of the police and courts needs to be reformed to accommodate migrants ignorant of English or of Australian law and custom; there is no reference to the role of migrant groups in upholding migrant rights (1976: 111–116).

Structures and activities have also become more differentiated during the seventies, and all three of the possible forms of structural response have accelerated. In the first place, with virtually no structural change, some organisations have become more aware of ethnic situations and more sensitive to ethnic needs simply because personnel now include numbers of individuals of migrant origin, many of them bilinguals. Second, established institutions have also developed special services and substructures for non-English-speaking clients or members: for example, the hospital interpreter service in New South Wales, to be described in Chapter 6. For the purpose of certain areas of institutional activity, ethnic groups have become organisation units in their own right: the Grants to Community Agencies scheme provides the main example; the possibility that ethnic schools run by ethnic groups should become responsible for teaching ethnic languages and cultures is also being canvassed by some proponents of multicultural education (see Chapter 4). Finally, new structures have developed specifically to serve migrants, ethnics or usually more particularly non-English-speakers. The most significant government initiative of this kind is doubtless the Telephone Interpreter Service.

The second of these three forms of structural response, the emergence of special services and substructures, calls for further discussion. In the welfare field new services, like the Commonwealth Grants to Community Agencies scheme (described below), the Richmond Ecumenical Migration Centre and CURA, developed to compensate for the neglect of migrants by existing agencies. The community health centres were intended to give migrants better access to health care than they receive from hospitals and the medical profession, but, as we shall see in Chapter 6, the health centres programme has become so emasculated that it provides no national substitute for regular health care.

For the most part, responses in established institutions have been kept to a minimum and conceived as short-term adjustments to a passing need. In very large measure, they have also been planned simplistically as responses to non-English-speakers, not as responses to migrants or ethnics. In practice this means that by providing information—and, less commonly, translations of applications and other kinds of form—in languages other than English, organisations expect to solve any problems that might arise in the access of non-Anglo-Saxons to services and resources. Helen Ferber's study of Victorian Citizen Advice Bureaux (CABs) illustrates how ill-based such expectations often are. She reports that:

In common with many other Australian services, the CABs seem to assume that the services they offer to everyone will be helpful to migrants provided they are advertised in foreign languages and interpreters can be called in if required . . . The bureau which appeared to have done most to publicize itself in Greek and Italian had only seven enquiries from non-English-speaking migrants during the first year of operation. (1977: 265)

Ferber's account of the services provided by the Good Neighbour Council of Victoria is also illuminating. The Good Neighbour Councils print information leaflets and advice about the services they offer in a number of languages, but at the time of Ferber's study in 1973 only one of three offices offering welfare counselling had a full-time member of staff speaking a language other than English; this was a Yugoslav welfare officer. In a one-month period about six months after this woman began work, the office where she was employed had 129 calls from Yugoslavs, while the other suburban office (also in an area of migrant concentration) had only 2 calls from migrants of non-English-speaking origin and the head office had a total of 135 calls in all (1977: 265–6).

The weak impact of responses limited to mechanical interpreting and literal translations of material produced in the first place for English-speakers is associated with the fact that no durable social relationships or telling experiences flow from such measures. Unless there is a specific decision to assess their impact (which has never happened in any significant case), they generate no feed-back and their value continues to be seen as self-evident and their use as un-problematic. However, once organisations go beyond this limited response to take account of the particularity of migrant experiences and of differences in ethnic interests, values and identities, then ambiguities, difficulties and unintended consequences abound. The role of bilingual and bicultural welfare professionals provides an example. In a paper called 'Social work with Greek migrants: a personal experience of the issues and dilemmas', Loula Rodopoulos says:

As a Greek social worker I have experienced immense difficulties in applying accepted casework techniques in my work with Greek migrants and question whether in fact I am justified in even attempting such application. (1975: 45)

Rodopoulos goes on to argue that—because Greeks have little under-standing of social work, look for practical help and expect professionals and officials to be directive—social workers cannot function effectively as counsellors for Greek migrants in the way they have been trained. Greek or not, social workers face the same frustration and confront the same intransigent situation. 'Solutions' to family problems come from the force of kin group pressures, not through changes in attitude resulting from the social worker's intervention. As Rodopoulos puts it:

any 'insight' provoking counselling sessions initiated by the social worker are, in real terms, meaningless to the family. (1975: 47)

In their study of family, community and welfare services in Melbourne, Jean McCaughey and Wendy Chew present a complementary picture, this time from the point of view of Italian families seeking help from the Italian welfare agency, CO.AS.IT. Some families got the assistance they needed from CO.AS.IT., but others

only wanted financial help in a crisis, and, like other agencies, CO.AS.IT. suffered from inadequate resources to meet the needs of families with no income. As a result these families were often dissatisfied with the help given. Some also resented the case work approach. They simply wanted what they regarded as enough money to meet their needs. They did not want to talk to a social worker about their problems. A typical comment of this group of families was: 'They were all talk, talk, talk, and not enough money'. (1977: 76)

Change in activities and structure can provide the new experience that generates new social knowledge, but a half-hearted, reluctant commitment to migrant interests repeatedly stifles the insight that would point to more radical responses. The Telephone Interpreter Service (TIS) provides a good example. Since this free service was established in 1973, it has been extended to all States except Tasmania. In the last two years, its use has expanded beyond all expectations. In addition to telephone interpreting, TIS operators arrange for community interpreters to attend in person in cases where the need cannot be met over the telephone. This latter function, only a minor component of the service as originally planned, has recently escalated and put TIS under severe financial strain. This very strain demonstrates the need for a general community interpreter service, a need asserted countless times over the years and reiterated by the Task Force on Co-ordination in Welfare and Health (known as the Bailey Committee, after its Chairman, P.H. Bailey). The first report of the Task Force recommended that TIS be returned to the Department of Immigration and Ethnic Affairs, linked with the translation service operated by that Department, and developed in co-operation with States, local government and non-government agencies as 'a comprehensive national interpreter, information and referral service available to all migrants, and to the community needing that kind of service' (Aus., Task Force on Co-ordination in Welfare and Health, 1977: 155).

Contrary to such recommendations and to evidence from the use of TIS, however, government policy is to contain the service, not develop it. Margaret Guilfoyle, Minister for Social Security, expressed the official view in a statement in 1976:

the TIS is under increasing pressure to provide a comprehensive interpreting and translating resource for the community at large. I am somewhat concerned at this development because the Service, being designed to fulfil a specific purpose, was never intended to meet general community needs for interpreting and translating. . . . TIS is not necessarily a substitute for facilities which other Government departments and instrumentalities that have frequent contact with migrants, and the community in general, should provide themselves. This applies equally to private industry and to professional groups like doctors and solicitors who might, for example, be thinking in terms of collectively seeking ways and means of meeting their own interpreting and translating needs. (Aus., Minister for Social Security, 1976: 5)

In other words, the ball goes back into the court of the very groups whose failure to do anything about communicating with non-English-speakers has forced the unwelcome expansion on TIS and whose collective thinking, when addressed to the issue, has rarely gone beyond the rhetoric of concern and a demand for *government* action.

An examination of how TIS resources are being used will dispel any remaining doubt about Commonwealth priorities. The geographical area covered by TIS is being expanded and ingenious technical innovations, like dual hand-sets, are being adopted to make the service more flexible. But the wage rate of community interpreters—who are paid on a contract basis to do telephone interpreting in languages not covered by the salaried staff, and to make community visits—has not changed since the service was introduced; it is approximately equal to the wages paid to domestic cleaners, and, according to the Minister, is not to be increased in the current financial year (Aus., Senate, Estimates Committee D, 8 September 1977: 177). In this respect, TIS practice simply repeats one of the most consistent themes in the past thirty years of response to non-English-speaking migrants: the exploitation of bilingual and multilingual migrants as unpaid or underpaid interpreters.[4]

If we shift focus from definers, definitions and practices and turn to a comparison of institutions with one another, the process of differentiation is again evident. Within the Commonwealth, as the Bailey Committee cautiously puts it, 'the services of many departments are deficient, having regard to the ethnic composition of the population' (Aus., Task Force on Co-ordination in Welfare and Health, 1977: 153). But response has occurred in areas for which the Department of Immigration was originally responsible: that is, the education of migrant children and adults, and migrant welfare. Limited and tardy though government initiatives in these matters have been, they have nevertheless contributed to debate, new knowledge and new structures. In other areas that have been repeatedly nominated as exerting a crucial influence on migrant settlement—health, employment, housing and access to social security benefits—but which were never (except temporarily and exceptionally) within the

Department of Immigration's orbit, the Commonwealth has responded to the migrant presence with abysmal indifference and neglect, still justified on the grounds of the old assimilability thesis. A comment made by the Department of Social Security to the Senate Standing Committee on Foreign Affairs and Defence during the Committee's inquiry into 'the plight and circumstances of Vietnamese and other refugees' illustrates the thinking that prevails in most departments:

> In some cases efforts are made to follow-up families who leave the hostel
> . . . while in others follow-up action is considered to be unnecessary and
> even undesirable. In taking this position the Department is prompted
> by the dangers of fostering long-term dependency relationships which
> militate against the successful settlement of these people. Efforts are
> made to encourage the former refugees to become fully integrated
> members of the community as soon as practicable. (Aus., Senate,
> Standing Committee, 1976: 85)

In an unusually outspoken and thorough report, the Senate Standing Committee rejected both the argument and the evidence put forward by the Department of Social Security: in reality, the Committee concluded, dependency was being fostered by *neglect* of the refugees' special circumstances and needs and, in place of efforts to encourage integration, there was general lack of concern for the well-being or future of the refugees.

In the most recent of a number of stringent critiques of employment services for migrants, the Review of the Commonwealth Employment Service (the Norgard report, after its chairman J.D. Norgard) found the Commonwealth Employment Service too often 'unable to overcome language barriers' and deficient in providing job and social security information in multilingual form ('[a]lthough this need has been known for some time'), and its staff in need of training to enable them to give effective help to migrant workers (Aus., Review of the Commonwealth Employment Service, 1977: 95–7).

Just as, within the Commonwealth, the job of responding to the migrant presence has been allotted to specific agencies (with other government authorities thereby absolved from responsibility and free to relegate migrant issues to the wastes of nondecision-making), so, between the Commonwealth and States, migration has been defined as the Commonwealth's burden and State-initiated response has been minimal (although some recent developments will be noted). The institutional areas in which there is the greatest discrepancy between potential and actual response are those which the Department of Immigration never entered in any serious way and which are primarily State responsibilities: that is, housing and health.

The process of allocating the response to migrants to selected agencies and absolving the rest from responsibility is repeated at the level of community service groups. Although the Commonwealth-financed Good Neighbour Councils were originally intended as co-ordinating bodies, they have had indifferent success in activating churches or other community groups to serve migrants or to extend their membership among migrants—and, to the limited extent that the Councils have played a role in the settlement of migrants of non-Anglo-Saxon origin, it has been through welfare and other services they have provided themselves.

If we leave aside the Good Neighbour Councils and look across the spectrum of voluntary community groups, we find a few that are specifically concerned with migrants and a majority that are over-whelmingly Anglo-Saxon in membership and clientele, and are un-responsive to the migrant presence, except for occasional token gestures of goodwill. The Melbourne study by McCaughey, Shaver and Ferber vividly documents this disjunction so far as welfare services are concerned, from the point of view of migrant families as well as voluntary groups. The family study found that most migrants in the sample fell into the group of 'vulnerable' families—not into the groups described as 'copers' or 'passive'—and were 'isolated and alienated from the surrounding community'. None of the twelve Italian families in this group 'had any contact with the municipal social worker nor had they any knowledge of local services' (McCaughey and Chew, 1977: 53, 73). In one suburb several Greeks, one a priest, the others mostly professionals, provided material and other help for the large Greek population—but they operated for the most part separately from the established community groups, which they saw as having little or nothing to offer Greek migrants (Shaver, 1977: 216). Ferber's account of Citizen Advice Bureaux (CABs) draws the same picture from yet another angle. Most CABs, she writes,

> do not understand what is involved in helping our second identifiable category of non-users [of the CABs]: those migrants most in need of information and help of all kinds, namely newly-arrived migrants who speak no English. (1977: 265)

The total spectrum of community groups is now becoming further differentiated to a significant degree as some ethnic and inter-ethnic groups expand their functions and their relations with other groups. The organisations that virtually all migrant populations formed at one time or another in the fifties and sixties were devoted principally to sociability, the maintenance of ethnic culture, religion and language, and the pursuit of political causes associated with their home countries —and they functioned largely in isolation from the Australian community (see Cox, 1975; Martin, 1972a). There were always of course many differences in group organisation from one ethnic population to another, but salient new sources of differentiation have emerged in the past few years. Most important have been the interdependent changes in function and in relations with established structures (government and voluntary): as some ethnic populations have developed welfare and service functions, they have attracted government resources and have become part of a community network. Thus they have developed a degree of organisation and expertise and a community role, which distinguishes them as much from other ethnics as all migrant communities were once distinguished from the established groups of Australian society. Table 2.4 provides a rough indication of the degree of differentiation among ethnic groups in terms of their access to the services of professionals of their own background.

It is important, finally, to take note of one factor that has been decisive in encouraging the various processes of institutional differentiation that I have described. This is the provision of government—principally Commonwealth—resources. Although I have not tried to measure precisely the relation between sources, resources and a differentiated response, a general trend can be suggested. Where the Government has not played a role as catalyst, co-ordinator or initiator, nor made available resources of money, personnel or expertise, response has been weak, slow and undiscriminating. The media are a notable example. Apart from providing radio and, since 1971, television English lessons, the Government has in the past played only one significant role, and that a negative one: to restrict the use of foreign languages in programmes and advertisements. ABC and commercial radio stations broadcast some cultural and information-giving programmes in languages other than English, and in 1973 the Commonwealth took the major—and among ethnic communities, highly acclaimed—step of introducing ethnic radio. In general, however, regular radio programming gives little acknowledgement of ethnicity in Australian society, and television even less. As A.J. Grassby said in *A Multi-cultural Society for the Future*, referring in particular to television:

> Where is the Maltese process worker, the Finnish carpenter, the Italian concrete layer, the Yugoslav miner or—dare I say it—the Indian scientist? Where do these people belong, in all honesty, if not in today's composite Australian image? Are they to be *non-people* . . . because they do not happen to fit the largely American-oriented stereotypes of our entertainment industry? (1973: 4)

In its 1976 report, the Advisory Committee on Program Standards of the Australian Broadcasting Control Board also deplored the fact that the media ignore minorities of all kinds. So far as ethnic minorities are concerned, the report said, the media do little to enhance inter-cultural understanding, to deal with problems of communication, or to spread information. By ignoring ethnic cultures, they deprive both

Table 2.4 *Ratio of ethnic professionals to ethnic population, Australia, 1971*

Ethnic origin	Number of professionals per 1000 population of same ethnic origin									
	Upper professionals			Lower professionals			Doctors,	Nurses,	Social and welfare workers,	Clergymen,
	Overseas-born	Australian-born	Total	Overseas-born	Australian-born	Total	Overseas-born	Overseas-born	Overseas-born	Overseas-born
German	10.1	2.1	12.2	46.0	5.9	51.9	1.3	4.7	0.4	0.3
Greek	1.0	1.9*	2.9	3.3	2.6*	5.9	0.1	0.1	0.0	0.3
Italian	1.5	1.3	2.8	5.7	3.0	8.7	0.1	0.2	0.1	0.1
Maltese	2.0	0.1	2.4	7.8	1.8	9.6	0.2	0.5	0.1	0.4
Dutch	8.4	0.4	8.7	37.0	3.3	40.3	0.4	5.1	0.5	0.8
Polish	12.7	3.8	16.5	22.3	8.0	30.3	3.4	1.8	0.2	0.5
Yugoslav	2.0	0.6	2.6	9.3	1.9	11.1	0.3	0.8	0.1	0.2
Total population			16.2			52.3	All doctors 1.3	All nurses 4.4	All social and welfare workers 0.4	All clergymen 0.7

*Numerator includes Cyprus.

Source: Aus., ABS, *Census* 1971. The total number or persons of a specific ethnic 'origin' has been arrived at by adding persons born in that country of origin to persons born in Australia with either (1) both parents born in that country or (2) mother born in that country and father born in a different non-English-speaking country. Ratios have then been calculated with the number of ethnic professionals in each occupational category as the numerator and the total number of persons of that origin, divided by 1000, as the denominator.

Anglo–Australians and ethnics of access to the 'rich diversity' of a plural society (Aus., Australian Broadcasting Control Board, 1976). Government has not tried—by its own example, by intervening through its controlling powers or by providing resources—to change this situation. Also, among the commercially controlled media, the goal of maximising audiences and profits continues to overwhelm attention to minorities, and even to subdue recognition of Anglo-Australian culture in favour of material imported from the United States.[5]

Where government has taken an active role of some kind, the effectiveness, range, subtlety and authenticity of response have varied greatly. One source of variation appears to be the degree of isolation, on the one hand, or of integration into established structures, on the other, of the agencies through which government influence and resources have been channelled. The point can be made by comparing the adult and child education programmes. The adult education programme has always been the responsibility of the Commonwealth Department of Immigration, or, since 1975, the Department of Education, but is administered and staffed through the State education departments. The core of the programme is, as it has always been, constituted of part-time classes, mostly conducted in school premises out of working hours. Innovations introduced in the past ten years are an attempt to meet some of the criticisms repeatedly levelled at these classes, but, as Table 2.5 shows, enrolments in the new full-time courses, in courses in industry and in the home tutor scheme are only 12 per cent of total enrolments. Moreover, while enrolments in what appear to be the least effective courses are going up, absolutely and proportionally, enrolments in full-time and industry courses went down between 1975–1976 and 1976–1977. The only students receiving a living allowance under the programme in 1976–1977 were the 3924 in full-time courses. The first full-time courses for students with little or no English were introduced at the end of 1977.

The only serious public examination ever made of the adult migrant education programme is contained in recent papers by the Victorian Migrant Education Branch (MEB) Staff Association and the New South Wales Association of Adult Migrant Teachers (*Migration Action*, 1976; Victorian MEB, 1976), and in a New South Wales Government report (NSW, Department of Education and Public Service Board, n.d. [1977]).[6] The Victorian statement points to a number of shortcomings: the confused distribution of responsibility between State and Commonwealth; the concept of migrant education as meeting a temporary need; the small number of students catered for; the inadequacy of student allowances; the fact that courses and materials assume literacy in the migrant's native tongue and lack the variety needed to meet the range of student needs; inadequate selection

Table 2.5 *Adult Migrant Education Program: number of students enrolled in courses, Australia, 1975–76 and 1976–77*

Course	1975–76		1976–77	
	Number	**Per cent**	**Number**	**Per cent**
Full-time				
Intensive	1 474	1.7	1 267	1.3
Accelerated	2 922	3.4	2 657	2.7
Part-time				
Accelerated	9 350	11.0	9 538	9.8
Advanced	2 968	3.5	3 270	3.4
Continuation	45 621	53.5	56 136	57.9
Special Program				
Radio/correspondence	16 723	19.6	16 538	17.0
Industry	2 293	2.7	2 088	2.2
Home tutor	3 947	4.6	5 510	5.7
Total enrolments	85 298	100	97 004	100

Source: Aus., Department of Education, unpublished information provided February 1978.

procedures for recruiting students into the more demanding courses (with the result that for many the experience is 'humiliating and soul-destroying'); and the lack of opportunity for teachers to contribute to the production of materials. A major factor in the perpetuation of these shortcomings has clearly been the isolation of the migrant teaching service:

> The M.E.B. staff have never known if they are really State or Federal employees, nor to where to turn to demand improvements in the program and in their conditions of employment, *for brick walls abound.* From one authority one may meet dumb silence, from another an ignorant shrug of the shoulders, from a third, a 'tut-tut', from another the suggestion that things aren't really so bad, and from everyone, but everyone, a rapid 'passing of the buck'. (Victorian MEB, 1976: 11; my italics)

The production of the Victorian statement is itself testimony to the claim that the newly formed Staff Association of salaried MEB teachers 'has been a catalyst for much of the re-thinking that has taken place' (Victorian MEB, 1976: 13).

The New South Wales report, by J.D. Gibson, a Project Officer of the Public Service Board, was commissioned in 1976 in response to the activism of the New South Wales Association of Adult Migrant Teachers. The enquiry seems to have been somewhat hamstrung by the fact that the Commonwealth was at the same time reviewing the

Adult Migrant Education Service (AMES) and the Commonwealth–States arrangements entered into in 1951, and never formalised, for the funding and administration of the Service. The Commonwealth inquiry has not been made public, but the New South Wales report was written with advance knowledge of the Commonwealth position; Gibson's recommendations, it is implied, would not cut across Commonwealth intentions. The New South Wales report is in fact more important as a political document, aiming to pour oil on troubled waters, than as a source of information about AMES. Indeed Gibson asserts the 'great need for a specific programme of evaluation' (NSW, n.d. [1977]: 11), which is the very thing one would have assumed his own investigation would at least initiate. Nevertheless, muffled behind Gibson's favourable account of the language–teaching activities of AMES, the problems come through patently enough: an internally fragmented organisation, cluttered with day-to-day administration, in poor communication with both the State Government and the Commonwealth, lacking a research capacity, and out of touch with its potential clients or the organisations that should be bringing migrants within its purview. Gibson does not make the point that he could have stressed: the courses that he judged to be particularly effective—the home tutor scheme, courses in industry, and classes for women—cater for approximately half the number of students taking radio and correspondence courses, 'which received least commendation' from his informants (NSW, n.d. [1977]: 25).

Overall, the teaching of English to adult migrants at the State level, and the production of materials in the Commonwealth Department of Education, have clearly suffered over the years from intellectual and structural isolation.[7] Not only has AMES developed as a largely forgotten Commonwealth outpost in the States, but the programme suffers from lack of the migrant participation—which could have been forthcoming if the medium of instruction had not been English alone, if bilingual teachers had been employed and if ethnic communities had been involved. Adult migrant education today remains in much the same situation as child migrant education in the sixties.

It is also instructive to compare the Australian Council of Social Service (ACOSS) and the Good Neighbour movement. ACOSS is a co-ordinating body, which receives a Commonwealth subsidy and provides the most thoughtful and carefully researched continuing critique on welfare matters in Australia. In recent years it has contributed to a more differentiated and authentic definition of migrant welfare in two ways: by placing migrant questions in perspective in terms of welfare policy in general, as in its submission to the Poverty Inquiry (ACOSS, 1973), and by conducting research and seminars on specific problems, such as the mental health of migrants (ACOSS, 1971, 1976) and interpreter needs (ACOSS, 1974). The strength of ACOSS's work clearly lies partly in its independence from government control and partly in its capacity to tap the experience of workers immediately involved in welfare practice. The Good Neighbour movement, on the other hand, is not an effective co-ordinator, provides a largely self-contained welfare service and serves English-speaking migrants best. Being well-endowed financially by the Commonwealth Government, it has succeeded in maintaining considerable immunity from community influences, while at the same time lacking the independence to develop as watch-dog or critic of government policy. It has promoted a bland, self-satisfied rather than a penetrating and discriminating picture of the migrant situation, and has long resisted proposals for an enquiry into its work (the most recent made by the Bailey Committee). However, it is now under scrutiny by the Review of Post-arrival Programmes and Services to Migrants, initiated by the Prime Minister in August 1977 and under the chairmanship of F. Galbally (known as the Galbally Committee).[8]

Politics and response in the seventies

The structural arrangements and processes that have been described in the previous section are the product of complex historical factors, and are not explicable in any direct sense in terms of the philosophies or policies of the political parties that have held office in the Commonwealth (or the States) during the seventies. It is important, however, to address ourselves directly to the question of whether Labor and Liberal Governments have promoted different definitions of the migrant presence and different responses to it. As a preliminary to the discussion of that question—which forms the conclusion to the present chapter—I should reiterate that I am dealing here only with the question of response to migrants *qua* migrants, not with the different and larger question of the way in which government policy in general has affected the experience or situation of migrants.

As we have already seen, from the mid-sixties onwards the Liberal Government became more active in dealing with the settlement of migrants—and the Labor challenge of 1969 and 1972, combined with an increasing awareness that the migrant vote might be worth cultivating, gave further stimulus to this activity. When in 1972 A.J. Grassby became Minister for Immigration under the new Labor Government, the Immigration portfolio burst forth as a dynamic and highly visible source of energy. However, Grassby was only at the beginning of establishing his new order when he lost his seat in the

1974 elections. E.G. Whitlam, again at the head of a Labor Government, took the opportunity to dismember the Department of Immigration, transferring passport control to Foreign Affairs, education to the Department of Education and social welfare to Social Security. What was left of Immigration was then amalgamated with the Department of Labor (see Price and Martin eds, 1976*a*: A6–12). Because the intake of migrants had already been severely reduced, there was a widespread feeling, both inside the bureaucracy and out, that the Government was curtailing its involvement in the immigration area in general. The Department of Immigration lost numbers both because of the transfer of functions to other departments and because staff voluntarily moved out of the public service or to departments with higher morale and a brighter future. When the Liberal Government again came into power at the end of 1975, the name of the Department was once more changed and the new title, Immigration and Ethnic Affairs, was intended to convey the Government's recognition of 'the special needs of migrant peoples' and its determination '[t]o fully overcome these needs and at the same time offer the maximum opportunity for ethnic groups to continue to contribute to Australian society in general' (Liberal and National Country Parties, 1975). To give substance to the new name, an Ethnic Affairs Office was established within the Department, but the question of the return of the former education and welfare functions became the subject of intense inter-departmental rivalry. Following the Bailey Committee's recommendations (1977: 158–9)—that the Migrant Community Services Branch of the Department of Social Security be returned to Immigration and Ethnic Affairs ('on the basis that the Department's functions are strictly limited to the post-arrival stage'), that Immigration also assume responsibility for TIS (but not for Grants to Community Agencies or Good Neighbour Councils), and that all functional departments should improve their capacity to serve migrants—the Government established the Galbally Review Group to assess 'the effectiveness of Commonwealth Government programs specifically directed at migrants', to examine general community Commonwealth programmes which have an impact on the social welfare of migrants, and to clarify 'the Commonwealth's role, and that of other spheres of Government, non-government organisations and the private sector, in the provision of services to migrants' (Aus., Review of Post Arrival Programs and Services to Migrants, 1977: 1).[9]

However, immediately following the further elections called by the Liberal Government at the end of 1977, a year before its three-year term was up, new administrative arrangements (transferring migrant welfare and adult education back to Immigration and Ethnic Affairs) were announced. In a letter of protest to the Prime Minister, ACOSS reiterated its position that 'migrants should not be segregated from the general community services in this manner' and went on:

> The decision is of particular concern to us, since it pre-empts the report of the Galbally review of post-arrival services to migrants. ACOSS, as well as other groups, have just presented submissions to the Galbally review on this very matter . . .
>
> The new arrangements will be confusing to migrants, who justifiably will not understand why in respect to certain services they are set apart from the general community. (ACOSS, 1977)

Confusion—not only on the part of migrants, by any means—has certainly been associated with the several re-organisations of the Department of Immigration and the re-packaging of migrant-related functions that have occurred in the past five years. The administrative disruption associated with these changes also seems to account for some features of Commonwealth operations during this period, although it is not possible to say how far other considerations—such as the general cut-back in Commonwealth expenditure, which began while Labor was still in government—were responsible, or to what extent the problems of re-organisation have provided a welcome rationale for delaying decisions and developments on which ministers or bureaucrats were in no hurry to commit themselves.

Indeed, Commonwealth commitment on migrant questions since Grassby went out of office in 1974 is probably best described as *non*-committal. Despite much huffing and puffing over the re-structuring, disbanding and re-forming of advisory committees—and several foreshadowings of fundamental re-thinking of the Government's role in migrant settlement and in dealing with ethnic questions (one example of which will be given)—no coherent policy has emerged. Instead, decisions affecting migrants are made primarily in consideration of other interests or simply are not made at all. It is not that one party has thrown out the policy of its predecessors in office in favour of its own, but that the lack of commitment to *any* policy—and reluctance or inability to think through the intellectual and administrative complexities involved in responding to the migrant presence—has led to stalling, timidity and the avoidance of controversy at all costs. In the context of the present study, this can best be illustrated by reference to the wary and hesitant way in which succeeding Governments have handled the results of official inquiries.

At the beginning of its brief 1970–1972 period of expansive concern with long-term questions of migration and population, the Department of Immigration not only established the National Population Inquiry and initiated a cost-benefit study of migration, but also decided to undertake the first nation-wide survey of migrant settlement. By the time the survey was carried out in 1973, Labor was in power; and by the time the results of the inquiry were ready for analysis, the Department had been dismembered and was seriously short of research staff. After a period during which the Poverty Inquiry was the only body to show any interest in examining the survey findings, the task of producing a report on the study fell to the Social Studies Committee of the newly formed Australian Population and Immigration Council (APIC), by which Labor had replaced the old Immigration Planning Council. By February 1976 when the Committee presented its report, the Labor Government had gone out of office and APIC was in abeyance, waiting to be reconstituted. The new Minister did not table the report until seven months later. (Somewhere along the line, something had happened to the sense of urgency, which in 1971–1972 had dictated that the survey would be cross-sectional instead of longitudinal 'in order to obtain results more quickly' [Aus., APIC, 1976:1].) The report received the minimum of publicity. Some of the survey findings undeniably called for serious attention from the Government, as it was originally intended they should do. But neither these findings—the most important related to the underutilisation of migrant skills and the crucial influence of knowledge of English on migrants' job histories and incomes—nor the general conclusion that 'migrants' disadvantages often persist well past the initial settlement period' (Aus., APIC, 1976: 128) prompted public expression of interest on the part of the Government.

The reception of the report of the Committee on the Teaching of Migrant Languages in Schools more directly illustrates how one Government's enthusiasm can become its successor's embarrassment. The Committee was established in 1974 by the Minister for Education in the Labor Government. By the time the Committee reported in March 1976, the Liberal Government was in power. The report was tabled in the Senate in December and debated in the House of Representatives in April of the following year as a 'matter of public importance' on the initiative of E.G. Whitlam, now Leader of the Opposition. Whitlam accused the Government of sitting on the report and tabling it 'on the last day . . . before the Christmas recess', adding:

> This needless and unforgivable delay prevented public study of the report and forestalled any debate on it in the Parliament. (Aus., House of Reps., *Parl. Debates*, Weekly Hansard no. 8, 1977: 1277)

Speaking for the Minister for Education in the Senate, R.I. Viner defended the delay on the ground that the Government was studying the report in the context of other related documents. He informed the House that

> within a few months—we cannot be more specific than that because of the magnitude of the task to be undertaken—a consolidated report will be possible. On the basis of that . . . the Government will give serious

consideration to the implementation of what is necessary in this area of the teaching of migrant languages in schools. (Aus., House of Reps., *Parl. Debates*, Weekly Hansard no. 8, 1977: 1279)

The consolidated report has yet to appear (January 1978), but in the meantime—as we shall see in Chapter 4—the thorough and considered Migrant Languages study has proved a potent fuel for ethnic and other pressure groups in their drive to have the teaching of migrant languages and cultures defined as a government, and particularly a Commonwealth, responsibility.

Although, as I have said, vagaries in Commonwealth response to the migrant presence in the seventies are not to be explained simplistically in terms of the differing migration and ethnic policies of the Labor and Liberal Governments, the two cases described in some detail hint at a far-reaching difference in political philosophy: Labor avowedly initiating, activist and interventionist; the Liberal stance precisely the opposite. The difference became explicit in the Migrant Languages debate, with the Opposition Leader referring to 'the ultimate abdication of Federal responsibility for our migrant communities' as 'another example of the real meaning of Fraser federalism', and the Liberal speakers emphasising that it was up to the schools and the States to decide to what extent and how the Committee's recommendations should be implemented. The example of Victoria in recruiting teachers from Greece, said one of these speakers, W. Yates, shows 'exactly what happened when one of the governments practising the new federalism started to work on this report' (Aus., House of Reps., *Parl. Debates*, Weekly Hansard no. 8, 1977: 1285).

Geoffrey Sawer interprets the 'New Federalism' of the Whitlam era as a weak version of what he calls, after the German, 'organic' federalism: the Federal elements consisting of 'a guaranteed *structure* of Regional government alongside the guaranteed Centre structure', with major policy made at the Centre, and administration and some local policy decisions carried out in the regions. Fraser Federalism is, by contrast, of the 'co-operative co-ordinate' kind. It represents a reaction against 'the centralising, welfare-spending and even mildly socialist "New Federalism" of the Whitlam period'. Its general aim

is to restore a greater measure of State autonomy, particularly in tax and spending choices; the method is to increase State access to taxation, in particular income taxation, and to reduce the volume of Commonwealth grants to States, and in particular the relative volume of conditional grants, and to make the conditions of conditional grants less detailed and less rigorously policed.

The 'federal system' aspects of the Fraser policy are, however, but parts of a broad economic and social policy; reduction of the public sphere, encouragement of the private sphere, economy, reduction in spending on welfare services and on the needs of disadvantaged minorities. (Sawer, 1977: 18, 19)

The implications of Fraser Federalism—and the 'broad economic and social policy' associated with it—are not at all clear, so far as official response to migrants is concerned. The philosophy is not, in any case, all of a piece and its implementation is not a straightforward matter of transferring power to the States, but a complex process of negotiation, bargaining and bullying which, up to the present time, has left strategic powers in Commonwealth hands (Wiltshire, 1977). In particular situations, pragmatism and considerations of immediate advantage often outweigh the influence of political philosophy in determining the decisions that are taken. Moreover, the intellectual labour of translating political philosophy into a migrant settlement policy has never been undertaken (the start made by APIC's Green Paper, *Immigration Policies and Australia's Population*, 1977, has still to be followed through), and government practice in this area shows much of the caution, 'fumbling, indecision and procrastination' which Sawer describes as characteristic of Fraser Federalism compared with its North American models (1977: 18). The present ambiguous situation is, however, likely to continue, because it keeps alive the possibility that any of the contending sections and objectives in the migrant field may ultimately attract government support and preserves the Government from open confrontation with critics— particularly ethnic critics—who would be likely to become vocal if Liberal philosophy were consistently applied to the matter of migrant settlement.

Nevertheless, some implications of Fraser Federalism are already coming into the light and some serious critics are already at work. Yates' commendation of Victoria for taking the initiative in recruiting Greek teachers points to one of these implications: the effect of Liberal policies in increasing differentiation of response to migrants at a number of levels. With no expansion of support for new and still experimental programmes, bodies that have already established a claim to resources are in a good position to keep and build on their advantages, while others fall farther behind—and some that might have secured a slice of a bigger cake lack the incentive even to get to the point of deserving it. The Grants to Community Agencies scheme provides the most obvious example. The scheme was established in 1968 under the Commonwealth Department of Immigration to make funds available to non-government agencies to enable them to employ welfare workers (originally only social workers) to assist migrant clients. Of the 50 grants at present in operation, 37 were approved during the first five years of the scheme's operation, 1968–1972, and only 1 has been approved in each of the last three years, 1975–1977. Because the number of grants was frozen by the Labor Government in 1975 and there is virtually no turnover in agencies funded under the scheme, groups that did not get in on the ground floor have little hope of doing so now. The bodies that have benefited from the scheme since the beginning are mainly welfare agencies attached to the established churches and Good Neighbour Councils. Only two ethnic agencies were funded in the first two years of the scheme (three, if the Australian Jewish Welfare and Relief Society is included) and only three have been added since then. Altogether these six agencies receive 11 of the 50 grants: 3 go to Greek groups; 1 each to German, Jewish, Turkish and Lebanese groups; and 4 to the Italian association CO.AS.IT., which also receives a subsidy from the Italian Government. There are more applications outstanding than there are grants in operation, and many of these are from ethnic communities that claim they could effectively use a social worker— although how many would be regarded as stable or organised enough to merit one is another question. Without the funds, professional expertise and participation in a welfare network (for which the scheme provides the only access), some of these communities will certainly abandon ideas of developing a welfare role.

It is likely, however, that Liberal policies are having their greatest differentiating effect at a regional level. This is the concomitant of the Liberal policy, which envisages, as Sawer puts it,

> with some justification . . . that many States will elect to do without a public activity, or a supervision of a private activity, or a welfare service, rather than find the requisite money themselves. (Sawer, 1977: 19)

Regional differentiation in welfare and education has particularly significant implications for response to migrants. (Employment remains too important a matter to be taken out of the Federal Government's hands.) The education aspect will be taken up in Chapter 4. So far as welfare is concerned, Adam Graycar argues that the Fraser Government has returned to the residual view of social welfare espoused by its Liberal predecessors. This view 'holds that social welfare institutions should come into play only when the normal structures of supply, the family and the market, break down'. The 'institutional' approach, which Labor attempted to develop, 'is based on a more innovative and aggressive approach to social malaise' and views social welfare bodies 'as major and permanent institutions rather than as residual agencies in industrial society'. Residual views are associated with the concept of individual deficiency as the cause of welfare problems; the institutional approach aligns with the concept of social problems as the product of systems and institutions. These contrasting approaches to welfare 'need different interpretations of federalism for their attainment':

> A residual view of welfare with a prime focus on charitable type cash payments fits well with a weak central government interpretation. Most of the ameliorative services are carried out by State Governments, and the Commonwealth writes cheques for various types of pensioners and beneficiaries. An interpretation of social welfare that goes well beyond income security to community functioning, and places emphasis on citizen involvement and citizen participation in quality of life issues, needs a federalism in which a strong central government can develop a national strategy in co-operation with its target population, i.e. communities themselves. (Graycar, 1977: 155)

The impact on minorities in general, and migrants in particular, of a residual, individual deficiency concept of welfare—associated with devolution of responsibility and cut-backs in public expenditure—is, quite simply, that initiating and long-term planning on a national scale disappears as a government function and the Commonwealth role is limited to activities it cannot avoid. What Bruce McFarlane wrote of the economic policy of the Liberals in 1968 aptly describes their social policy today: 'change is not initiated it is reluctantly conceded' (quoted in Catley and McFarlane, 1974: 1). The case of the Telephone Interpreter Service, already recounted, illustrates the point. That the Commonwealth accepts that these policies will accentuate differences bewteen the States is made explicit in the report of the South Australian Working Committee on Interpreting and Translating. The Committee reports information given by the Commonwealth Public Service Board that, with regard to the development of interpreting and translating services, the 'Commonwealth will liaise with States individually i.e. what happens with New South Wales won't affect South Australia' (SA, Working Committee, 1977: Appendix 2).

It can of course be argued that devolution allows State and local government authorities to pursue whatever welfare policies they wish: the Commonwealth, in other words, is imposing neither a residual model nor any other. But in practice this is largely a hollow option. The major reason is that local authorities are severely constrained in dealing with welfare problems generated by national institutions and practices (Graycar, 1977: 159). Where, for example, Commonwealth practice results in the downgrading of income security for low-income earners (Harris and Grewal, 1977), State and local authorities (and voluntary associations) are left with only one alternative: to provide short-term 'band-aid' income support. Another reason is that—partly as the result of the States' reluctance to assume major responsibility for unpopular taxing decisions (Mathews, 1977), and partly because the Commonwealth retains significant controls over money-raising and spending (Sawer, 1977)—the States do not in fact have enough financial leeway to go their own way in the enormously expensive health and welfare fields.

Despite these constraints on State and local authorities, the room left for State initiatives by the curtailment of Federal welfare responsibilities (and specifically the abandonment of the AAP) seems clearly to be associated with increased regional differentiation so far as migrant welfare is concerned. Following on action begun by its Liberal predecessor, the Labor Government in New South Wales is developing a vigorous programme of response to migrant/ethnic issues under the aegis of the Ethnic Affairs Division in the Premier's Department, the Ethnic Affairs Commission and other functional departments (such as the Health Commission, whose hospital interpreter scheme will be described in Chapter 6). No other State is as active, but Victoria and South Australia have taken some similar initiatives. The other States show little sign of using their newly acquired powers in the interests of migrant well-being. So far as local government authorities are concerned, neither Whitlam's attempt to bypass them through establishing a new regional structure for the AAP nor Fraser's implementation of devolution has changed their structure, functions or control of resources significantly (Harris, 1977; Robbins, 1977; Wood, 1977). They continue to reveal an immense range of variation in terms of their welfare role, allocation of funds to welfare, professionalisation and efficiency (see Aus., Task Force on Co-ordination in Welfare and Health, 1977: 32–5, 50–2). Commonwealth policies may intensify and certainly will not 'rectify' the situation reported in a national survey carried out by the Department of Immigration in 1974: according to this survey the contribution of local government authorities

> to the settlement, welfare, and integration of immigrants appeared, in general, to be uneven, unco-ordinated, and lacking explicit integration with other programmes. Action to rectify this appeared desirable. (Aus., Department of Immigration, 1974: 25)

During the fifties and sixties there was little competition for the job of defining the meaning of migrant in Australian society, and Commonwealth-inspired definitions of their essential assimilability held sway—despite the occasional scepticism of the press, claims from academics that things were more complex than official views suggested, and the silent rejection of that definition by migrants themselves. The situation now is very different. The last of those consensus-building occasions, the Australian Citizenship Conventions, was held in 1970 and since that time—except for the somewhat illusory impression of agreed-upon ends and self-evident means created by the Grassby reforms 1973–1974—the Commonwealth definition has lost its former certainty and single-mindedness. The distribution of migrant functions between several government departments has contributed to this process, but even within the Immigration Department core the old self-confidence about who migrants are and what the role of government is in migrant settlement has gone. Official advisory bodies have added their diverse and not always mutually consistent views (cf. Aus., APIC, *Immigration Policies and Australia's Population*, 1977, and Aus., AEAC, *Australia as a Multicultural Society*, 1977). Official inquiries, most notably the National Population Inquiry and the Commission of Inquiry into Poverty, and new statutory authorities, particularly the Schools Commission and the Office of the Commissioner for Community Relations, have disposed of simplistic, monolithic definitions by giving substance to the diversity of migrant characteristics, experiences and situations. State Governments are also beginning to produce their own interpretations of the migrant presence, as Chapters 3 and 4 will illustrate. Outside government, political parties, voluntary associations (with ACOSS as their most articulate spokesman), churches, trade unions, ethnic communities, academic and a range of other groups all offer something to the construction of social knowledge about migrants in Australia.

The three major definitions that now jostle each other in public discourse derive from three different periods in the history of response to migrants during the past thirty years: from the fifties and early sixties, migrants are assimilable (without undue strain on themselves or undue change on the part of the Australian community); from the late sixties, early seventies, migrants are people with problems (mostly seen as arising from some inadequacy or unsuitability within themselves); from the mid-seventies, migrants are a minority pressure group with rights to power and participation (Storer ed., [1975]; Martin, 1976). The first two definitions emphasise the transient, marginal status of newcomers as *migrants*; the third conceives of culturally diverse groups as established, legitimate structures within Australian society—*ethnic* comes to the fore as an appropriate term to convey the claim to dignity which this definition implies.

NOTES

1. In a review of *Arrivals and Departures*, C.A. Price (1967) asserted that Jupp 'completely misunderstands the Good Neighbour Councils' and rejected Jupp's assessment of Good Neighbour work. Sharp disagreement about the value of the movement continues. In its final report on *The Departure of Settlers from Australia*, 1967, the Committee on Social

Patterns of the Commonwealth Immigration Advisory Council noted that 'most opinions' expressed to the Committee were that the movement 'was not sufficiently dynamic—that it was a potentially rather than an actually valuable force for promoting migrant welfare' (Aus., Immigration Advisory Council, 1967: 52). My own research in a New South Wales country town in the early fifties, in Adelaide, covering the period 1949–1970, and in Melbourne in 1970–1971 (Martin, 1965: 27; 1972a: 101–5; 1975b: 205) confirms the emphasis on work with British migrants and the difficulties which, in these places at these times, the movement had in making impact on the well-being of non-English-speaking migrants or involving migrant communities in settlement activities. The only substantial study that has been made of Good Neighbour work is contained in an unpublished manuscript by M.J. Kelly (1974). Kelly's detailed history of the movement in South Australia, Victoria and New South Wales, up to the early 1970s, shows much variation in both time and place in the scope, direction and intensity of Good Neighbour work. Information provided by Kelly on the New South Wales Council in the fifties indicates what was probably a common reason why Good Neighbour work concentrated on British migrants: because Italians and Greeks were not assisted migrants, the Council was not informed of their arrival by the Department of Immigration and they were not included in 'welcome parties and activities'. The Council considered this problem in 1957, but resolved to continue to print welcome cards only in English. Kelly comments: 'It was not until quite a few years later that the importance of being able to communicate with migrants in their own language became generally accepted' (1974: 312–3). Kelly also documents the fact that during the sixties work with British migrants continued to be more systematically organised than work with non-English-speakers (1974: 434–46). The Councils were originally intended as co-ordinating bodies not as direct providers of service. However, in the lacunae left by the churches and other voluntary associations they found themselves involved from time to time in direct service, though lacking the trained staff to make this work effective and put it on a continuous basis. Contact worker schemes, which themselves had a chequered history, represented an attempt to provide direct service to migrants, but Kelly's data on contact workers show that in each of the three States about 60 per cent of them were Australian- or British-born (1974: Tables 15, 16, 17, 18). With the advent of the Grants-to-Communities Agencies scheme in 1968 (see page 74), the Councils gained access to additional resources specifically designed to develop their direct welfare role, but most social workers employed by Councils under this scheme have been English-speaking. Further reference to the Good Neighbour movement and to the present review of its work appears on pages 81–2.

2. Dr Price has provided the following note in explanation of Table 2.1. *Method A* = SDs/SAs, i.e. persons saying they were former settlers and were now departing permanently (SDs) as a proportion of persons arriving, saying they were settlers. SDs is an incomplete estimate of settler departures as many former settlers leave, saying they are Australian

residents intending to come back—but never do—and were never settlers but visitors.

Method B = Deficit/SAs, where Deficit = difference between settler arrivals (SAs) and net gain (e.g. 10 000 Italians may enter Australia in a given period, calling themselves settlers, but there are only 8000 more Italians in Australia at the end of the period than at the beginning; the deficit of 2000 = settlers who have left, no matter how they describe themselves on leaving). Deficit covers most settler departures in normal conditions.

Method C = SLg/SAg, where SLg = settlers leaving, and SAg = settlers arriving, after allowing for time lag and often adding in estimates of visitors who decide to stay on as settlers, and deducting estimates of persons who enter as settlers for the second or third time.

3. From his study of the response of the Catholic Church to migration since the Second World War, Frank Lewins concludes that 'the Catholic bishops have not influenced thinking in the political and social realms but, rather, have consistently followed periodic shifts of thought in these realms. As such, the bishops' migration policy is not policy at all but a "moving with the wind of change", in political and social milieus' (1977: Abstract).

4. Following upon a recommendation by a Working Party of COPQ (August 1974, published 1977), the Commonwealth Government established a National Accreditation Authority for Translators and Interpreters (NAATI) in 1976. The objectives of NAATI are to:

> Establish the standards and conditions leading to professional status, and in so doing develop translating and interpreting in Australia to meet community needs.
>
> Develop the basic infra-structure for the emergence of a national self-regulatory professional body in the expectation that this body would, within 5 years, assume responsibility for the profession, including accreditation.
> (Aus., Minister for Immigration and Ethnic Affairs, 1977).

A year later, in November 1977, NAATI announced a nation-wide survey of interpreters and translators: 'a questionnaire for people wanting accreditation by NAATI would be supplied to professional associations, employer bodies, training institutions and relevant Commonwealth and State departments for distribution to applicants . . .' The information received would help to establish procedures for accreditation (Aus., NAATI, 1978). Meantime, apart from a small number of State Government initiatives (e.g. by the Education Department, Victoria, the Health Commission and the Ethnic Affairs Division of the Premier's Department, New South Wales), employment opportunities for interpreters and translators have expanded very little and some newly established training courses have been abandoned or reduced in scope. NAATI is potentially a 'boost' to interpreting and translating resources in the community (as the Minister's news release described it), but reduction in the levels of government spending and the operation of Fraser Federalism are more important in *limiting* such expansion than NAATI can be in *encouraging* it. COPQ's Working Party clearly foresaw the possibility of changes of form rather than substance when it concluded its 1974 report with the warning:

Members wish to stress that the foregoing discussion and conclusions can achieve little or nothing unless steps are taken to create proper employment opportunities for qualified interpreters/translators. Students cannot otherwise be enrolled, with propriety, in such specialised courses. Moreover it will only be as a result of the lead being taken by the Australian and State public services in insisting on interpreters/translators in their employ being adequately qualified that the community will come to require similar standards being maintained outside government service. (Aus., COPQ, 1977: 32)

The Public Service Board at present has under review a revised schedule of fees for community interpreters, with provision for indexation.

5. In 1977 a short-lived public row emerged over the Commonwealth's decision to discontinue funding for two access radio stations, which had been giving radio time to certain ethnic groups, and to bring ethnic radio directly under government control. Subsequently, the Commonwealth established an independent statutory authority, the Special Broadcasting Service (SBS), to provide multilingual and other special broadcasting and television services. SBS began operations in January 1978; it runs the two ethnic stations 2EA (Sydney) and 3EA (Melbourne). The committee advising SBS on ethnic broadcasting is the National Ethnic Broadcasting Advisory Council (NEBAC), appointed in February 1977. However, much activity in relation to the media is at present concentrated on the possibility of developing ethnic television. In March 1978, the New South Wales ECC was preparing a submission to the Commonwealth 'for consent to operate Australia's first foreign language television station in Sydney' (*Weekend Australian*, March 4–5), while the Commonwealth was considering a report on the cost of trial stations in Sydney and Melbourne which 'could be expanded to a fully commercial system' (*Age*, March 2). Already in December 1977, 'The owner of a Sydney videotape production company [had] approached the Federal Government with a proposal to provide multi-lingual television' (*Sydney Morning Herald*, December 29).

6. In February 1978, after this book went to press, the Good Neighbour Council of Victoria made a submission on the Adult Migrant Education Program to the Minister for Immigration and Ethnic Affairs. The submission, researched and written by the Council's Community Education Officer, Peter J. Wilkinson, consists of a thorough and authoritative overview of the operation of the programme, an evaluation and a set of precise recommendations. It is a model of informed criticism and no brief summary could do justice to it. Here I can simply note that Wilkinson backs up a stringent critique of the Program with detailed documentation of: continued underspending of budgeted funds, on the one hand, and shortage of places, courses and administrative back-up and under-payment of teachers, on the other; anomalies and confusion throughout the programme, in terms of eligibility and selection of students, payment of living allowances, teachers' salaries and allocation of funds to different centres; totally inadequate advertising and promotion of courses, teacher training and materials. The ultimate evidence for the failure of the programme is that it reaches only a small fraction of non-English-speaking migrants: no one knows what proportion, but Wilkinson's figures give about

5 per cent of eligible migrants enrolled in full-time courses in 1970–1975 (Wilkinson 1978: 57), and he endorses an overall estimate that, 'less than 20 per cent of migrants are touched' by the programme (1978: 44), which discriminates against those who need it most. See also Note 8.

R.C. King, Professor of Education at the University of Wollongong, New South Wales, is at present carrying out a 'Migrant Education Television Research Project, 1976–1978': a study 'of the effectiveness of current programs . . . leading to a study of psychological and sociological characteristics of immigrant groups vis-à-vis future policy and planning concerning use of media in migrant education' (Aus., Department of Education, 1977a: 139).

7. 'It is well known that specialist personnel working on materials development at the Language Teaching Branch in Canberra have very limited liaison with classroom teachers in State capitals. On the other hand, when innovative and creative programs and materials have been developed by classroom teachers, their work has not been well supported or encouraged in terms of refining, editing, publication or distribution' (Wilkinson, 1978: 61).

8. Wilkinson's report on the Adult Migrant Education Program (Wilkinson, 1978), referred to in Notes 6 and 7, is clearly an example of the kind of critique that has rarely come from Good Neighbour Councils in the past. It is, however, consistent with the argument advanced here that this paper is a joint publication of the Good Neighbour Council of Victoria and the Ecumenical Migration Centre, Richmond, a long-standing and insistent critic of government immigration policies and programmes, and of the Good Neighbour movement. Recent upheavals in the Good Neighbour Council of Victoria are described in Faulkner (1977) and Matheson (1975, 1977).

9. The report of the Galbally Review was tabled by the Prime Minister (in ten languages) on 30 May 1978 (Aus., Review of Post Arrival Programs and Services to Migrants, 1978). The main thrust of the Review's recommendations, which were accepted *in toto* by the Government and include the disbursement of $50 million largely additional funds over the next three years, is to give expression to the Government's Federalism policies so far as migrant settlement is concerned. Although this does to some extent involve the 'change of direction' to which the Review refers, the impact of the report is primarily to consolidate existing trends in the division of responsibilities and to affirm existing priorities—with two exceptions: the termination of funding for Good Neighbour Councils and the allocation of funds to one major new initiative, a $7.3 million pilot ethnic television station, with provision for commercial participation.

In the education of children and teaching adults English, the Review's recommendations strengthen the Commonwealth's established responsibilities (with $16.8 million—of the $20 million devoted to education—set aside for English teaching for children and multicultural education in schools, the effects of cuts made by the Liberal Government in Schools Commission funds over the past two years, and anticipated in the future, are now offset). In welfare, the recommendations will re-orient and focus (but not change in any dramatic way) the comparatively meagre welfare responsibilities that the Commonwealth has assumed over the years; the proposal that $12 million should be devoted to initial settlement programmes is also in line with the higher priority the Commonwealth has given to the immediate post-arrival stage of migrant settlement.

Overall, when associated with general cuts in welfare spending for the whole community, the combination of a number of the recommendations—the Commonwealth moving away from direct welfare service towards a largely consultative and information–giving role, the provision that the extremely limited additional funds ($1.5 million) allocated to the welfare areas defined as 'areas of special need' (law, income security, employment, health) and 'special groups' (young children, women, the handicapped, the aged) be spent on a cost-sharing basis with the States after the first year, the requirement that funds for self-help projects undertaken by ethnic and voluntary organisations be on a 'once-only' basis—is likely to leave migrants, and groups working with them, rather better off for advice and information but, in the long run, worse off for resources and a stable supply of services.

3   Child Migrant Education in the Fifties and Sixties

Education is the only clearly identifiable area in which there has been a comprehensive nation-wide response to the presence of non-English-speaking migrants in Australia. The scale and institutionalisation of this response derive from the active involvement of the Commonwealth Government, which has funded and promoted the education of adult migrants since 1947 and child migrants since 1970 (see Aus., Department of Education, 1976*b*). For adult migrants, education has always meant simply learning English. The thrust of child migrant education has been and still is the same—but a continuing accumulation of challenges, from a variety of sources, to English-language-dominated approaches received the blessing of the Schools Commission in 1975. Several different, and to a degree incompatible, concepts of migrant education now compete for legitimacy and resources. In the past, response was directed to giving migrant children the minimum language skills needed for them to communicate in a monolingual society. This was accomplished with the minimum of structural change in education departments or schools; the commonly used term 'withdrawal classes' for migrant English classes signifies that the system has been kept intact by the device of taking teaching staff and migrant children out of it. Changing perspectives involve more differentiated modes of communication (as for example through bilingual education), a substantial development of the knowledge response (multicultural education for all children, for example), and structural changes (entailing, for instance, participation of ethnic communities in the school's operations and diversification of school personnel). In embryonic form these perspectives have been around since the fifties; as they are institutionalised, the term 'migrant education' becomes increasingly inappropriate. It is more correct to say that response to the education of migrant children is contributing to changes in educational thinking in general. At the same time, the practice of education in the classroom reflects changing perspectives very unevently indeed.

I shall approach the history of child migrant education by asking: who have been the definers of migrant education problems, what definitions have they offered and what solutions, and in what ways has educational practice changed in recognition of the presence of migrant children? The sources used to answer these questions are the items listed in H.F. Willcock's 'Bibliography of the Education of Migrant Children 1945–1975' (1976) and published and unpublished material produced since 1975. In response to a request from me, 69 of the individual authors listed in the 'Bibliography' wrote accounts of their engagement with migrant education and I have drawn on that most informative material too. (The accounts are referred to as the Migrant Education Questionnaires.)

An analysis of the 417 items in Willcock's 'Bibliography' appears in Tables 3.1–3.3. Writings on child migrant education were meagre up to 1965, sustained a higher level in 1966–1969, increased substantially in 1970 and again in 1971, and continued at a relatively high rate up to 1975. (Individual authors accounted for about 80 per cent of the items in both the pre-1970 period and in 1970–1975; following a negligible contribution in the earlier period, the Commonwealth published 9 per cent of items in 1970–1975.) Victoria's pre-eminent position stands out strongly from an analysis of the place of publication of all items: over the whole period 52 per cent of items were published in Victoria, three times as many as in any other State. Over two-thirds of the 301 items with a named individual as author (excluding editors and 'official' authors) were written by school or tertiary teachers. Table 3.2 shows the increasing contribution of tertiary teachers after 1967, both absolutely and relative to school teachers.

The definers of the fifties and sixties

The themes that dominated teachers' thinking about migrant education up to the mid-sixties were clearly stated in 1951 in an article by J.B. Cox, headmaster of a primary school in a migrant holding centre. Cox described his staff as teachers who 'have no special training for this work, nor do they use any foreign language, but they have met their peculiar problems with commendable initiative, patience and skill' (Cox, 1951: 31). 'No information' was available about the previous schooling of the children, who were of diverse European origins and mostly had 'negligible' English on arrival. Cox describes the supportive attitude of teachers and the central place of English teaching:

the child must learn to think in English from the start . . . English is to be the basis of all instruction. It is the avenue to mutual understanding. It is the key to the success of the whole immigration project . . . English

Table 3.1 *Place and year of publication of 417 items in Child Migrant Education Bibliography, 1950–1975*

Place of publication	Year of publication																										Total	%
	50	51	52	53	54	55	56	57	58	59	60	61	62	63	64	65	66	67	68	69	70	71	72	73	74	75–6		
Victoria					1	1	1			1	1		1	1	1		1	3	10	7	16	37	14	34	42	43	215	51.6
New South Wales							1	1	1		2		1	1			2	6	3	5		3	10	19	10	8	73	17.5
Canberra										1								2		1	7	8	8	17	8	19	71	17.0
Western Australia									1		1		1			1	3		2				2	2	3		16	3.8
South Australia	1	4				1														1	2		2	3			14	3.4
Queensland											2	1		1			1					1	1	1	1	1	10	2.4
Tasmania																						1	1	2			4	1.0
Overseas						1			1			1						1			1		1	4	3	1	14	3.4
Total	1	4	0	0	1	3	2	1	3	2	6	2	3	3	1	1	7	12	15	14	26	50	39	82	67	72	417	100.1

Source: Analysis of items contained in H.F. Willcock, 'Bibliography of the Education of Migrant Children 1945–1975', in Price and Martin eds, 1976*b*.

Table 3.2 *Occupations of 301 item-authors of items in Child Migrant Education Bibliography, 1950–1975*

Occupation	Year of publication

Occupation	50	51	52	53	54	55	56	57	58	59	60	61	62	63	64	65	66	67	68	69	70	71	72	73	74	75–6	Total	%
Tertiary teacher		1				1											2	6	6	6	5	13	13	17	24	26	120	39.9
Teacher		1					1									1	7	4	2	6	5	5	16	7	4	17	76	25.3
Higher education administration										1	2		1									2	1			1	8	2.7
Lower education administration													1					1			1	3		1			7	2.3
Research officer																			1		4	4	1	1		2	13	4.3
Non-teacher professional																4			1	1	2	2	6	6		5	27	8.9
Other						2											4				2	7	1	8	5	2	31	10.3
Unknown							1		1				1	1	1						1		2	6	4	1	19	6.3
Total	0	2	0	0	0	3	2	0	1	2	3	1	3	1	1	3	6	9	11	12	17	35	30	56	49	54	301	100

Source: See Table 3.1. An 'item-author' is the author (or, in the case of items with more than one author, the first author) of an item with a named person as author. Each such item is counted once. Because some persons were authors of more than one item, the number of 'item-authors' is greater than the number of authors. Thirty items entered in the Bibliography under the name of editors and 'official' authors (e.g. P.R. Lynch, Minister for Immigration) are excluded.

Table 3.3 *Occupations of 188 authors of items in 'Child Migrant Education Bibliography, 1950–1975*

Occupation	Year of publication																											Total	%
	50	51	52	53	54	55	56	57	58	59	60	61	62	63	64	65	66	67	68	69	70	71	72	73	74	75–6		
Tertiary teacher		1					1				1							1	1	1	3	3	5	10	16	13	56	29.8
Teacher		1					1						2					7	3	2	5	3	4	12	7	13	60	31.9
Higher education administration									1	1											1	2	1	1	1		8	4.3
Lower education administration													1						1				3	1			6	3.2
Research officer																						3	2	1	1	2	9	4.8
Non-teacher professional														1						1		1		4	4	3	14	7.4
Other						2											2					3		3	4	2	16	8.5
Unknown										1	1			1					1		1	1	2	6	3	2	19	10.1
Total	0	2	0	0	0	2	2	0	1	2	2	0	3	2	0	0	2	8	6	4	10	16	17	38	36	35	188	100

Source: See Table 3.1. Each author is counted only once, in the year of his most recent publication. Editors and 'official' authors are excluded, as in Table 3.2.

must be spoken to the pupils and by them, all day and every day, in every activity, in school and out of it. (Cox, 1951: 32)

The procedures used in the classroom and in other activities like play, sport and singing, to which much importance was attached, were directed unambiguously at 'influencing' the child, teaching him to understand and obey orders and, in general, to 'fit into our school life and later into our society' (1951: 32). The phrase 'fit into' was repeated as the leitmotiv of Cox's article. Problem children were children who didn't fit in. A concentration on Australian life and tradition would help new arrivals 'to learn the significance of all that we honour and respect' (1951: 32). The language and traditions that the children brought with them were not mentioned. Parents were referred to only in the context of 'problems' encountered.

The emphasis on learning English, on discipline and conformity continued in subsequent writings, and the pre-eminence of the *teacher's* definition of the situation was mostly taken for granted (see, for example, Coles, 1967; Smart, 1967). Even the most open-minded discussions were suffused with the assumption of a one-way flow of wisdom and authority from teachers to migrant children and their parents. In an insightful article published in 1962, for example, G. Strauss described his experience in a Melbourne high school in these words:

> We simply asked the parents of problem children to come and see us. This is still being done and constitutes our most powerful disciplinary device. In these interviews we very often located the source of the trouble, and as the majority of parents were co-operative and eager to further their children's education, we had a great deal of success. In some cases, one or both parents altered their shifts of work to facilitate closer supervision of youngsters who misused their spare time. One growing boy was actually removed from the over-protective hands of a well-meaning but misguided mother and handed over to the stricter guidance of his father. In other cases, study routines and home supervision were arranged. We realized that prevention was better than cure and decided to call meetings to warn the parents of the consequences of certain lacks in the home . . . we found that once the parents had been alerted, once we had warned them of the various dangers, the occasions for wrongdoing were restricted. (Strauss, 1962: 100–1)

The complete lack of appropriate materials was a recurring theme from the early fifties. What teachers repeatedly asked for were materials both for teaching English and for occupying the attention of children who could not join in regular classroom work. These demands gained their force from the anxiety of staff who were unprepared to cope with non-English-speaking pupils and from the way in which the presence of these children threatened the teachers' competence to carry out the classroom role for which they *had* been trained. Some teachers tried to use overseas publications or the materials produced by the Commonwealth for adult migrant classes; others adopted the experimental books, few in number and of very limited value, that were prepared in the Victorian and New South Wales Departments of Education in the sixties. None of this was seen as anything but an ineffective stopgap, and by the end of the sixties the lack of suitable materials had emerged as one of the teachers' major grievances.

During the post-war period, most school systems began to provide special teachers for backward and handicapped children. It was therefore understandable that, whether teachers saw children of non-English-speaking origin as one type of slow learner or (which was less common) as a distinctive group, they sought solutions to the problems that these children posed through the provision of special teachers and segregated classes or lessons. The earliest record of a request for special teachers is contained in a letter written in 1954 from the Victorian Teachers' Union to the Victorian Department of Education. In common with other statements of the period, the request is justified by reference to the disadvantages suffered by Australian children and the way in which migrant pupils jeopardise the teacher's normal work.

> I have been requested to ask that the department appoint special teachers in schools where needed to give instruction in English to New Australian children.
>
> The increasing number of New Australian children in certain schools is making a very grave problem for class teachers. The normal class teaching is affected by the inability of the New Australian children to speak, write and understand English to a satisfactory standard. It is impossible for teachers to give the necessary time to these children when they have large classes.
>
> The problem is particularly acute in some areas and schools, and we would suggest that the appointment of specialist teachers for the purpose asked would not only be of benefit to the New Australian children, but also enable normal instruction to proceed with the other children. (VTU, Schubert to Secretary, Education Department, 15 October 1954)*

To educational administrators, the significance of the influx of migrant children lay above all in the additional numbers they contributed to total enrolments and to the size of the handicapped or slow-learner segment of the school population in particular. Migrant children represented simply one more source of strain in an overtaxed system. Education would be fulfilling its assimilationist function to the extent that migrants were indistinguishable from other pupils. Sporadic attempts on the part of teachers to convince administrators that

---

* The unpublished files to which reference is made in this chapter are listed on page 218.

migrant education needed to be confronted as an issue in its own right met with a negative or stalling response. Lack of initiative on the part of administrators reflects the general crisis in education, but there were also more far-reaching grounds for the general malaise among educational bureaucracies in the years after the war. According to R.T. Fitzgerald,

> Cultural, professional and administrative factors thus operated against the diffusion of new thought and practice in the school systems. At the top, the constant concern of departmental officials with routine tasks gave them little opportunity to reflect on the need for reform. They also lacked the research facilities to plan and evaluate alternative approaches or to experiment with new methods. They did not have the means of communicating changes in policy and practice effectively to the schools; nor could they readily induce teachers to reconsider existing procedures. (Fitzgerald, 1973: 60)

The only State to attempt any systematic approach to the education of non-English-speaking migrant children during the fifties was South Australia. In 1956, a committee of teachers under the chairmanship of the Inspector of Primary Schools, N.L. Haines, surveyed the situation of migrant children in State primary schools. Its findings (called the Haines Report) touched on all the issues in migrant education that were to become matters of concern in other States during the following ten to fifteen years. For the purposes of the survey, 'migrant children' were children who were experiencing difficulty with English, and Haines warned that it was hard 'to make a really accurate check of these children as head masters differ on what constitutes backwardness' (SA, Department of Education, 1956: 2). The returns from the 102 schools contacted revealed 1460 migrant children, as defined. (In 1956, primary school went up to seventh grade and accounted for the great majority of South Australian school children.) Each school was apparently making an *ad hoc* adaptation to the presence of migrant children as best it could and without benefit of previous experience, its own or anyone else's. Attitudes and action emerged as immensely diverse, with the sharpest differences and the greatest uncertainty revolving around the question, should children with little or no English be segregated for all their schooling until they could cope with normal classes, or for English lessons only, or not at all?

Clearly there were also differences in practice—and perhaps discrepancies between what was believed to be educationally desirable and what was in fact done—in terms of the grade level in which migrant children with inadequate English were placed. A number of headmasters referred to problems with older children in junior grades, and the figures collected by the Committee showed that many children were placed in grades well below their age level: eight-year-olds, for example, ranged through grades 1 to 4, nine-year-olds from 1 to 5, ten-years-olds from 2 to 5, and eleven-, twelve- and thirteen-year-olds from 3 to 7. Grades 3 and 4 contained children with an age span of seven years.

Other issues drew similar comments from a number of the head-masters: the need for teaching materials; the desirability of training teachers for work with non-English-speaking children, or at least of selecting teachers with sympathy and understanding; and the danger of children developing 'bad work habits' and settling into patterns of idleness if 'left to their own devices' in large classes. One headmaster referred to the need for printed material to be made available to parents in their own languages. The school returns consistently revealed the assumptions that migrant education meant teaching English, that assimilation was the ultimate goal, and that 'national groups' in community or school hindered assimilation and were therefore to be discouraged. There was also a number of references to the problems presented by Greek and Italian children in particular, problems that were usually attributed to the fact that the native language was spoken in the home and that the ethnic communities to which the families of these children belonged gave no stimulus for the learning of English.

The Haines Report was perceptive and wide-ranging. It concluded with the recommendations that: special classes for teaching English should be established; children should be placed in normal classes as soon as they had mastered enough English; and teaching materials, modelled after those developed for adult migrant classes, should be prepared for use where there were only a few migrant children and no special class was possible. By the time the matter had been dealt with by the usual bureaucratic procedures and the South Australian Director of Education conveyed his recommendations to the Minister, there was no mention of special classes and the proposals had been pared down to two: schools with a large number of non-British migrants should 'be staffed as liberally as possible in order to enable the children to receive special help in the learning of English'; and the Committee be asked to make more specific recommendations on materials (SA, Director to Minister, 9 January 1957). The Minister endorsed the recommendation regarding materials, but side-stepped the question of staffing with the instruction that the Deputy Director should 'raise this matter at the Citizenship Convention, discuss the principles involved with Commonwealth Officers, and ascertain the practice adopted in other States, after conferences with their represent-atives in Canberra' (SA, Minister to Deputy Director, 17 January 1957). Haines subsequently produced a report on materials along the lines suggested and the Deputy Director recommended that work should proceed on the proposed assignments, pointing out that they could be prepared by teachers and produced by the Technical Correspondence School (SA, Deputy Director to Director, 22 February 1957). The task, in other words, could be accommodated without disturbance to existing practice or structures.

In describing the South Australian experience to a conference on the study of immigrants held in Canberra in 1960, Haines outlined how the Committee had gone on to develop work assignments, had laid down guide-lines for teachers (including advice against segregating migrant children), and at one school had established a model for dealing with the situation where there were large numbers of migrants. At this school, St Leonards, two specialist teachers had been appointed and migrant children were taken out of their normal classes for a period each day 'for tutorial work in English' (Price ed., 1960: 158).

By 1963 the number of special classes in South Australia had fallen to four and by 1964 only one class was in operation (SA, Asst Superintendent Primary Schools to Superintendent Primary Schools, 19 January 1965). The Department continued to keep the situation of non-English-speaking children under review through surveys of various kinds. However, the Committee appears to have been disbanded and the promising work begun in the late fifties subsided without having influenced the approach to migrant teaching in other States.[1]

The steps taken as a result of the Haines Committee's work appear to have met the most urgent problems in South Australia. There is no evidence of teacher agitation over migrant pupils in the following years and in the early sixties the South Australian Department was apparently satisfied that its original initiatives had accomplished all that was needed. In the process by which the experience of South Australian teachers in direct contact with migrant pupils became transformed into social knowledge and then absorbed into prescriptions for action, the interpretation of what was actually happening in schools became highly simplified and the policy recommendations accordingly narrow and technical. The administrators succeeded in re-defining the changes that were needed in such a limited way that the necessary adaptations could be made without causing more than a ripple on the surface of the existing system: provision of a few extra staff in problem schools and the production of some assignments through the use of already available resources and according to familiar procedures.

In Victoria, the Teachers' Union's request to the Education Department for special teachers, referred to previously, elicited a soothing reply:

In general, it has been found that migrant children acquire a working knowledge of English in a comparatively short time and, if these children are given some attention by the class teacher, they create no serious problem. It is considered unwise to segregate migrant children from Australian children as contact with the latter hastens the acquisition of ability to speak English.

A special class for migrant children was established in one of our larger schools but was later abandoned as experience proved that it was unnecessary. *In any case, the present acute shortage of teaching staff prevents the appointment of special teachers for this purpose.*

The question of providing greater assistance to teachers in this regard is being investigated. (VTU, Secretary, Education Department, to General Secretary, VTU, 25 October 1954; my italics)

The Victorian Teachers' Union, however, persisted in pressing the matter, and in 1958 carried out two surveys in response to the Director's request for information in support of their case. The second survey, the Union claimed, revealed that seven schools had among them 22 grades containing 10 per cent or more of children 'seriously handicapped from language point of view'; four schools reported 7 grades in which the proportion was over 25 per cent. The figures were collected in somewhat haphazard fashion, but there was no basis on which they could be challenged and they served the purpose of backing up a number of concrete recommendations, including: more help from the Psychology Branch of the Department; the appointment of a 'Supervisor of Migrant Teaching' in the Primary Division; and a special course of training for teachers appointed to schools with 20 per cent or more children of non-English-speaking background—plus the provision of 'remedial readers', the appointment of teachers in remedial English, and extra staffing for such schools (VTU, 'Migrant Education Conditions', n.d.). These recommendations became the basis of the Union's policy in the following decade. The Victorian Department, however, remained unresponsive and sceptical, warding off pressures to take action by reference to the teacher shortage, and by asserting both that responsibility lay with the Commonwealth and that the needs of migrant children were being adequately met.

The administration of the New South Wales Education Department seems to have been subject to less harrassment from teachers, and put off its critics with bland assertions that all was well. In 1958, for example, in response to requests for special reading materials, the Director-General, H. Wyndham, stated that the 'great majority' of the 2000–3000 non-English-speaking children entering the schools each year made 'such rapid progress with the language that they have little need for special reading material'. He went on to say that the children most in need of help were those in schools with large numbers of non-English-speaking children and those with special difficulties in learning English. The Department had already taken steps to supply special materials to two schools with high migrant densities, while, with reference to the child with special difficulties:

> you may be assured that, as in the past, every newcomer with a particular or personal problem will receive special assistance to the limit of the resources available, including the free use of the many clinical and remedial services provided by this and other Departments. (Wyndham, 1958)

In other words: to the extent that migrant children constituted a problem, the problem was individual-psychological (not structural) and could be handled by existing services.

The regular response of the New South Wales Department to requests and complaints about staffing in schools with large enrolments of non-English-speaking children was consistent with the view that migrant children could and should be absorbed into the established school system:

> the Department does not propose to appoint specialist teachers for the instruction of non-English speaking migrant children. Favourable consideration in general staffing, however, is given to those schools where the enrolment includes a high proportion of migrant children. (NSW, Director-General to General Secretary, NSW Teachers' Federation, 5 December 1961)

A further expression of departmental policy in 1966 firmly placed non-English-speaking children in the category of children with learning difficulties. In response to a request from the New South Wales Teachers' Federation for the appointment of 'especially trained remedial teachers to schools where class loads exceed 30 pupils or where there is a large percentage of migrant children' (NSW, Lancaster to Director-General of Education, 18 August 1966), the Director of Primary Education observed:

> The Department does not recognise the 30 class size nor the developing outlook that class teachers have the services of a remedial teacher for teaching the retarded and slow. Our outlook is that teachers do their own normal remedial work. (NSW, Director of Primary Education, memo, 29 August 1966)

The 1959 Queensland survey and the Dovey Report

The only comprehensive survey of the educational experience of migrant pupils carried out anywhere during this period confirmed the view that they were being smoothly absorbed into the established school system. This was an inquiry covering all State schools in Queensland in 1959 (Queensland, 1961). It produced information on the geographical location, distribution in grades by age and performance of 25 882 children born overseas or with one or both parents overseas-born. The results showed that migrant children, defined in this way, were concentrated in the metropolitan area and were slightly older than other children in the same grade. Although the survey was conducted with care; the analysis of the data largely obscured the facts that nearly half the children covered had one Australian-born parent and that children of post-war migrants of non-British origin constituted only a quarter of the total population.

The report of the Queensland survey claimed that migrant pupils performed as well or better than their peers. Performance was assessed in terms of the proportions of migrant children who were placed in the top, second, third, fourth of bottom fifth of their class at the last examination. However, in a system where some pupils are in grades below their age level and/or all pupils are streamed into classes of different ability levels within the one grade, such a method of calculating performance can be highly misleading, because the various fifths that are combined to produce a composite result are not comparable. If in fact the distribution of ability among migrant children is similar to the distribution for the rest of the school population, then the migrants, when placed because of inadequate English in classes with younger children or children of lower ability, are likely to rise to top places in some subjects, like mathematics or craft (see Caldwell, in Price ed., 1960: 152).

The one set of data that the Queensland report gives on the schooling of children of non-British origin (Table 12) indicates which birth place groups were the oldest, on average, in each grade. The report misinterprets these data: it states that 'children of Russian and Italian parentage are generally the oldest in the respective grades' (Queensland, 1961: 17), whereas the table actually shows that children of Greek mothers were most commonly the oldest in their grade and that Italian or Greek children were the oldest or second oldest in eight out of the twelve grades in the Queensland system.

The report also noted that 'The higher the grade, the greater the disparity between average age of migrants and the state average', and drew the important conclusion that 'many children of migrants are too old to consider completing four years of secondary education' (1961: 17). If migrant children were

> to enjoy the benefits of a full secondary education and possibly further education, they should be placed as nearly as possible in grades corresponding to their age groups. Otherwise it may be impracticable for them to complete secondary courses. (Queensland, 1961: 22)

Attention to the implications of this statement and careful analysis of the Queensland data would have alerted educationists to trends that were beginning to become more evident in other States than in

Queensland, with its comparatively small number of post-war non-British settlers. However, as noted previously, the data were sometimes distorted. They were also presented in a blanket, undiscriminating way that minimised their value and concealed the differences between the situations of children of English and non-English-speaking background. By the time these findings were incorporated into the first report on *The Progress and Assimilation of Migrant Children in Australia* by the Commonwealth Immigration Advisory Council, at whose request the Queensland Department of Education had carried out the survey, their significance as a source of reliable information and a basis for critical assessment of the experience of migrant pupils had altogether disappeared (Aus., Immigration Advisory Council, 1960).

The Advisory Council's first report (there was never a second) should have been a milestone in the systematic co-ordination of knowledge about migrant children and in the development of policy in terms of what was actually happening in schools. It was based on a nation-wide inquiry on pre-school children, school children, young workers, social participation and delinquency. Its findings concerning school children derived largely from questionnaires completed by a sample of teachers in each State—and many of the conclusions were presented in quantified form, such as 'most young migrants—about 97 percent—settle down well to life in Australia' (1960: 7), or 'Migrants have a better [scholastic] record than Australians—in 47 percent of the small classes; in 56 percent of the medium size classes; in 51 percent of the large classes' (1960: 15). Because the methodology of the inquiry and the interpretation of the information collected were quickly and thoroughly discredited (Price ed., 1960), we cannot look to the report for acceptable evidence on the situation of migrant school children at the end of the fifties. However, the inquiry holds considerable interest as a statement of the prevailing perspective on migrant children and on policies appropriate for incorporating them into the educational system. As Mr Justice Dovey, the Chairman of the Special Committee that conducted the inquiry, said at the Australian Citizenship Convention 1960, where the report was presented:

> It is not only our report, it is the report of literally thousands of Australians throughout the length and breadth of this land. (Aus., Department of Immigration, ACC, 1960: 41)

The content of this perspective (pertaining to education, which formed the main substance of the report) can be briefly summarised: migrant children have adjusted well, are above average in scholarship and present no problem of absorption (that is, non-conformity); such problems as do arise, either with parents or children, result from lack of knowledge of English and evaporate when English has been mastered, which, for the children, happens 'fairly quickly'; parents should therefore be encouraged to speak English in the home; 'national groups' among school children, though not 'a major problem', are undesirable because they hinder 'the children's integration in the school community and their progress' (1960: 19, 21). The Committee's proposals for promoting the adjustment of migrant pupils ranged from the provision of English classes for children on shipboard on their way to Australia, to the organisation of campaigns by clubs and other formal groups to encourage migrant children to join and assume their share of the leadership. The Committee acknowledged the value of maintaining migrant traditions, but its suggestions for achieving this —that all children should study the countries of origin of migrants and that bilingual families should be preserved—had none of the force, conviction or concreteness of the assmiliationist-oriented proposals, and indeed, as one speaker at the Convention pointed out, were inconsistent with them (Aus., Department of Immigration, ACC, 1960: 41).

The Dovey Committee acted as a gatekeeper and legitimating agent: it screened out information that ran counter to prevailing views and confirmed the wisdom of current policies. It lulled disquiet about the experience of school children of non-English-speakin origin and the problems of teachers; it exaggerated the scope of provisions for teaching English in schools and the extent to which children were in fact mastering the new language (1960: 18–19). In a sense it was the wrong kind of milestone: the kind that says, 'you are well along the right road, keep going as you are, the end is in sight and no misadventures are likely to befall you on the way'. Academic criticism of the inquiry probably did not penetrate far beyond the universities, but it combined with the soporific effect of the report itself to damp down the work of the Committee and to keep the question of the education of migrant children off the agenda of Citizenship Conventions for three years.

Teachers had supplied the basic information that the Dovey Committee used in reaching its conclusions about migrant school children. If, as the critics maintained, these conclusions were misleading in their bland optimism, the report might have been expected to arouse a reaction from the teaching profession. As part of his evaluation of the inquiry, the demographer J.C. Caldwell did refer to the dissatisfaction of Canberra and New South Wales teachers— especially teachers in secondary schools and the poorer urban areas —with the form of the schools survey and the interpretation of the results. But (as Table 3.2 indicates) the early sixties marked the lowest ebb in teacher interest in migrant education and the only serious public response from a teacher was an article published in 1962 by G.J. Hughson, the principal of a Canberra high school. Hughson questioned the Committee's assertions about migrant children's high level of scholarship, at least so far as secondary students were concerned, and illustrated how the schools questionnaire was biassed to exaggerate the proportions of more competent pupils; he also gave a rounded and perceptive picture of how migrant children and their parents saw and responded to the school situation (Hughson, 1962).

Changes in perspective in the late sixties

By the mid-sixties there was evidence of a quickening of interest in the question of the schooling of migrant children. As migrant education came to be widely perceived as a *problem*, it was at first in terms of themes that had been present, though only sporadically articulated, in the thinking of teachers and other observers since the end of the forties. The crust of complacency was cracked with familiar tools, and it was not until this process was well advanced that the focus of attention shifted from migrant education to the larger question of education in an ethnically diverse society.

One set of influences that helped to produce changed perspectives in the sixties came from the explosion of interest in education in general and from a shift in orientation among educators from a system-centred to a child-centred philosophy, with an attendant increase in school and teacher autonomy. With these changes the education of migrant pupils was more likely to be viewed from the perspective of the children themselves, in their unique school situation.

Public controversy over the continuance of large-scale immigration also emerged at the end of the sixties and the education of migrant children became a focus for criticism of existing policies, particularly criticism of Liberal Governments by the Labor Opposition in Victoria and the Commonwealth. Figure 3.1 shows both the increased attention to child migrant education in State and Commonwealth legislatures in this period and the predominant position of Victoria in bringing the issue into the political arena.

At the same time, in the schools themselves, the changing composition of the migrant population was undermining the kind of well-entrenched stereotypes that the Dovey Committee had confirmed. Until the early sixties most migrant children came from the families of refugees and other settlers from eastern and northern Europe. Children from this background, seen to be (and perhaps in reality) highly motivated and high-achievers, were the source of a somewhat romantic image of above-average performance and successful adaptation. This image persisted to distort understanding of the actual experience of the very different population of children that predominated in the schools by the late sixties. As Table 3.4 shows, the period 1961 to 1971 saw a major decline in the actual numbers of

Figure 3.1 *References to child migrant education in Commonwealth and States Legislatures 1950–1974*

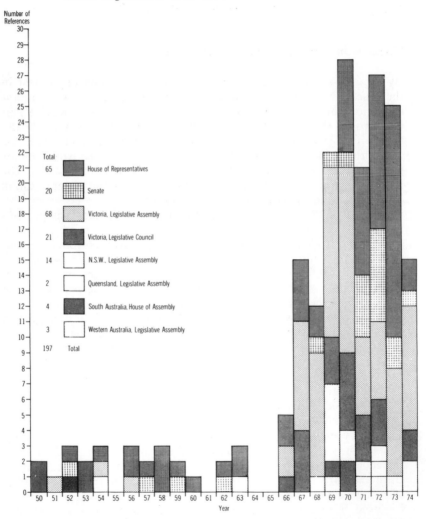

Source: H.F. Willcock, 'Bibliography of the Education of Migrant Children 1945–1975' in Price and Martin eds, 1976.

children from northern and eastern Europe (from 62 503 to 25 683 for the five-to-fourteen age group) and an increase, both in absolute numbers and proportionately, of children from southern Europe and a variety of Middle Eastern and Asian countries, which during that period came into prominence as source countries.

A large segment of this new child migrant population belonged to the families of unskilled and semi-skilled workers, with little formal education, who had settled in the inner suburbs of Melbourne and Sydney (see Burnley, 1974). These communities came to be labelled as ghettoes. Being concentrated in schools that were, in any case, the worst victims of an impoverished education system, made migrant children more visible than they had been in the fifties. High transfer rates of migrant children between schools, accompanied by wide fluctuations in enrolments (conditions that once affected only those schools near migrant hostels), were now part of the general city-school scene. High rates of staff turnover intensified the problems of inner-city schools and of the migrant children who formed a large proportion of their student body (see Elliott, 1977).

By the end of the sixties, then, a number of disparate influences had combined to create an awareness of the educational problems of children of non-English-speaking origin. At this point, Victoria began to stand out as the State with the most vigorous and innovative approach, a position that it retained for about ten years. Already in 1965 at Fitzroy High School, an inner-city school with an increasing enrolment of Greek, Italian and other non-English-speaking children, an Italian and Greek-speaking teacher had been appointed full-time to tutor pupils who needed help with English. From this beginning, a 'crash course' of twelve weeks of classes—involving children from a number of neighbouring schools—was developed in 1967 (Manley, 1967; Elliott, 1977).

The 'Fitzroy experiment' attracted a good deal of publicity and helped to marshal community support for the efforts of a number of teachers, counselling staff and parent bodies bent on serious examination of the situation of migrant children and determined to goad the Education Department into action. One of these catalysts was Alison Goding, a social worker in the Psychology and Guidance Branch of the Education Department, with a wide personal and professional knowledge of the experience of migrant children. In her words:

It was a voluntary organization, the Victorian Council of School Organizations (VICCSO), which brought before the public the serious problems of migrant children attending inner suburban schools which were ill-equipped and unprepared to meet their needs. In 1967 a survey undertaken by this body, of sixty-eight schools within a five mile radius of Melbourne showed that more than one third of the pupils were

Table 3.4 *Birthplace by age of 5–14-year-olds, Australia, 1947–1971*

Birthplace	5–9 years						Age group: 10–14 years					
	1947	1954	1961	1966	1971	1947	1954	1961	1966	1971
Australasia	601 078	825 003	980 875	1 080 869	1 101 427	530 168	645 980	890 332	979 039	1 087 119
United Kingdom and Ireland	1 148	25 491	25 503	44 523	66 035	1 487	20 831	44 587	48 195	73 509
Germany	48	20 025	5 389	2 838	2 861	203	3 346	20 000	5 714	3 621
Netherlands	17	7 840	8 100	3 043	1 773	43	5 290	14 412	7 971	3 525
Poland	43	917	524	522	189	150	1 184	1 139	1 014	640
Greece	44	899	2 808	4 207	5 027	145	549	3 811	5 738	6 687
Italy	74	7 813	9 383	7 642	7 814	405	4 298	19 283	13 479	11 554
Yugoslavia	16	475	1 659	2 026	7 425	76	899	1 772	3 148	7 366
Malta	25	3 054	2 627	2 539	1 207	34	1 690	5 398	4 442	2 768
Other Europe	167	5 459	4 491	3 855	6 341	369	5 372	8 448	5 684	6 733
Other countries	1 323	5 761	6 162	10 832	20 156	1 603	4 741	10 802	12 024	22 835
Total	603 983	902 737	1 047 521	1 162 896	1 220 255	534 683	694 180	1 019 984	1 086 448	1 226 357

Source: Aus., ABS, *Censuses*, 1947, 1954, 1961, 1966 and 1971.

migrants, with two schools having an enrolment of more than 70% of migrant children, 1,170 of whom were unable to speak English adequately. A seminar organized by the Victorian Council of School Organizations in the same year was entitled 'Problems of Inner Suburban Education'. Speakers stressed that both migrant children and Australians suffered from language deprivation and called for special provision for meeting their needs. (Goding, 1973: 67)

At the end of 1967, the Victorian Education Department appointed Allen Humphries as the first 'Co-ordinator and Adviser on Migrant Education' in Australia. Advisory committees for primary and secondary education were set up in 1968 and 1969, and in 1968 a series of four-day training courses in teaching English was inaugurated and the first full-time advisory teacher appointed. The Psychology and Guidance Branch established its own working committee and began producing teachers' notes on the cultural background of particular migrants groups (Goding, 1973).

The most important product of this period of activity in Victoria was in fact the reflection and discussion involved. In the process of experimenting, collecting information and exerting pressure on government authorities (Commonwealth as well as State, as we shall see), those concerned explored what could and should be done with an intensity that had no parallel in other States. The outcome was not consensus—indeed, every effort had its critics—but a deepened knowledge of the actual situation in schools and a sharpening of concepts and aims. One long-term product has been the building up of the unique body of published material on the experience of schools and their migrant pupils, which forms a substantial proportion of all writings on child migrant education.

The role of the Commonwealth

By the late sixties another major influence was appearing on the scene. This was the growing involvement of the Commonwealth.[2]

At the beginning of the post-war migration scheme, the Commonwealth had set up a programme for teaching English to adult migrants. The Commonwealth Office of Education, established in 1945, was at first responsible for all aspects of this work. But in 1951 the Commonwealth handed over to State departments of education the supervision and conduct of all English classes within Australia. Until 1952 the Office of Eudcation also acted as a liaison between the Commonwealth Departments of Immigration and Labour and National Service, on the one hand, and the States, on the other, in organising schools in migrant centres, and in 1950 and 1951 it published special notes to help the teachers of 'New Australian' children in State schools (Aus., Commonwealth Office of Education, *Annual Reports*, 1948–1966).

Such ambiguity as may have existed in these early years about the future of Commonwealth responsibility for teaching English to migrant children was, however, soon dispelled. The Commonwealth continued to confine the teaching of English on board migrant ships to adult classes, which older children could attend; where there were classes for children, they were run by unpaid volunteers. Representations made in 1949 and 1950 by the Catholic Church for help with providing buildings, equipment and staff for Catholic schools in migrant centres led the Commonwealth to confirm its policy that the education of migrant children was a State matter and that Commonwealth assistance was limited to providing buildings, for the use of government schools only, in migrant centres.

On the wider question of the education of children of non-English-speaking settlers once outside the Commonwealth-controlled ships or migrant centres, the Commonwealth also remained unmoved, despite grumblings from the States, like P.P. Inchbold's complaint in the Legislative Council of Victoria in 1952. The Education Department, he said:

> is pleased to receive migrant children into its schools and to watch the wonderful progress they make. But the fact is that they are crowding out Australian children, to a degree, and in the matter of educating migrant children, the State has received little assistance from the Commonwealth Government. Federal and State Ministers should hold consultations on Australia's migration policy. (Vic., Leg. Council, *Parl. Debates*, Vol. 239, 1952: 1551)

Relying on an argument that has a familiar ring today, the Liberal Government claimed that moneys allocated to the States took account of population increases: if migrant children were exacerbating the crisis in education, that was the outcome of State decisions and remediable by the States if they so wished. 'The need for special and additional measures for migrant children' was not yet acknowledged (Aus., Department of Immigration, *Migrant Education Programme 1970–71*, 1971: 2).

By the end of the sixties, however, the Commonwealth had assumed a new role in relation to education in general and changes in policy towards the education of migrant children followed. Pressure on the Commonwealth Government to involve itself in alleviating the crisis in the schools increased at the beginning of the decade, and education was a major issue in Federal elections from 1963 onwards. During the 1963 election campaign the Prime Minister, R.G. Menzies, announced the Commonwealth's first scheme for direct aid to schools, the science laboratories programme; the second major Commonwealth involvement came in 1968 with the school libraries programme. Both schemes won substantial political support for the Liberal Government. Further initiatives could be expected to pay off and were in any case demanded by the continuing failure of State Governments or Catholic schools to cope with the mounting costs of an education system acceptable to changing and loftier community standards.

Although the education of migrant children was one issue of increasing concern, it was not at first self-evident that the Commonwealth would enter this area of the States' domain. Its other main initiatives in education had been preceded by the compelling arguments of the Academy of Science's statement on the supply of scientific and technological manpower and the Murray Committee's recommendations on science education, and stimulated by the organised campaign of the Libraries Association (see Smart, 1975). No such weighty influences were operating to draw the Commonwealth into the area of child migrant education.

There were, however, influences of a different kind. In the fifties and early sixties, community groups and individuals had made sporadic and abortive efforts to attract Commonwealth attention to migrant school children. Then, from about 1964, a steady flow of representations began. They came from all over Australia and for the most part had no connection with each other. Some were formal approaches through members of parliament to the Department of Immigration or Education and Science (which was established in 1966 and absorbed the Office of Education). Others originated in informal discussion. An observation made by a Canberra teacher to a member of the Senate, for example, led the Commonwealth in 1964 to take the opportunity provided by regular conferences of officers-in-charge of adult migrant education to enquire from the State authorities about difficulties experienced by migrant children. Most representations came from practising teachers or principals in charge of schools with large numbers of migrant children (particularly schools adjacent to migrant centres), but there were also letters from Good Neighbour Councils, Parents and Citizens Associations and academics. Some of these approaches aimed to make the Commonwealth aware that there was indeed a problem in the education of migrant children; some appear to have followed fruitless efforts to stir the State departments. Others asked for specific help, particularly for teaching materials. A few reported experiments in teaching migrant children, made recommendations for dealing with the problem or solicited Commonwealth support for some new method of teaching English. Occasionally there were requests from research workers for information: an inquiry from a university lecturer preparing a paper on bilingualism, for example, led the Department of Immigration to attempt an estimate of the number of non-English-speaking children in Australian schools.

The appointment of B.M. Snedden as Minister for Immigration in December 1966 coincided with this accumulation of pressures. Snedden had been educated in an 'international (that is, multi-ethnic) school' in Perth, an exceptional enough experience in Australia in the thirties, and had served as an Immigration officer in London and Rome in 1952–1954. With this background, he saw himself as unusually qualified for his new portfolio and proceeded to use his joint position as Minister for Immigration and Leader of the Government in the House to confirm the Department of Immigration's expanding functions and social impact (Snedden, personal interview, 1976). His active interest in child migrant education brought a new focus and stimulus to the Commonwealth's concern with the question. Almost immediately after becoming Minister, and in response to an unofficial approach from an acquaintance in the Victorian Education Department, he asked his Department for a review of the current situation. He appears not to have been greatly impressed with the bland account that he received in reply and noted on the report:

> Thank you. This statement is factual, as I asked, but contains no assessment of sufficiency or result or whether more should be done. Are we—or is anybody presently able to provide this assessment. If so please let me have it. If not we should consider ways of obtaining it. (Aus., Department of Immigration, Education of Migrant Children, Part 2, File 67/71547, Armstrong to Snedden, 25 January 1967)

In an attempt to meet the Minister's request for an assessment, the Department made further inquiries from the States and again conveyed the view that the question was neither serious nor urgent. There was no suggestion from the States that they could not cope—however, a problem 'in varying degrees' did exist, and the States were likely to be understaing it. We could follow up, suggested the Secretary, P.R. Heydon, 'when the resources of our survey team will permit' (Aus., Department of Immigration, Education of Migrant Children, Part 2, File 67/71547, Heydon to Minister, 10 March 1967). Snedden accepted the proposal that the matter be followed up and again showed some scepticism about the picture that the report conveyed: in the paragraph on South Australia, he underlined the sentence, 'It is stressed, however, that the number of non-English speaking students who enrol in high school is small', and wrote in the margin, 'Are there many who don't go *because* their English is not good enough?'. He was not satisfied that enough was being done. When the officers of his Department reiterated the limited role of the Commonwealth so far as the education of children was concerned, he retorted that times had changed:

> The Minister considers that these days the Commonwealth is able, in agreeing to provide funds for projects, to ensure that they are spent by the States in just the way the Commonwealth desires. He thought that there should be exploratory discussion with the Commonwealth Department of Education [and Science]. (Aus., Department of Immigration, Education of Migrant Children, Part 2, File 67/71547, H. McGinness, minute, 20 April 1967)

Snedden's initiative led to a period of significant contact between members of his Department (involving also on occasion officers from Education and Science) and the Victorian teachers and school counsellors who were by this time mounting a strenuous campaign on the question of migrants in schools in that State. Among other things, officers of the Department observed the language-teaching experiment at Fitzroy High School and in August 1967, at the invitation of the Victorian Education Department, attended a meeting to evaluate this innovative programme. Following informal discussion about the possibility of Commonwealth support for the expansion of courses of this kind, the Victorian Minister for Education eventually, in May 1968, requested the Commonwealth to supply (free of cost) copies of the *Situational English* series, developed for the adult education programme, for use in Victorian schools. Treasury, however, threw cold water on Snedden's readiness to comply and he was reluctantly forced to turn the request down.

The Department adopted a much firmer stand on the question of child migrant education during this period, and began to prepare the ground for public support of Commonwealth initiatives. The education of migrant children had been a recurring theme at Citizenship Conventions in the 1960s (see Harris, 1973), but the nation-wide scope of the problem was first systematically spelled out, and official, wide-ranging involvement foreshadowed, in the background paper written, at Heydon's invitation, for the 1968 Convention by the sociologist, Jerzy Zubrzycki. After outlining the disadvantages suffered by children of non-English-speaking background, the abysmal inadequacy of measures taken in the State departments to deal with the problem and the lack of research, Zubrzycki concluded:

> What seems to be called for is a special educational policy for migrant children . . . what [this] implies is the realization that the problem calls for bold and necessarily costly measures. (Zubrzycki, 1968: 24)

As Heydon had foreshadowed in March 1967, the Department also initiated moves to inquire into the precise extent of English-language problems. The results of these inquiries would justify Immigration's position both to the Commonwealth Government and to those States that still did not recognise any special deficiencies in the schooling of migrant children. As the one important migrant-receiving State that had undertaken no official survey of migrant children at any time, nor developed more than an embryonic acknowledgement that migrant children might experience difficulties, New South Wales was the obvious choice for these sensitive investigations. In December 1967, therefore (following discussions with Heydon), the Secretary of the Department of Education and S ience, A.H. Ennor, requested the Director-General of Education in New South Wales, H.S. Wyndham, to arrange a conference early in 1968 to consider studies of the adult English programme and the educational needs of migrant children.

The first New South Wales survey was carried out in 1968, the second in 1969. The final report, published in 1971, began by pointing out that there were no existing data on the problems of migrant children because of 'the long-standing official practice of not identi- fying migrant children statistically in routine returns lest this be construed as discrimination' (NSW, Department of Education, 1971: 5). The first survey, covering all primary and secondary schools in New South Wales, both government and non-government, identified 5 per cent of the total school population of nearly one million children as migrants. Most were in primary schools and they were distributed between the government (73 per cent) and non-government (27 per cent) systems in almost the same proportion as the total school population. About one-third (16 000) of all those identified as migrants was reported as having an English-language handicap, the proportion handicapped decreasing from 37 per cent in grade 1 to 8 per cent in the final year of secondary school.

The 1969 survey of a sample of government and non-government schools was designed to explore English-language difficulties more thoroughly. The main groups of children with difficulties were of Italian, Greek and Yugoslav origin. The major difficulties reported were reading and comprehension. Most children with an English- language handicap came from homes where English was rarely or never spoken. About a third were in a lower grade for their age or in a slow-learning grade. The great majority of primary children with difficulties had entered the school system in kindergarten or grade 1, and most secondary pupils handicapped by inadequate English had entered at primary level.

The research methods used in the New South Wales surveys made rigorous interpretation of the results almost impossible. The only guidance in filling out the questionnaire given to school principals was that 'migrant children' were those 'from a non-English speaking background (excluding Asians)'. In the words of the report:

the matter of identification of whether a child was a migrant or not was left to each principal's discretion. In view of this policy of identification, the figures should be regarded as underestimating rather than over-estimating the situation. (NSW, Department of Education, 1971: 6)

Pupils 'with English difficulties' were simply those with 'school work affected' and no attempt was made to indicate the criteria to be used in assessing 'progress' or in measuring the particular types of difficulty —reading, writing, speaking and comprehension—on which information was sought. The potential value of the 1969 survey was not realised because it covered only children with 'English difficulties', and there was no way of knowing how the characteristics of children with or without difficulties compared. The text in general takes no account of this crucial deficiency. It implies, for example, that the evidence supports the proposition that English-language difficulties and lack of progress are often the result of English not being spoken at home (1971: 32)—whereas, without information on the home languages of children *without* difficulties, it is not possible to establish this association. Interpretation of the data on the nature of difficulties is also confounded by the method of data analysis: data on pupils are analysed for each of the four difficulties separately and the extent of multiple difficulties is not examined (although the raw data would apparently have made this possible).

These methodological aberrations, however, did not detract from the impact of the findings. At the Citizenship Convention in January 1970, Olive Nichols, District Inspector of Schools for the Sydney city area and editor of the Departmental publication, *English for Us*, drew on the results of the two surveys to substantiate a case for the development of a language-teaching programme and other services to migrant children. 'The first essential', she concluded, 'is possibly the setting up of a branch to organise and co-ordinate at both school and community level' (Nichols, 1970: 9).

During 1968 and 1969 the New South Wales Government came under pressure from individual schools, the Federation of Parents and Citizens' Association and the Good Neighbour Council to take positive steps—including steps to secure funds from the Commonwealth—for the education of migrant children. It seems likely that much of this pressure was stimulated by the knowledge that Commonwealth-inspired surveys were being undertaken and the anticipation that the Commonwealth was about to extend its responsibilities into this area. At first, these pressures met with as little response as had the sporadic approaches made during the preceding years. However, apparently following the appointment of a new Director-General in January 1969 and the appearance of an interim report on the 1968 survey in March, the Department's attitude changed. As the new Director-General,

D.J.A. Verco, wrote to J. Maclean, the General Secretary of the Federation of Parents and Citizens' Associations, in September 1969:

> As a result of the information obtained from the above investigations a much more positive approach to the promotion of more rapid learning of English by migrant pupils is possible . . . As new information from research investigators comes to hand present policy will be extended and varied to improve the teaching of English as a foreign language in this State. (NSW, Department of Education, Verco to Maclean, 9 September 1969)

A small number of specialist teachers were appointed during 1969, but migrant education did not become a major public issue in New South Wales, as it did during the same period in Victoria. By January 1970, when the Commonwealth and States met—at the Commonwealth's instigation—to develop plans for a Commonwealth-funded programme, Victoria was acknowledged as the only State where any serious attempt was being made to deal with the education of migrant children or the problems of schools with large numbers of pupils from non-English-speaking background: 338 pupils were being taught English in withdrawal classes and teachers were receiving some in-service training. But the Victorian representative went on to emphasise that

> only the first stage of the problem—the oral problem is being treated. Not much at all is being done for the second stage of the problem— the literacy problem. (Aus., Department of Education and Science, notes on meeting, 21 January 1970: 5)

In none of the other States was the education of migrant children a matter of public concern at this time. The South Australian representative at the January 1970 meeting was N.L. Haines, who referred back to the scheme developed at St Leonards Primary School in 1958, which, he said, was still in operation. Withdrawal classes were being used at St Leonards and in a number of other primary schools. There were no organised classes in secondary schools, but if staff were available a teacher would be freed to take a group of migrant children.

The representatives of Queensland, Western Australia and Tasmania reported some experimental attempts in individual schools to give migrant children special language instruction, but, as the Queensland representative put it: 'Schools generally handle their problems according to their own resources' (Aus., Department of Education and Science, notes on meetings, 12 January 1970: 5).

The January 1970 meeting also discussed the particular areas which needed additional resources in each State. The one area agreed upon by all the States was the production of teaching materials. Development of teacher training and the need for accommodation were mentioned by most States. New South Wales, Victoria and South Australia proposed that additional staff should include social workers.

Further consultations followed the January 1970 meeting and in April 1970, P.R. Lynch, who had followed Snedden as Minister for Immigration, announced that funds were to be provided to inaugurate a programme of child migrant education in government and independent schools. The funds were to cover:

> The salary costs of teachers employed to teach migrant children in special classes and the necessary supervisory staff; special training courses for teachers in the method of teaching English as a foreign language; the provision of approved capital equipment of the language laboratory type for special classes; and the provision of suitable teaching and learning materials. (Aus., House of Reps., *Parl. Debates*, Vol. 67, 1970: 1521)

The Commonwealth itself would assume responsibility for teacher training and for producing suitable materials. There was no mention of accommodation.

Legislation to authorise these expenditures was contained in the Immigration (Education) Bill brought before the House of Representatives in May 1970 and deriving from the immigration provision of the Constitution. The second reading debate was deferred until February 1971 and the Act came into force in March. The Bill included provisions for expanding the adult education programme and these occupied more of the members' attention than did the new child education measures. Debate on the child programme did, however, elicit information from individual electorates, particularly in the poorer city areas, confirming the urgent need for help to migrant children and teachers. The Labor Opposition supported the Bill in principle, but chastised the Government for taking so long to introduce the school programme and for not providing capital funds for classrooms. Speakers on both sides acknowledged that the current shortage of teachers could hinder the implementation of the programme. Debate on the Bill provided an opportunity for a broad consideration of the whole immigration programme.

The Ministerial Statement of April 1970 referred to a five-year programme, with an expected annual expenditure of $1.5 million (Aus., House of Reps., *Parl. Debates*, Vol. 67, 1970: 1522). By the time of the second reading, the Minister acknowledged that the 'rate at which the child migrant education programme has developed since it was announced in April of last year has in fact exceeded expectations', but he still envisaged that 'peak requirement for special teachers could now be reached in the next financial year and that it should not be greatly in excess of 400' (Aus., House of Reps., *Parl. Debates*, Vol. 71, 1971: 168–9).

The Child Migrant Education Program was seen originally as a limited commitment, like the science laboratories and libraries schemes: once the backlog of remedial work with children already in the schools had been taken care of, new enrolments would be catered for as a matter of routine at only a fraction of the expenditure required initially. It soon became clear that noone knew what the dimensions of the need for English instruction were at the time the Program was initiated, and that the scope and necessary duration of the enterprise were seriously underestimated. Even in the first year of operation, 1970–1971, the Program cost $1.8 million instead of the anticipated $1 million.

One important source of error in calculations of likely demand for English teaching lay in the definition of 'migrant'. On the basis of the New South Wales surveys, it was anticipated that about one-third of all migrant children would be handicapped because of English-language difficulties. As we have already seen, no exact definition of 'migrant' was adopted in these enquiries. But in extrapolating from New South Wales to Australia as a whole to arrive at a figure of 44 000 in need of English classes, official estimates appear to have taken 'migrant' to mean 'born overseas, other than in the United Kingdom'. Had the definition of migrant children included both overseas-born children *and children born in Australia* of parents from non-English-speaking countries, then instead of 44 000 the estimate of demand might have been more like 132 000 (that is, one-third of the 400 000 children who were aged five to fourteen at the 1971 Census and whose mother was born in an overseas country other than the United Kingdom and Ireland). The limited interpretation, however, got the scheme off the ground without the opposition that a more realistic definition—implying a more substantial financial commitment—would doubtless have aroused.

NOTES

1. There had, however, been some contact between South Australia and Victoria. The Haines report refers to a member of the committee, R.H.O. Milway, during a visit to Melbourne, making contact with Mr Greening, a Staff Inspector of the Victorian Education Department. Milway stated: 'From my conversation with Mr Greening I gathered that, in Victoria, a similar problem to ours exists but that little has been done in the matter' (SA Department of Education, 1956: 6). Haines also showed a pilot copy of the work assignments at the 1960 Canberra Conference (Price ed., 1960: 157).
2. Most of the evidence on which this section is based comes from files of the former Department of Immigration, which were with the Department of Education in 1975 when I was granted access to them.

4   From Migrant to Multicultural Education in the Seventies

The Child Migrant Education Program (CMEP) was explicitly based on the definition of child migrant education as a problem of communication, located in the individual migrant child. A simple solution befitted this simple definition: change the migrant child—by teaching him English—and no other changes would be needed. Although the implementation of this aim did in fact involve also knowledge and structural responses, there is still some basis for the assertion that the established educational systems never comfortably digested CMEP, and that the trends of thought that now are changing the whole concept of migrant education owe little to CMEP except insofar as it has provided a stone for advocates of change to sharpen their weapons on. This is, however, an over-simplified assessment of the role of CMEP, as a closer examination of the programme in terms of communication, knowledge and structural change will show.

What was not foreseen at the beginning was that CMEP would 'flush out' children whose educational difficulties were being ignored or being accepted as irremediable or as a sign of backwardness. The expected levelling off in demand did not occur. Instead, CMEP generated its own clients and expanded from year to year. As Table 4.1 shows, the number of teachers working under the programme increased from 246 to 2291 between 1970 and 1976; the number of children in special classes from 8800 to 90 810; the number of schools from 199 to 1407; and expenditure from $0.1 million to $13.1 million for the last full year of operation. In 1973, in response to widespread criticism of the physical conditions in which withdrawal classes were being held, in hallways, washrooms and storerooms, the Government amended the 1971 Act to give the Commonwealth authority to include 'portable class-rooms' in the capital equipment for which it could make funds available under the provisions of the Act.

The awareness and demand created by CMEP did not come automatically, however, and administrators often had to work hard

Table 4.1   Child Migrant Education
                              Program, Australia, 1969–1975

Financial year	Number of special teachers*	Number of children in special classes	Number of schools qualifying for assistance	Expenditure ($m)
1969–70 (4th quarter only)	246(164)	8 800	199	0.1
1970–71	546(408)	21 000	440	1.8
1971–72	929(774)	34 800	663	3.3
1972–73	1136(967)	43 300	828	5.1
1973–74	1508(1308)	57 746	1013	8.3
1974–75	2095(1891)	85 689	1252	13.1
1975–76†	2291(1970)	90 810	1407	10.4

* Figures in brackets represent the number of equivalent full-time teachers.
† First half only.
Source: Aus., Department of Education, *Migrant Education Program 1975–76*.

to bring schools into the programme. As one departmental official said
in an interview in 1975:

> The general philosophy has been that 'they pick it up' [that is, English];
> so it's a 'sitting next to Nelly' idea; you pick it up and that's that. [There
> are] any amount of schools now where although we made a survey and
> found that there are x number of migrant children—quite enough to
> justify a migrant teacher—they still don't apply for a teacher.

Because—even within States—there has been no standard procedure
for assessing a migrant child's need for English teaching nor any regular
attempt to collect information on the numbers of such children, by States
or nationally, there is no way of calculating what proportion of all
children with inadequate English was represented by the 91 000 in
special classes at the end of 1975. On some criteria, the shortfall may
be as high as two-thirds, which is the figure the Schools Commission
arrived at from a survey of non-governmental schools (Aus., Schools
Commission, 1975: 124). On the criteria used in a national study of
literacy and numeracy, about 40 per cent of 14-year-olds who needed
remedial instruction in reading had not received it (Bourke and Keeves,
1977: 173). On *any* criteria, a shortfall certainly exists.

Teaching English under CMEP

The teaching of English as a second language (ESL), as developed
under CMEP and as still most widely practised, is based on the view

that different processes are involved in learning first and second languages. Courses are highly structured and take the form of a developmental sequence of units. Teachers are warned that it will be difficult for them 'to modify to any significant extent the teaching order of particular items without creating additional linguistic difficulties for themselves and their pupils' (quoted by Tenezakis, 1977: 7). The Language Teaching Branch (LTB) of the Commonwealth Department of Education has the responsibility of producing the course materials that embody this approach. It began working on a course for eight- to twelve-year-olds in 1971 and launched the first set of units in this course, called *Learning English in Australia*, in 1974. The LTB is currently working on an *English Development Course* for second phase learners, ten years and older.

The LTB works in Canberra and is not in close touch either with schools or with the general operation of the child migrant education programmes. It has little knowledge of how the units it produces are actually used in schools, nor of the wide range of materials that individual teachers and State bodies are themselves producing for teaching English to migrant children. The '10+' course is being developed by course writers who are language or special-subject teachers but who, for the most part, have no experience in teaching English to migrant children. 'The writing team worked almost in isolation until the first trialling of material took place in November 1976' (Millbank, 1977: 7). Because materials are so long in the making —about three years from inception to the first products becoming available in schools—and because the type of course produced is such that, once the pattern is established, there is little scope for change, the work of the LTB has not been responsive to the volatile situation that has developed in the States in the past five years.

The course *Learning English in Australia* was prepared for use in withdrawal classes, and the *English Development Course* is designed to be used the same way (Millbank, 1977). Withdrawal classes involve the withdrawal of children from the normal teaching programme into classes where they receive regular instruction in English, usually in groups of five to ten for one or two periods a day. Withdrawal classes normally consist of children of mixed origin and are taught by teachers who have qualified for the job by taking a short training course and who rarely have any knowledge of the languages spoken by their students.

It is hard to document exactly how the withdrawal system works in practice. Margaret Jackson, an ESL teacher in Sydney, gives some hint of the tensions it can create: in describing a new system of parallel English classes, she comments, 'We wish to report on the enormous advantages we have found in this new system . . . Previously, a large amount of energy was spent in justifying withdrawal to both the girls themselves and other teachers' (Jackson, 1977: 15). These remarks imply the common criticism that the withdrawal system has not become an integrated part of the school's operations, but this criticism should not deflect attention from the fact that it has come to fulfil very specific functions in school organisation. Because the selection of students for withdrawal classes relies on no standardised procedures, and because the scheme does not provide for all who might be judged eligible, there is much scope for teachers to use criteria other than English ability in deciding which children should or should not be chosen. The system thus provides a safety valve for classroom teachers, enabling them to hive off children who present discipline problems or who are simply the most visible outsiders in the class, and therefore the most uncomfortable reminders of any inadequacies teachers may recognise in their own work. The withdrawal system can also absolve the classroom teachers from the obligation to respond to the needs of non-English-speaking children, and encourages the situation where ESL teachers become responsible for all problems associated with migrant children, whether these problems have anything to do with English teaching or not (Millbank, 1977: 5).

Some cogent criticisms of the withdrawal system relate less to its demerits as a method of teaching English than to the philosophy underlying it and its social implications. Dealing with the question, 'The migrant child and the remedial child: are they necessarily the same?', Tony Knight claims that segregation into any kind of special or remedial class stigmatises the child and makes him or her vulnerable and powerless.

> Once set in motion, these remedial careers have an institutional logic that can be predictive within a student's school life, especially if he/she is not able to re-negotiate stigmatised and institutionalised reputations. (Knight, 1977: 22)

In his perceptive study, *The Schools*, Barry Hill gives examples both of the kind of situation Knight is talking about and of something rather different. At 'City Girls' there was a 'migrant centre', where migrants with poorest English had English classes while the rest of the class did General Studies. The scheme, says Hill,

> was perfectly pleasant, even if their class was a converted storeroom. But it didn't work. There was a stigma attached to being extracted for a special group. The instruction was divorced from most of their more meaningful class work. (1977: 79)

At 'Working Boys', on the other hand, Hill found that withdrawal classes provided 'a haven from the rest of the school': ' "No one calls us wogs here", a Greek boy tells me' (1977: 132).

At a more fundamental level there has been criticism of the official approach to ESL for its reliance on behaviourist theories of language learning, with the concomitant emphasis on the interference of the first language on the second, habit formation, the avoidance of error and sequential development (Millbank, 1977; Tenezakis, 1977; see also Claydon, Knight and Rado, 1977). The Department of Education acknowledges such criticisms and is adopting a more flexible approach in its *English Development Course* (Aus., Department of Education, 1976b). However, it has not engaged in serious debate on the issues involved, nor contributed to the development of theoretical insight into second-language learning. Consistent with its concentration on the technology of producing materials, the Department has never evaluated the effectiveness of ESL teaching; neither has it tried to test any of the assumptions on which the programme is based.

Several small-scale academic inquiries have, however, helped to fill this gap. One of the most theoretically interesting of these is Maria Tenezakis's study of language use and comprehension among monolingual English-speaking children compared with children whose first language was Greek. Tenezakis concluded that interference from the Greek children's first language did not explain such minimal differences as were to be found between the two groups; the structure of English itself appeared to be more important than contrasts between English and Greek. Whether the Greek students had or had not attended ESL classes or received instruction in Greek had no relationship to their performance in English. In both the Australian and Greek groups, the significant differences in performance were related directly to grade: higher-grade children did better than first graders. The results also suggest that, for both groups, the level of cognitive development is significantly related to the level of linguistic performance, and Tenezakis interprets this as contradicting the behaviourist assumption that learning a language is a kind of habit formation. Her research supports an alternative approach to second-language learning: that 'genuine communication', as compared with rigid instruction in correct usage, enables the individual to move from what Piaget calls 'assimilation', where 'errors' betray the persistence of mother-tongue structures, to 'accommodation', where the language structure is continuously modified by what is assimilated (Tenezakis, 1977).

CMEP teachers

As part of its commitment to migrant education, the Commonwealth Government assumed responsibility, in collaboration with the States, for training special teachers to teach English to migrant children and acquainting these teachers with 'the cultural backgrounds and specific linguistic difficulties of the major ethnic groups' (Aus., Department of Immigration, 1973*b*: 21). Training has normally consisted of a four-week in-service course; up to mid-1975, 2444 teachers had been trained under this programme. There has never been an overall assessment of migrant teacher training.

While, in the first years of CMEP, these training courses filled a need that was not being met elsewhere, they are often criticised for concentrating too much on language. A more widespread criticism is that they are too short and superficial. At best, they often come too late: in answer to the Migrant Education Questionnaire, a member of one State department of education, with many years experience in the field, wrote:

> The training of Child Migrant Teachers needs upgrading. It is almost non-existent. It should be a specialized training, of at least one year full-time . . . The present situation is farcical. Migrant teachers rarely have any previous experience nor training in migrant education, yet are required to commence duty after *one day's* induction . . . After some months or up to a year as a migrant teacher, they are given four-six weeks' training. As I have been involved with their training course, I have become aware of the frustrations of untrained but enthusiastic migrant teachers, who invariably state that they needed the course *before* they commenced teaching migrant children! Then they wouldn't have made so many errors of judgment, nor been so ignorant and confused.

The success with which CMEP teachers were incorporated into the State education systems varied from State to State, but the common overriding factor was the low priority given to the appointment of special migrant teachers when teachers in general were in short supply. This meant that, in a situation of shortage, the teachers available for migrant education were often those whom, as one administrator put it, 'nobody else wants'. It also meant that ESL-trained teachers were not necessarily allocated to migrant teaching. Neither was there any career structure for ESL teachers.

The overall result of the manner of recruitment and training of teachers of English to migrant children, and of the position they occupied in the State departments, was that they were marginal to the schools and the teaching profession and had little incentive to see their function in anything but the narrowest, technological terms. Their status was generally low and their voices were not heard in high places. A 1975 report on schools of high migrant density gave guarded expression to a situation that teachers themselves often described much more forcibly: one panel of advisers, said the report, observed that 'at least in the schools they had visited, special English teachers usually had fairly low recognition from their peers, thus making effective liaison difficult' (Aus., Department of Education, 1975: 22).

Emphasising the value of in-service training courses, one Departmental officer commented in an interview that the participants 'gain a great deal from one another; group interaction is tremendous; migrant teaching can be a very lonely type of existence'.

Forces for change in the seventies

At the time when CMEP was introduced, the only relevant term in common usage was 'migrant education' and the only relevant definition of 'migrant education' was teaching English to children who were of non-English-speaking origin and who had *learning problems*. What was once 'migrant education' now means many different things to different people. The field has become a microcosm of 'the intellectual cross currents' which Barry Hill sees as characterising the education scene in general, with its 'concatenation of critics' advocating a 'variety of reforms' (1977: 150). But, instead of the polarisation that Hill describes (between those who think schools worth reforming and those who want to do away with them), migrant education looks more like a harbour full of sailing boats on a sunny day: on close inspection, some are competing in a regular race, others are engaged in private little *ad hoc* battles, a few verge on collision though apparently unaware of each other's existence, some go their own independent way, alone or in agreeable company.

The shores surrounding this picturesque if disorderly array need to be briefly sketched in. Education has been more affected than other institutions by emerging definitions of Australia as a plural, multi-cultural or polyethnic society and has experienced the impact of radical claims for 'ethnic rights, power and participation' (Storer ed., n.d. [1975]).

Political events of the seventies have also entailed wide swings in the fortunes of migrant education. When Labor won office at the end of 1972, it continued to support initiatives already taken by the Liberal Government at the beginning of the seventies—the most important of which were CMEP, the sponsorship of academic research and the development of testing procedures for non-English-speakers—and embarked on a somewhat hectic series of inquiries and developments of its own. Those initiatives associated with the new Schools Commission, founded in 1973, have had the most continuing and far-reaching impact, but others—such as the Task Force surveys carried out in each State in 1973 and the Committee on the Teaching of Migrant Languages in Schools (the Committee on Migrant Languages), set up in 1974—have also been significant. Labor's curtailment of government expenditure in 1975 and the tougher restrictions introduced after the Liberal Party won power again at the end of that year (combined with the Liberal Federalism policy) have resulted in some embryonic developments being delayed or stifled for lack of funds —for example, bridging courses for ethnic teachers, exchange of teachers between Australia and Italy, and the introduction of new courses on migrant and multicultural studies in teacher-training institutions (Aus., Department of Education, 1976*c*: 88). Within the limitations of their own functions and budget, however, a number of Commonwealth authorities the Department of Education, the Schools Commission, the Education Research and Development Committee and the Curriculum Development Centre—are all actively involved in the area of migrant-multicultural education, which now has an impetus that is independent of any one agent.[2]

Recent demographic changes also have implications for migrant education. An estimate of the size of the young population of non-English-speaking origin is given in Table 4.2, which groups 0–19-year-olds according to twenty-five ethnic-language categories. Because of the high rate of migration at the end of the sixties and the heavy decline since 1971, the great majority of children of migrant parents are now Australian-born and most of them know some English when they first enrol in school. Also, partly because migrant birth rates (like those of Anglo-Australians) have declined sharply in recent years, and partly because all children are now tending to stay longer at school, a greater proportion of migrant children is now in secondary school than formerly—and at this level there is an accumulation of children whose ability to benefit from secondary education is limited because of their poor primary education. Thus, in both primary and secondary school, there is more demand for language-development courses for second-phase learners and less for the kind of elementary teaching of English that formed the original thrust of CMEP.

School populations have also changed in other ways. Because migrants arriving at the end of the sixties and in the early seventies were distributed over a greater number of source countries than in the past, schools with children from twenty to thirty different birth places are now not unusual, and they present students and teachers with a situation different from that which existed in schools with high concentrations of a particular ethnic group. A complementary set of new questions has also arisen in relation to small ethnic communities: with current negligible rates of immigration, these groups will remain small and the question of how to meet the educational needs of *their* children—few in number and widely scattered in the schools—will become more insistent, replacing the earlier concern over concentrations of large numbers of Greek, Italian and Yugoslav children.

Table 4.2 *Estimate of young population of non-English-speaking origin, by origin and age, Australia, June 1976*

Ethnic origin	Age group				
	0–4	5–9	10–14	15–19	Total
German	13 820	16 585	15 580	14 705	60 690
Scandinavian	1 325	1 145	1 760	1 155	5 385
Dutch	14 835	15 125	16 145	16 025	62 130
French	1 515	1 520	2 040	1 890	6 965
Swiss	280	330	645	500	1 755
Baltic	1 135	1 390	1 655	2 030	6 210
Russian	1 305	1 615	1 840	2 340	7 100
Polish	4 215	3 205	4 505	6 210	18 135
Czechoslovak	1 050	925	1 160	1 450	4 585
South Slav	24 280	20 530	18 660	16 255	79 725
Italian	37 670	44 895	49 445	43 035	175 045
Spanish	7 995	6 890	6 460	5 265	26 610
Greek	28 720	34 960	27 320	21 095	112 095
Maltese	11 475	10 840	9 735	11 400	43 450
Arabic	14 350	9 650	7 005	7 675	38 680
Turkish	3 460	3 470	2 980	2 195	12 105
Chinese	6 525	7 015	6 560	8 380	28 480
Indian etc.	7 460	6 805	6 145	9 640	30 050
South-east and East Asian	4 990	4 180	3 905	5 685	18 760
African and Mauritian	2 270	2 065	2 205	3 000	9 540
Oceanian (excl. New Zealand)	4 275	5 195	4 005	4 095	17 570
Hungarian	1 780	1 925	2 315	2 840	8 860
Estonian and Finnish	1 100	990	1 050	1 460	4 600
Rumanian	200	215	415	495	1 325
Israel ·	860	670	510	655	2 695

Source: C.A. Price and P. Pyne, 1976.

The issue of the education of children of non-English-speaking origin has undergone another notable change since the beginning of this decade. At that time the level of public and official discussion of the question was uninformed and there existed no coherent, comprehensive statement of theory, philosophy, policy or practice. Such discussions and commentaries as were to be found tended to be parochial in outlook, revealing no knowledge of anything apart from the personal experience of the writer, and they rarely penetrated beyond a small local readership. This situation has now changed, with T.W. Roper's 1972 *Bibliography on Migration to Australia from Non-English Speaking Countries with Special Reference to Education* as the most clear-cut bench mark.

Inquiries and committees sponsored by the Commonwealth have

made a substantial contribution to the development of a better informed body of opinion. *Education News*, published by the Commonwealth Department of Education, gives regular coverage to issues of migrant-multicultural education. *Polycom: A Bulletin for Teachers of Non-English-Speaking Migrant Children*, published by the Education Department of Victoria, is the most professional of the State publications. In New South Wales, the *Child Migrant Education Newsletter* has been refurbished and promises to provide a forum and channel of communication in that State. The three bibliographies and digests on immigration produced by Charles A. Price at the Australian National University give a comprehensive coverage of literature on education up to 1975 (Price ed., 1966 and 1971; Price and Martin eds, 1976a and 1976b).

Recently founded organisations specifically committed to ethnic interests have facilitated continuity of debate and discussion to a degree that was not possible previously. The most notable of these have been mentioned in previous chapters: the Ecumenical Migration Centre at Richmond, Melbourne, which publishes the quarterly, *Migration Action*, and houses the Clearing House on Migration Issues, a resource and publication centre that now provides a documentation service called Chomi Das; the Centre for Urban Research and Action, Fitzroy, Melbourne; the Australian Greek Welfare Society, Melbourne, which publishes the *Greek Action Bulletin*; and the Ethnic Communities Councils in Melbourne, Sydney and Adelaide.

The more vigorous role taken by ethnic communities in the past few years is indicated in a survey of responses to the Committee on Migrant Languages' call for submissions. Of 126 'useful' submissions received, 62 per cent were from 'ethnic-Australian' associations and a further 10 per cent from 'ethnic-Australian' individuals; in all, they represented views from 24 different ethnic groups. J.J. Smolicz and M.J. Secombe, who analysed the submissions, comment:

> Such high level of ethnic response represented a new development in Australia. Until recently, ethnic groups had been reluctant to express publicly their desire to maintain their ethnic languages or to discuss the ethnic schools they had established. (1977: 2)

As we have already seen from the analysis of items listed in Willcock's 'Bibliography' (a contribution to the third in the Price series), writings on migrant education increased dramatically in the seventies. Further information on recent trends in authorship of publications can be obtained from the 69 answers to the Migrant Education Questionnaire. Expansion in the role of academics and tertiary institutions, and the decline in the relative importance of teachers and schools, is indicated by a comparison of respondents' occupations and employers in terms of the period of their first interest in migrant education: when respondents are ordered into three groups according to period of first interest, the percentage of teachers from universities and Colleges of Advanced Education in the group increases from 21 to 29 to 40, while the percentage of teachers declines from 43 to 38 to 10. Similarly, the percentage of respondents employed by tertiary institutions or Commonwealth education authorities increases from 21 to 29 to 45, while the percentage employed in State education departments declines from 39 to 29 to 25.

A profile of what might be called the active contemporary definers —the fifty-nine people whose first publication appeared between 1970 and 1975—shows that 56 per cent were born in Australia, 19 per cent in the United Kingdom or Ireland and 25 per cent elsewhere. Also, 61 per cent had some knowledge of a language other than English and 29 per cent knew two or more other languages. One-third was university teachers, one-fifth teachers in Colleges of Advanced Education, 12 per cent were school teachers, 17 per cent were non-teaching professionals, and the remaining 18 per cent worked as administrators, students and in a variety of other jobs. One-third had become first interested in migrant education before 1966, one-third during 1966–1969 and one-third since that time.

The end of CMEP

The end of what might be called the CMEP period was officially signified in the first report of the Schools Commission, established by the Labor Government in 1973. In this report, published in June 1975, the Commission recommended that CMEP be discontinued and that 'funds for child migrant education should be provided to the States through the General Recurrent Grants Program of the Schools Commission' (1975: 130). This policy change came into effect in January 1976. It meant that henceforth the States received a block grant for 'Migrant and Multi-cultural Education' and that these funds could be used at the discretion of the States for teaching English to migrant children or for a variety of programmes directed at ethnic or Australian children or both. In addition, it was envisaged that migrant children and high-migrant-density schools would benefit from the Specific Purpose Disadvantaged Schools Program. Although the Commonwealth Government has not provided the promised level of funds for the Schools Commission for 1978, the guidelines it issued in June 1977 advised the Commission to continue its programmes for migrants, and in allocating funds for 1978 the Commission has given highest priority to the 'protection of programs specifically directed towards more equal educational opportunities', including funds for disadvantaged schools and migrant and multicultural education (Aus., Schools Commission, 1977a: 8–9, 27).[1]

Already, before 1976, schools with concentrations of migrant children were drawing on the special resources provided through the Schools Commission's Disadvantaged Schools Program. How little impact CMEP was making on schools of this kind was revealed in the Inquiry into Schools of High Migrant Density, sponsored by the Commonwealth and carried out in New South Wales and Victoria in 1974. There were some positive findings, but the report of the Inquiry shows clearly that response to the presence of migrant children in these schools was minimal. Apart from CMEP, 'the usual school programs are designed for Australian children and make no concessions to the particular needs and backgrounds of migrant pupils' (Aus., Department of Education, 1975: 6). Although, the report continued, not all migrant children of non-English-speaking background were impeded in their education by language difficulties, 'in the schools visited it is believed that the great majority were in fact in this category' (1975: 9). In a number of schools library facilities were poor or non-existent:

> the almost universal lack of appropriate books either in English or in ethnic languages was considered [by the advisory panels] to be a very serious deficiency. Major omissions were bilingual dictionaries, phrase books and reading material in which structural grading as well as vocabulary control were taken into account. (1975: 16)

Teachers were not adequately prepared to work in schools of this kind and there was much indifference and even intolerance towards migrant children (1975: 21–22, 29). The Committee of Inquiry saw little evidence 'of any meaningful communication between schools and local employers or any other interested members of the community', and in general 'the school tended to operate in a vacuum' (1975: 27). The burden of the Committee's final 'overview' was that most of these schools continued to function in a 'narrow, assimilationist mould' and tried 'to make the migrant children fit into a pattern which was determined before any migrant pupils were enrolled in the schools' (1975: 29). The phrase 'fits into' echoes the words of J.B. Cox in 1951 (see page 89).

Current issues

The wide-ranging investigations of the Inquiry into Schools of High Migrant Density signified a transformation in Commonwealth definitions of child migrant education. The question now at stake clearly went far beyond the individual problems of children who did not know English.

To clarify exactly what these more encompassing concerns at present involve, it will be useful to distinguish five main issues: teaching English, bilingual education, community languages, multicultural education and ethnic schools (see Nicoll, 1977; Matthews, 1977). Critics of the English-teaching emphasis of CMEP are commonly also supporters of bilingual education, the teaching of community languages in schools and multicultural education for everyone. They are more vocal than the 'traditionalists', who want to keep ESL teaching as the central core of the enterprise and are often sceptical of the wisdom of encouraging ethnic languages and cultures.

However, although ESL advocates now often appear on the defensive, they continue to dominate what actually happens in schools, for various reasons: they include the majority of CMEP teachers, most regular classroom teachers and most educational administrators; the structures established under CMEP also remain largely intact, because no education system was ready to replace them at the time CMEP ended. The practice of ESL has, however, become varied and the extent of this variation itself differs from State to State. In most States, for example, 90 per cent or more of ESL teachers in government schools still teach in withdrawal classes (Aus., Schools Commission, 1977b). In South Australia, however, as the outcome of an official policy of education for a multicultural society (Steinle, 1976), the figure is less than 25 per cent, and ESL teachers are increasingly seen 'as resource people available to the whole staff, capable of assisting with planning language programmes, modifying curriculum and up-grading the sensitivity to language of other teachers' (Giles, n.d. [1977]: 7)—a development also appearing in embryonic form in other States. With the establishment of migrant education centres in Brisbane, Adelaide, Melbourne, Canberra and Sydney, some new arrivals are now able to attend full-time intensive language courses before being thrust into the normal school situation. Highly welcome as this alternative to the conventional in-school withdrawal class approach is, it in turn raises the problem of the transition from 'the supportive and intimate atmosphere of the language centre' (Giles, n.d. [1977]: 8) to the much more demanding conditions of the normal school. The centres also run the first regular programmes designed for adolescent arrivals, and for these students they are in effect an alternative to brief attendance at a regular school, or no schooling at all.

In practice, then, for the great majority of children English learning is still a self-contained activity, unconnected with the rest of their school education, and most classroom teachers see migrants' learning difficulties as someone else's problem. But this perception is increasingly challenged as the problems of second-phase learners become more apparent because of higher retention rates (for all students and, it seems likely, for migrant students in particular, see Martin and Meade, 1978) and the influx into secondary schools of children from the immigration peak years of the sixties. Rosita Young predicts that, 'although specialist English language teachers may be needed initially in particular areas, the emphasis in future must be on individual teachers being able to diagnose and remedy English language difficulties of second-phase learners' (1977: 6). However, though many academic and professional definers agree with the Schools Commission's view that classroom teachers should be able and willing 'to provide special language assistance and to adapt programs to the varying backgrounds and experience of students' (Aus., Schools Commission, 1976: 31), there is little evidence that teachers in general subscribe to this view or see themselves as competent to take on such a responsibility. Neither the training of new teachers nor in-service education provides the background that would enable more than a small fraction of classroom teachers to do so effectively.

Although the teaching of English to adult migrants and the education of migrant children—which still also predominantly means teaching them English—represent the major item of Commonwealth expenditure on migrant settlement, little attention has been paid to the theory on which programmes are based, to the explication of policy aims or to evaluation. Uninformed debate becomes further blurred as the question of bilingual education enters into the discussion. The argument in favour of bilingual education (in the narrow sense, as distinct from community language education, although the terms are often not distinguished in this way) owes much to overseas, particularly American, experience. It rests strongly on the principle, as Marta Rado has put it, 'that the school takes the learner from where he stands, builds on and develops what he already knows, and certainly does not waste it' (1976: 46). But beyond this basic principle, the modes and aims of bilingual education are diverse (see Clyne, 1977). One important distinction refers to the aim of producing bilinguals, on the one hand, or monolinguals, on the other. In the latter case, as 'the learner becomes more efficient in the second language, the first language is phased out . . . bilingual education is used as a technique to enable the learner to make the transition from the first to the second language more effectively' (Rado, 1976: 3).

Fully bilingual education—in the sense that teaching takes place through the medium of two languages—is in fact very rare (see Clyne, 1977, and Aus., Department of Education 1976c: 30–31, for descriptions of some programmes in operation). One of the few well-developed programmes is the Italian Bilingual Project being carried out in several primary schools in Adelaide. It involves the participation of bilingual teachers, teacher training, the importation and development of materials, and consultation with parents (Giles, n.d. [1977]). Support for bilingual education seems to come mainly from primary schools, where the advantages to the school of programmes that cater systematically for children who enrol with little or no knowledge of English are immediately apparent. At the secondary level, bilingual education has two different emphases. On the one hand, it can be aimed at continuing the bilingual education begun at primary school to produce balanced mature bilinguals. On the other hand, it can cater for non-English-speaking migrant children who enter an Australian school for the first time at adolescence and who therefore do not have the command of English needed for conceptual development at secondary level. Bilingual education enables these children to continue mastering the content and concepts of particular subject areas through their mother-tongue, while learning English at the same time. The Multilingual Project developed in Victoria by Marta Rado, providing student-centred social science courses in English and seven other languages, serves this purpose for ten- to fourteen-year-olds (Claydon, Knight and Rado, 1977).

Bilingual education is not always distinguished from the teaching of community languages, but programmes of this latter kind do not necessarily involve teaching regular subjects in any language other than English, and they may be directed either at the ethnic child or take the form of fairly undemanding enrichment experiences for a mixed Anglo-Australian-ethnic class. A submission from the New South Wales State Multicultural Education Committee (SMEC, a voluntary body of individuals and representatives of groups) to the Commonwealth Minister for Education in July 1977 illustrates some of the ambiguities surrounding the definition of community languages. SMEC requests the Commonwealth to fund a pilot programme, 'for the teaching of community languages and cultures'. Although the submission asserts the benefits which *all* children would receive from such a programme, the intention is to carry out the pilot in schools of high migrant density and—while it is proposed to give some in-service education to all teachers in the selected schools—the main item in the proposed budget consists of the salaries of 'community language and culture teachers'. The emphasis of the proposal is clearly on what are seen as the needs of the migrant child (SMEC, NSW, 1977).[2]

SMEC's proposals grow directly out of the findings and recommendations of the Committee on the Teaching of Migrant Languages in Schools. In its final analysis the Committee seeks to relate bilingual education, the teaching of community languages and what it calls 'intercultural education' into a coherent framework and policy. It favours bilingual education, particularly to overcome the difficulties of children of migrant background who enter school knowing only their parents' mother-tongue. Secondary schools should offer a much wider range of community languages for all students and opportunity for students of ethnic origin to study their own language and culture.

In practice, children of non-English-speaking origin are more likely to have the chance to develop competence in their mother-tongue through language courses—at day schools, ethnic schools or at centres like the Saturday School for Modern Languages run by the Victorian Education Department—than through bilingual education in the full sense. But at the present time these opportunities are meagre indeed. As the Committee on the Teaching of Migrant Languages has shown, a far greater proportion of the resources devoted to language teaching goes to traditional foreign-language subjects—mainly French and German—than to teaching languages currently spoken in Australia. The survey of schools conducted for the Committee in 1975 revealed that only 1.4 per cent of the 231 592 children from bilingual homes in New South Wales, Victoria and South Australia were studying their native language and that only 78 out of the total of 670 courses taught at the 546 primary schools teaching modern languages were catering for these children. At the secondary level, the survey found 98 684 children from bilingual homes, with 10 per cent studying their native language; these students were being taught in 708 of the 2269 courses offered at the 1269 secondary schools teaching modern languages (Aus., Department of Education, 1976c: 18, 39). The only widely taught migrant languages were Italian and Greek, the languages of half the children from bilingual homes—few other ethnic children had the opportunity to study their native tongue at school.

The opportunity and incentive for students to become proficient in languages other than English are affected by the status of that language as a matriculation subject and its availability at tertiary institutions, which in turn affect the supply of teachers qualified to teach it. Table 4.3, reproduced from the report of the Committee on Migrant Languages, shows the wide range of variation among States (in their acceptance of ethnic languages at matriculation level) and among languages (in their acceptability). (See Note 6.)

Intercultural education is the third cornerstone of the framework laid out by the Committee on Migrant Languages. What the Committee means by intercultural study is indicated in its statement about the nature of Australian society and about inter-group relations:

> In our developing multicultural society, a major concern of education
> is to help children understand and appreciate others not only as
> individuals but also as members of various ethnic groups with their own

Table 4.3 *Languages available at higher certificate/matriculation level, by States, 1976*

Language	NSW	VIC	QLD	SA	WA	TAS	ACT	NT*
Chinese	x	x		x	x		x	
Czech.		x						
Dutch		x		x	x	x		
French	x	x	x	x	x	x	x	x
German	x	x	x	x	x	x	x	
Hebrew	x	x	x	x	x			
Hungarian		x						
Indones/Malay	x	x	x	x	x	x	x	x
Italian	x	x	x	x	x	x	x	x
Japanese	x	x	x	x	x	x	x	
Latvian		x						
Lithuanian		x		x				
Modern Greek	x	x		x			x	
Polish		x				x		
Russian	x	x	x	x	x	x	x	
Serbo-Croat.		x						
Spanish	x	x		x	x		x	
Ukrainian		x		x				

* In the Northern Territory students may in principle study by correspondence any language offered in South Australia, but in 1976 only the three languages indicated were being studied.
Source: Aus., Department of Education, *Report of the Committee on the Teaching of Migrant Languages in Schools*, 1976: 54.

languages, beliefs, customs, ambitions and aspirations. All peoples have a history, characteristics and individuality of their own, and require to be accepted and respected in their own right. (1976c: 25)

Intercultural study should be part of every child's education at the primary level; it should be emphasised more than at present at secondary level, where the intercultural factors in all appropriate subjects need also to be brought to the fore. 'Intercultural studies could be made more meaningful by some language study' (1976c: 116), but they do not depend on a knowledge of languages.

The position on intercultural education taken by the Committee on Migrant Languages affirms the policy of the Schools Commission, laid down in its first report of June 1975 and reiterated in its two subsequent reports of July 1976 and August 1977:

The multicultural reality of Australian society needs to be reflected in school curricula—languages, social studies, history, literature, the arts and crafts—in staffing and in school organisation. While these changes are particularly important to undergird the self-esteem of migrant children they also have application for all Australian children growing up in a society which could be greatly enriched through a wider sharing in the variety of cultural heritages now present in it. (1975: 125)

In 1976 the Commission reaffirmed that the special funds for 'Migrant and Multi-cultural Education' provided in the General Recurrent Grants Program did not 'have to be used to employ teachers who will work only with migrant children', and added: 'It would be disappointing if the patterns established under the previous Child Migrant Education Program . . . were to impede the development of [such] varied approaches' (1976: 32).

With the kind of support that the Schools Commission and the Committee on Migrant Languages are giving to the teaching of community languages in schools and to multicultural education, it is becoming increasingly difficult to clarify the role of ethnic schools. During the fifties and sixties the only social knowledge available about ethnic schools consisted of negative comments from teachers who believed that after-hours classes retarded the migrant child's progress in regular schooling; ethnic communities, for their part, were reluctant to draw attention to what they correctly saw as an unwelcome activity from the point of view of the Australian community, and guarded their schools from public scrutiny and the risk of outside interference. Two sources now provide fuller information about ethnic schools: M.P. Tsounis's study of Greek schools, published in 1974, and the inquiries of the Committee on the Teaching of Migrant Languages. A substantial increase in enrolments in ethnic schools—which the Committee estimates at 50 000 for the whole country—has been accompanied by a vigorous campaign on the part of some ethnic groups, particularly the Melbourne Greeks, for public support (see, for example, Deliyannis, 1975; Economo, 1975; Greek Orthodox Community, 1973 and 1974; Moraitis, 1974; Tsounis, 1974).

Four distinct definitions of the role of ethnic schools are now being advanced. The first is the legacy of earlier antagonism or scepticism on the part of teachers in the regular school system and defines ethnic schools as harmful competitors for the child's time and attention. In the present climate this is not a position that anyone is anxious to be publicly identified with; its currency is to be inferred from the fact that ethnic schools are not taken seriously, not from evidence that they are openly attacked. The second definition acknowledges the right of ethnic communities to seek to transmit their cultural heritage through ethnic schools, but sees no place for these schools in the established educational system and denies that they have any claim on public funds.

From the third point of view, ethnic schools can be integrated with day schools to play their part in the teaching of community languages and in multicultural education. The Committee on Migrant Languages gives mild support to this position, largely, it seems, as a transitional arrangement because 'it will be several years before Australian schools can meet any substantial increase in the numbers of children desiring language study, and hence a pooling of all the relevant resources . . . from government, non-government and ethnic schools within a given area is indicated' (1976c: 113). The Committee suggests that financial support for ethnic schools could be justified in some circumstances, but it finds the resources and standards of ethnic schools generally inadequate and concludes that 'they are often too isolated from the mainstream of social, cultural, and intellectual life to contribute their proper share to the development of a multicultural society' (1976c: 113). The Committee's conclusion that 'the vast majority of migrant parents and groups expressed the view that they would welcome the introduction of their languages and cultures in the day schools' (1976c: 113) is confirmed by the activities of vocal groups like SMEC, which in April 1977 organised a large public meeting in Sydney in support of Commonwealth funding for teaching community languages in the schools (ECC of NSW, *Newsletter*, June 1977).

Finally ethnic schools, as the agents of ethnic communities, may be defined as the appropriate bodies to take responsibility for teaching community languages and cultures on behalf of the education system as a whole, which implies that they should be publicly funded. Only a fifth of the relevant seventy submissions to the Committee on Migrant Languages supported separate ethnic schools. This 'was the policy advocated by most *small* ethnic groups who saw it as the only realistic way of having their languages taught in Australia' (Smolicz and Secombe, 1977: 18), and the Committee endorsed it in the case of such groups. The SMEC, New South Wales, has a strong representation of ethnic communities, and reported in its submission to the Commonwealth that a working party for the establishment of a Federation of Ethnic Schools in New South Wales had been set up 'so that a representative body will be able to speak for all ethnic schools in the State' (1977: 7). However, SMEC is in line with the recommendations of the Committee on the Teaching of Migrant Languages when it proposes that ethnic school funds—a quarter of the requested total of $2 million—should be given primarily for teaching the minority ethnic groups 'not catered for in the community language programmes in schools' (1977: 10).

South Australia has probably come closer than any other State to giving public acknowledgement to the educational role of ethnic schools; in that State about seventy ethnic schools receive a government subsidy and have access to rent-free accommodation in the day schools (Giles, n.d. [1977]: 15). However, in a recent account of the

South Australian scheme, J.R. Giles, then Assistant Director of Schools (Curriculum), expressed some misgivings:

> We believe that they [ethnic schools] are good things, but professionally we get a bit uneasy about the standard of teaching which is often pretty grim (although there are splendid teachers as well). (n.d. [1977]: 15)

With important exceptions, teaching in ethnic schools is uneven and often poor, the curriculum is commonly geared to religious or other sectional interests within the ethnic community, the drop-out rate is high and little appears to be learnt. In the past the schools themselves have often been short-lived. The discrepancy between what ethnic groups hope the schools will achieve and their actual impact is a recurring theme in the thinking of migrant communities (Johnston, 1972; Martin, 1972a; Tsounis, 1974). It seems clear that very substantial resources would be needed to bring teaching and materials up to standards acceptable in regular schools. If such aid were forthcoming, it would almost certainly be a factor in differentiating ethnic groups from one another, because some would use it effectively to strengthen their own organisation while others would be internally divided over its use and/or find that they could not maintain the control they wanted and meet externally imposed standards at the same time.[3]

Conclusion: differentiation and conflict in a multicultural society

During the first twenty years of post-war migration, a few isolated teachers and others saw the question of the education of children of non-English-speaking origin as a problem in its own right, detached from the overall crisis in education and the provision of remedial teaching for backward pupils. In the fifties and sixties some of these people, driven by the sense of urgency created by day-to-day experience in schools, made their own *ad hoc* and unco-ordinated attempts to respond to the needs of migrant children. They experimented with teaching strategies, constructed materials, tried to inform themselves and others about the migrants' cultural background, and—an essential ingredient in their attempt to cope with a situation that they often felt was beyond them and in which they lacked outside support—they developed their own explanations about what strategies succeeded in the education of these children and why.

These efforts were spasmodic, lacking in continuity, dependent on the enterprise of a few individuals and easily snuffed out. They contributed as little to cumulative understanding of the situation of migrant children as did the few official inquiries of the period. Yet attention to the most important of these inquiries—the Haines study in South Australia in 1956, the Queensland survey of 1959 and the Dovey report of 1960—could have alerted educational authorities to almost every issue that became a matter of concern in the seventies: the placing of children in grades below their age level, with the ensuing implication that few would ever complete secondary school; the lack of teaching materials; confining migrant education to teaching elementary English; the concentration of large numbers of migrant children in particular schools; differences among children of different ethnic backgrounds and in particular the inability of the schools to educate many Greek and Italian children. These early inquiries, like the scattered observations of the teachers, also foreshadowed a number of the themes that became important in the response to migrant children when it eventually occurred: the merits of withdrawal classes or intensive courses for children of different ages; the advantages of bilingualism; the possibilities of multicultural education; the desirability of all teachers—not only special English teachers—taking responsibility for migrant education; the role of bilingual teachers and ancillary staff.

With the advantages of hindsight it is of course easy to see what might have been incorporated from the experience of this early period into the cumulative body of social knowledge. Earlier chapters try to explain why so little was learnt. One reason was the lack of any theoretical structure, other than the assimilationist model, within which to organise observation and experience about migrants and migrant-Australian interaction. The educational bureaucracies also played a crucial part. They expressed the temper of the times in refusing to confront the fact that the presence of migrants of non-English-speaking origin had in fact changed the nature of the schools and the scope of their own role. Captive to rigid, inflexible structures and overwhelmed by an increasing discrepancy between their resources and the community's expectations, they simply denied that the experience of migrant children or their teachers was any different from anyone else's. As Fitzgerald has put it, 'Despite the special problems of the post-war period, the school systems managed to operate on familiar and socially acceptable terms' (1973: 163).

The history of child migrant education in Australia is thus a story of abortive beginnings and forgotten insights. What appear as recent contributions to social knowledge are in part the rediscovery—painfully and late—of lost understandings. The difference is that there are now regular, legitimate channels through which definitions from diverse sources can penetrate into educational policy, at the most general level, and into schools, at the most particular.

An array of teachers, educational administrators and experts, teacher educators, academics, parents and ethnic communities, separately and in various combinations, claims a share in this defining process, and most educational systems have avoided committing themselves formally to any particular position. In producing a policy on migrant-multicultural education, South Australia is the only State to have attempted an official resolution of varied definitions (Steinle, 1976). In New South Wales a network of individuals linking the Department of Education, the Ethnic Affairs Commission and the non-government Ethnic Communities Council is at present working towards the development of an official policy, though the established bureaucracy seems less than enthusiastic. Victoria's failure to develop an official policy seems to be both cause and effect of a decline in initiatives and productive debate in that State.

There has been some structural change that invovles more than superficial and isolated rearrangements along established lines. In form, this change has involved the development of new substructures and roles within the administration of education authorities—State, Commonwealth and Catholic—new teaching functions in schools, new modes of communication and co-operation and new courses of teacher training. In some States and in the Catholic system this change virtually began after the introduction of CMEP; in others CMEP stimulated developments that were already under way.

So far as the production of materials and development of curriculum are concerned, Commonwealth resources have encouraged the diversification of agencies involved, while at the same time continuing to support the traditional work of the Language Teaching Branch of the Department of Education. This encouragement has come through innovation grants made directly to schools and through the work of the Curriculum Development Centre (CDC), a Commonwealth body established in 1973 to promote and co-ordinate curriculum development on a national scale.[4]

At the school level, there has been less structural change than the flurry of conferences, papers and curriculum programmes might suggest. As the uncertainty and frustrations of the transition from CMEP to the Schools Commission's Migrant and Multi-cultural Education Program indicate, the school systems as a whole are by no means dedicated to the major structural changes that the proposals of more enthusiastic advocates of migrant and multicultural education would require.

M.J. Elliott's study of four schools with large migrant enrolments in the inner Melbourne suburb of Fitzroy shows how uneven and stumbling the response to migrant students continued to be up to the mid-seventies, and to what an extent classroom teachers were still trying to deal with the presence of migrant children on an *ad hoc* basis and in isolation from one another. In one of the schools studied, the lack of co-ordination reflected in the range of teachers' levels of understanding and awareness of children's language difficulties, their attitudes about the intellectual capabilities of migrant students, and the variety of syllabuses which focused on a child's language development in various ways, illustrates one of the major impediments in the evolution of an agreed set of concepts, theories and programs for child migrant education in Victoria as a whole during the last decade. Not only was there lack of co-ordination about ideas and practice concerning the education of migrant children within one school, but also there was very little co-ordination and interchange of ideas about migrant children between schools. (1977: 146)

The unwillingness of the States to establish a career structure for staff engaged in migrant education has always been a symptom of grudging commitment to solving what they saw as a temporary problem, which was not their responsibility anyway. Career opportunities are still extremely limited. Of far-reaching importance in schools, however, is the differentiation in the composition of school staff that has resulted from the introduction of non-teacher personnel —still defined as 'ancillaries'—into the school situation.

Teachers, counselling staff and others with direct contact with migrant children have for years been emphasising the need for bilingual ancillary workers to support school staff. Education systems began to respond to these demands about 1975, partly as the result of funds for this purpose being provided through Schools Commission programmes, partly as a by-product of a general relaxation of traditional constraints on school staffing. In Victoria, for example, legislation introduced in 1974 to permit school councils to employ teacher aides led to the appointment of bilingual aides in some schools of high migrant density, their salaries paid under the Disadvantaged Schools Programme of the Schools Commission. The fact that these 'ethnic aides' are not recruited, trained or employed by the Department of Education, together with the inevitable initial lack of definition in the roles they were expected to fulfil, created some difficulties in their incorporation into the school system. Somewhat similar structural problems seem to have been responsible for the meagre impact of a scheme to train bilingual welfare officers to work in schools, initiated by the Commonwealth Department of Immigration in 1972, and taken over by the Department of Social Security in 1974. The fact that the training and employment of these welfare officers are the responsibility of a body other than the State authority that controls the schools in which they work has clearly counteracted their usefulness and the schools' capacity to absorb them. By contrast, an interpreter service introduced by the Department itself in 1976 has been well received and is being effectively incorporated into the system.[5]

Teacher-education bodies have in general put up a strong resistance

against changing their programmes in response to the ethnic diversity
of schools or concepts of multicultural education, and their resistance
has been the easier to sustain because they are to a considerable degree
isolated from productive contact with schools, curriculum developers
or community groups. The Curriculum Development Centre, for
example, is beginning to support the development of multicultural
materials in a variety of enterprising ways, but the impact of its work
on school practice is likely to be attenuated because it has no formal
access to teacher-training bodies and therefore no means of ensuring
that teachers have the knowledge and skills to make effective use of
what it produces.

In the early seventies, it is true, a number of universities, teachers'
colleges and other tertiary institutions did introduce courses on the
teaching of English as a second language, and some teacher-training
courses added units on migrants and cultural pluralism. But the mode
of response of training bodies to the expectation that they should 'do
something' about migrant education often testified to a long experience
of absorbing pressures with the minimum of 'disruption', that is, of
structural change. Hank Overberg provides an example:

> In 1972 my own institution didn't have a migrant studies program, but
> then the boss recognised that the trend was in this direction and we did
> have a multicultural society didn't we?'
>
> A literary historian, untrained in sociology, psychology or linguistics,
> I was asked to mount a multicultural program with a year to develop
> the necessary expertise, my eligibility determined by my being the only
> migrant on the staff . . . Now, when asked what effort is being made,
> the boss says, 'We've got Overberg', and this also enables him to obtain
> funds from a multicultural source. 'We've done out bit. There's Overberg,
> he's palpable'. (Victoria, Education Department, Migrant Resources
> Section, 1975: 27)

Sober evidence that the education systems still carry a heavy burden
of the nondecision-making thinking of the fifties and sixties appears
in the report of a National Seminar for Teacher Educators, organised
under the auspices of the Committee on Migrant Education of the
Immigration Advisory Council in 1974. The aims of the Seminar were
to examine the possibility of changes in teacher education that would
give teachers a better understanding of the background of various
ethnic groups; to point to strategies for dealing with multilingual
classes; and 'to enable teachers to improve the knowledge and
understanding of all children in regard to the influence which
immigration has had on the character of Australian society' (Aus.,
Department of Education, 1974b: 5). In the event, no consensus on
any of these issues emerged among the seventy-five participants, and
in her Foreword to the published report the chairwoman, Barbara
Falk, noted that the 'suggestions for action were few and scattered'

(1974*b*: 4). No agreement was reached about the value of pluralism, the response, if any, that the educational system was required to make in a multicultural society or the role of ethnic schools. On the question of teacher training, there was, among other views, strong support for the established practice of confining training for migrant education to limited and specific functions:

> It was suggested that existing teacher-training courses already instilled the general principles and that the only specific requirements for migrants were the technique of teaching English as a second language and appreciation of bilingual education. (1974*b*: 18)

If these currents of indifference and antagonism reflected the thinking of numbers of teacher educators only three years ago, it is little wonder that many of the teachers they trained are ill-prepared to take initiatives in migrant and multicultural education or to respond constructively to the initiatives of others.

Most ESL and migrant-multicultural programmes in tertiary institutions are still short-term electives within general training courses, but by 1976 graduate diploma courses specialising in ESL teaching or ethnic studies were available in New South Wales, Victoria and South Australia (Aus., Department of Education, 1976 *a*). The extent of student interest in these courses has not, however, been matched by the readiness of education systems to give appropriate postings to teachers with such specialised training, and there has been some frustration and disillusionment on the part of teachers as a result.

Non-utilisation of the skills of migrant teachers represents a still more unwarranted waste of resources that could be used in migrant education. Teachers trained in non-English-speaking countries have found it extremely difficult to gain registration in Australia and until recently there have been no opportunities for retraining. In 1975, however, in collaboration with State authorities in Victoria and New South Wales, the Australian Department of Education inaugurated a series of retraining programmes, known as 'bridging courses for ethnic teachers'. The courses include intensive English-language instruction followed by teacher training of one or two years, and qualify the participants to teach in primary schools. Nineteen graduates are at present employed in Victorian schools as classroom teachers; future graduates may be appointed to disadvantaged schools as supernumaries to work with children of their own ethnic background (Victoria, Education Department, 1977). Reduction in Commonwealth support for migrant teachers undertaking bridging courses has, however, curtailed any further expansion. Teacher-exchange programmes provide another means of expanding teaching resources. A scheme for the exchange of Italian and Australian teachers has, however, been shelved '[m]ainly for budgetary reasons in both Italy and Australia' (Aus., Department of Education, 1977: 45).

While the subject of migrant and multicultural education remains to a considerable degree submerged beneath the debate and conflict over standards, curriculum, open schooling, classrooms, public examinations, school autonomy, school-parent and school-community relations, and similar matters that few schools can avoid confronting, there is an increasing tendency for advocates of change in these areas of common concern to try to harness ethnic-multicultural interests in support of their own case. As in the case of Overberg's boss, access to new sources of funding, expertise and power—flowing in various degrees from the Schools Commission, the Curriculum Development Centre and some State departments—is releasing unsuspected reserves of imagination and enterprise. Smolicz and Secombe's analysis of submissions to the Committee on Migrant Languages shows what a thoughtful and substantial response can be called forth—in this case, mostly from ethnic groups—when it looks as though government is likely to make significant decisions about the allocation of resources (Smolicz and Secombe, 1977).

Paul Nicoll's study of the operation of the first two years of the Schools Commission's Disadvantaged Schools Program in government schools in New South Wales documents another aspect of this process whereby migrant-multicultural issues are becoming incorporated into the activities of established organisations. This is the case where a pressure group adopts the migrant-multicultural cause to enhance its power in negotiating with government. Nicoll argues that the New South Wales Teachers' Federation's hard-hitting attack on the Education Department's financing and administration of disadvantaged schools was part of a long-term strategy aimed at: securing a public inquiry into education in the State; the establishment of a New South Wales Education Commission; increased expenditure on education; and a 'redefinition of professionalism in education, meaning greater teacher control of education'. By 1974, says Nicoll, the Federation

> realised that the Schools Commission access to resources and support of educational ideas shared by Federation (prominent among which was the provision of extra resources for the disadvantaged) offered new prospects for greater teacher involvement in the planning and administration of education at all levels. (Nicoll, 1975: 31)

Federation policy of securing better staffing for disadvantaged schools, says Nicoll, rested on industrial not educational considerations, for the Federation did not question 'whether more teachers automatically lead to better education'. Neither did it acknowledge the existence of class and cultural barriers between teachers and community (Nicoll,

1975: 25, 26). The interests of the Federation diverged from the interests of the disadvantaged in general, and the ethnic disadvantaged in particular, especially over the question of who should control the schools:

> Federation's assertions of absolute teacher control of schools and the restriction of parents to a consultative role are not likely to reduce working class alienation from school, nor lead to the creation of joint home-school action in order to change patterns of under-achievement. (Nicoll, 1975: 32)

Since Nicoll's study, the Teachers' Federation has adopted a much more explicit role as spokesman for ethnic interests in education, particularly with the organisation of a major conference on 'Education in a Multi-Cultural Society' in 1976 (NSW Teachers' Federation, 1977), but ethnic families—as distinct from vocal ethnic leaders—remain too cut off from the life of the school for their role to have become a serious issue.[6]

A largely invisible element of 'identity struggle' has, however, been present in the relations between schools and ethnic parents since the fifties, as the schools have tried to impose *their* definitions of proper language use on 'unco-operative' migrant families. Describing the situation as seen by teachers of Greek children in Sydney at the end of the sixties, Eva Isaacs says:

> Reports from teachers at schools containing a large percentage of Greek pupils showed that Greek children suffered severe handicaps in the acquisition and development of English language skills because of their attendance at Greek school and their parents' insistence on Greek being spoken at home; all this they regarded as a threat to their teaching efforts. Indeed, many considered the language barrier to be the major obstacle to the children's success and achievement at school. (1976: 1)

In her own research carried out in 1970, Isaacs found that speaking English at home was a 'conflict area' between parents and school, with some parents seeing the teachers' attempts to encourage children to speak English at all times 'as a threat to the maintenance and preservation of the Greek language' (Isaacs, 1976: 96). Because in the past migrant parents themselves have contributed almost nothing to social knowledge about the education of their children, their reactions to the schools' attempts to define what should be going on in their homes have rarely come to the surface. Research like Isaacs' is now yielding a differentiated picture of parents' reactions: while some ethnic parents resent the schools' devaluing of the ethnic language and culture, others think differently. M.J. Elliott quotes a principal of Fitzroy High School, where Italian and Greek had been taught for many years, as stating in 1976 that 'it would be wrong to pretend that bi-lingualism has been a total success': The principal's paper went on:

There has been considerable resistance to the study of their own ethnic languages by a large number of students, even when they have been taught by well-qualified and capable native-language teachers and in 1976 there have been serious doubts about the ability of the school to continue to operate these classes which are just a little more popular than French. (Miller, quoted by Elliott, 1977: 346)

To some migrant parents, the schools and a command of English are the crucial medium through which their ambitions for their children will be realised. Parents with this view did not need to be convinced that their children should speak English at home, but in their turn they now present a problem as retention of the mother-tongue is re-defined in positive terms. As Michael Clyne puts it in a recent paper:

It will be necessary to re-educate the public as to the value of bilingual education programs, which may fail if they do not have strong parental and community support. Many Australian teachers have been trying to persuade migrant parents for years that their children will not succeed at school unless they speak and hear nothing but English, and one cannot expect parents to accept the change of policy without an explanation. (1977: 9)

There are also incipient struggles over the definition of proper schooling. The expectations of some ethnic parents that schools should exercise custodial functions and mirror the authoritarian structure of the family are disappointed even in school situations that are 'traditional' in Australian terms, but come into sharp collision with the ideas and practices of 'progressive' approaches to education. In answering the Migrant Questionnaire, an Italian teacher described his own experience of a school that was one of the pioneers of bilingual and multicultural education:

Around this time [early 1970s] there was a great conflict emerging between the progressive teachers, mainly centered in the inner city schools, and the migrant parent . . . I started to perceive that migrants were being used for other purposes than educational . . . It was obvious that Italian parents were worried at the course being taken by events engineered by [progressive teachers who] kept stressing one side of the argument which suited their interest . . . [at this school] the indigent group, the helpless ones, the poor ones, the hopeless ones were the Australian students and not the Italian or the Greek. Of course the migrants were of more interest and power and therefore used to achieve a new school building . . . these people stressed or exaggerated reports about migrants, especially about Italians. I had the impression that migrants were kept illiterate to justify their theories.

For an Italian to describe migrant parents as 'of more interest and power' than Anglo-Australians—and so a potential resource for established groups or new groups trying to get a foothold in the educational power structure—is a remarkable sign of the times. At least officially, ethnic communities are now accepted as legitimate voices in the definition of migrant and multicultural education and as legitimate participants in the wider school-community education scene. Up to the present time, however, ethnic communities have made no more effective efforts than anyone else to examine the educational implications of a commitment to ethnic identity: that is, the crucial question of how migrant children's interests (in terms of conventional performance and skills criteria or in terms of developing 'the capacities which enable people critically to confront experience, to make sense of the world and confidently and rationally to act upon it', Aus., Schools Commission, 1976: 7) are articulated, supported, denied or otherwise affected by their sense of ethnic identity.

Two factors have been fundamental in making the construction of social knowledge about education in a plural Australia a more lively and productive enterprise in the past few years, but the further influence of both is at present under threat. One factor is that the experience of teachers, students and parents is beginning to be systematically incorporated into the picture. The mediators or catalysts in this process have been mainly academic researchers and Commonwealth-sponsored committees of inquiry.[7] The remarkable efforts made by the Schools Commission and the Committee on Migrant Languages to consult directly with associations, schools and individuals, and to obtain information and views from the whole spectrum of interested parties, represent major instances of the Commonwealth's role.

Until recently, research related to the education of children of non-English-speaking origin was for the most part politically motivated, in the sense that it was geared to produce hard data that would force or allow some authority to take some kind of action. This being the case, it is not surprising that the knowledge thus generated has been highly selective: the Greeks are the best organised pressure group of all the ethnic communities and we know more about Greek children than about any others; the problems of inner-city schools with a high migrant density are the most visible and are now well documented, while there is little information on the experience of children in schools of low migrant density in the cities or in isolated rural areas (see Aus., Department of Education, 1974*a*: 12–13; Aus., Immigration Advisory Council, Committee on Migrant Education, 'Interim Report', 1974: 7–9). New South Wales and Victoria, with the largest concentrations of non-English-speaking migrants, present the most apparent educational problems, and it is in these States that the recent upsurge of research and writing has occurred. In the last few years, however, there has been a considerable expansion of academic research geared less to the instrumental goal of stimulating immediate action and more to long-range and theoretical problems. Some of this research has been prompted by questions raised by government authorities, such as the Immigration Advisory Council, and most of it has been funded from Commonwealth sources. A list of current projects and researchers appears in the Department of Education's *Directory of Education Research and Researchers in Australia* (Aus., Department of Education, 1977*a*).

The cumulative effect of the policies of the present Liberal Government, however, is to reduce the funds available for official inquiries and for research (theoretical or applied, action research) on the part of the bureaucracies themselves, schools and community bodies, and academics. One likely result is that organised groups—like ethnic associations and progressive educationists—with views already well-formed and consistent with their broader interests, will dominate the scene and the voices of the majority of parents, students, teachers and others, who take no part in organised action, will continue to be inaudible or blurred. A likely related outcome is that the first efforts now being made to document the diversity of experience—from one ethnic population, one school situation, and so on, to another—will slow down and the present tendency for the prominent Italians and Greeks to be taken to stand and speak for *all* ethnic groups will be consolidated.

The second critical factor in enlivening and deepening social knowledge on these questions in the past few years has been, quite simply, the experience of changes in school practice. Some of these changes—like the increase in some States of school autonomy—are independent of the question of migrant and multicultural education; others—such as the availability of materials from the Curriculum Development Centre (the Social Education Materials Project) or the school-generated innovations funded by the Schools Commission—are the direct result of decisions for action in this particular area. From whatever source, opportunities and requirements for change in school practice have immensely increased the number of people who have been faced with the occasion to think about these issues and develop their own constructs of what education in a plural society involves. Conferences, meetings, training courses and the production of documents encourage communication among this expanding population and transform personal or parochial experience into social knowledge. It is sometimes claimed that there is indeed too much talk and too little action—but in the Australian context, productive interplay between social knowledge, theoretical knowledge and educational practice is only in its infancy. Without resources and opportunity for this interplay to go on, thinking—divorced from practice—is likely to revert to the stereotyped form that public knowledge about 'migrant education' took in the fifties and sixties.

NOTES

1. Since 1976 Commonwealth funds to the States for migrant education have
   been disbursed under the provisions of the *States Grants (Schools) Act
   1976* and the *States Grants (Schools Assistance) Act 1977*, instead of, as
   previously, under the restrictive provisions of the *Immigration (Education)
   Act 1971*.

   The Schools Commission's *Report for the Triennium 1979–81* was tabled
   in April 1978, while this book was in press. The Commission describes
   change since 1976 as 'developing slowly and unevenly'. There is 'confusion
   both about the ramifications of accepting a multicultural philosophy and
   about the possibilities of transferring various interpretations of it into
   reality. There is also uncertainty about what are legitimate claims against
   the nominated sums provided' (1978: 103). 'While some systems have begun
   to take advantage of the more flexible use of funds permissible since 1976
   ... major changes have, in most systems, barely begun ... the Commission
   continues to be concerned at the rigidities of organisation persisting in
   several systems whereby special attention to second language learners
   remains segregated from the mainstream of school organisation and
   programs' (1978: 107–8). In response to this situation, and in acknowledgement of its conviction that 'Special English language assistance to
   migrant students remains the most pressing need to be met' (1978: 106),
   the Commission is more directive than previously about how nominated
   funds for migrant and multicultural education in the General Recurrent
   Grants Program are to be spent: the employment of extra ESL trained
   teachers and their use in a variety of situations; 'the employment of
   interpreters, translators, bilingual welfare officers, teacher aides and
   school/community liaison workers'; the encouragement of bilingualism;
   changes in curriculum 'to acknowledge the dual cultural experience of
   second language learners'; 'the initial expense involved in experiments
   which allow some schools to cater especially for second language learners
   with a common mother tongue' (1978: 107). For the first time, the
   Commission recommends a special fund to support community languages
   ('in schools where local demand can be demonstrated') and multicultural
   education initiatives, but its role is to provide 'an impetus' to the work
   of school systems, which remain responsible 'for basic and continued
   funding' in these areas (1978: 109). The Commission also recommends that
   schools should make greater use of funds provided under the Services and
   Development Program 'to sensitise regular teachers to cultural difference'
   and to increase total skills and resources for teaching English as a second
   language (1978: 108). It seems clear that the overall impact of the report
   is: to affirm that both newly arrived and Australian-born children will
   continue to maintain at a substantial level the number of children whose
   first language is not English; to reassert the primacy of English language
   competence; and to play down somewhat the Commission's role in fostering
   recognition of 'the multicultural reality of Australian society' in the
   education of 'all Australian children', as expressed in its report for the
   previous triennium (1975: 125).

2. Bernadette Kelly's unpublished thesis, 'The Ethnic Communities Council Education Sub-committee: A Migrant Action Group In a Multi-cultural Society' (1977), contains a detailed account of the preparation of the SMEC submission.

3. The New South Wales Department of Education has provided funds for ethnic schools in 1977 and 1978. Evidence that ethnic schooling (if not all ethnic schools) is being taken more seriously than in the past is also seen in the support of the Commonwealth funding body, the Educational Research and Development Committee, for two studies of ethnic schools: one by M. Tsounis (not yet published) and one on 'Migrant definitions of ethnic schools', to be carried out by two sociologists, Frank Lewins and Paul Kringas. The Jewish day schools constitute the model of what some individual members of migrant groups would promote if resources were available. On the Jewish schools, see Bullivant (1977), Medding (1968) and Medding ed. (1973). The Greek Orthodox Archdiocese of Australia (Victorian Branch) is at present seeking funds to establish a full-time Greek Day School.

4. In its April 1978 *Report for the Triennium 1979–81*, the Schools Commission says: 'The policies governing production of suitable materials for the teaching of English as a second language are in need of review'. The Commission commends the work of the CDC, but notes the need to co-ordinate its work with that of the language teaching section of the Department of Education (1978: 108–9).

5. The Educational Research and Development Committee of the Commonwealth Department of Education is at present sponsoring a research project, under the direction of June Hearn, comparing the incorporation of these interpreters into the Victorian Education Department and the New South Wales Health Care Interpreter Program, referred to on pages 176–7.

6. B. Kelly's study of the New South Wales Ethnic Communities Council Education Sub-committee (ECCES) indicates that involvement with the Teachers Federation was a potentially divisive issue within the ECC. Some ECC members 'felt that the Teachers Federation should not use the ECCES as another pressure group', although most 'see the involvement of Teachers Federation as desirable' (1977: 68). At the beginning of 1978 a crisis erupted over the decision of the Teachers Federation to oppose the plans of the Department of Education to establish a Saturday School of Community Languages in Sydney, on the ground that community language teaching should be expanded in high schools. The Federation's position reflected its concern that employment opportunities for trained teachers should not suffer because of support for extra-curricular language training. The Department and the Federation, however, reached agreement on the staffing of Saturday schools, which opened in four centres in March with an enrolment of 1400 secondary students in School Certificate and Higher School Certificate classes. The crisis appears to have led to a range of rapid changes dissolving within three months (at least formally) three hard centres of resistance (besides the Federation) within the New South Wales system: the Department of Education expanded the teaching of community languages in primary and secondary schools (setting aside

$2 million of Commonwealth funds for the purpose) and initiated a survey of 'all secondary teachers to ascertain skills and desires of teachers to engage in expanded language programs' (NSW, Minister for Education: 1978); the Board of Senior School Studies approved of all Saturday School languages as Higher School Certificate subjects with syllabuses from Victoria where none exists in New South Wales; the University of Sydney resolved to extend the number of languages acceptable as matriculation subjects.

7. Table 3.3 shows that school teachers and tertiary teachers each accounted for a little less than a third of the 188 individual, non-official authors represented in the 'Bibliography'. The figures reflect the growing interest of University staff in migrant education after 1971 and the increased dominance of academic definers over teacher definers. Most academic authors were, however, in faculties of education; many had first become interested in migrant education as teachers in the sixties.

5 Defining Migrant Health

The institutionalised health care of the community is the responsibility of the medical and associated professions, government health departments and other statutory bodies, and public and private hospitals. Although it has been acknowledged for over twenty years—both within these organisations and outside—that migrants have special health care needs, knowledge about migrant health remains meagre and superficial.

Sources of information

The subject of migrant health did not appear on the agenda of any of the eighteen Australian Citizenship Conventions held between 1950 and 1970. In the early years the only migrant health matter that aroused interest was the question of the health standards applied by the Commonwealth in selecting migrants. At the 1956 Convention, the Minister for Immigration, H.E. Holt, answered criticism of selection procedures by presenting figures to show that migrants suffered less than non-migrants from tuberculosis and mental illness: in other words, overseas screening was effective (Holt, 1956: 24–5).[1] The alternative view—that Australia might offer a home to the infirm and disabled—was rarely heard. Even when the chairman of the 1952 Convention, Richard Boyer, referring to the 'hard core' of war-time refugees still in Europe, said that

> he could have hoped that Australia could set aside the obvious national interest of concentrating on the economically useful and have made a specific gesture, purely for the love of God, to that small remaining section of aged and ill, limbless and economically useless people

he blunted any impact his words might have had by adding immediately:

> The reluctance has not been on the part of our Governments or responsible officials. I well know the heaviness of heart with which Ministers and members of our mission have turned down people whom they know we Australians as a nation would not accept. (Boyer, 1952: 28)

146

In later years passing references to matters of health appeared occasionally in other contexts, but were never taken up in subsequent discussion. Migrant youth was a central theme of the 14th Convention in 1963. The discussion group allotted the topic, 'Physical health of migrant youth, including sporting activities and national fitness', focussed on the declining health of young people in general and the inadequacy of sports facilities and financial support for national fitness programmes. Migrants needed encouragement to take part in sporting and recreational activities. However, like most other delegates at the Convention, the members of this group put their money on national service. In the chairman's words:

> There was almost unanimous support within the group for the re-introduction of national service training—not necessarily in the previous form—for both girls and boys, to be provided separately, and for a minimum period of six months. (Aus., Department of Immigration, ACC, 1963: 40)

At the last Convention in 1970, a swell of dissent broke the smooth surface of self-congratulation that had predominated in previous meetings. The Liberals had won the 1969 election by a narrow margin and the Leader of the Opposition, E.G. Whitlam, took the opportunity given by the opening of the Convention to berate the Government for failing to follow through 'the full consequences' of the immigration programme, particularly in matters of health, housing and education. On the health question, he had little to say apart from a reference to the comparatively low rate of medical insurance among migrants, thus foreshadowing the only migrant health matter that was to attract attention over the next few years. But the main thrust of Whitlam's address was that Australia would have increasing difficulty in attracting and keeping migrants if general standards of community well-being —second-rate, he claimed, in comparison with the countries from which migrants were being drawn—were not improved. Two other speakers (one of them was H.J. Souter, secretary of the Australian Council of Trade Unions) referred to the need for interpreters in hospitals and in medical consultations (Aus., Department of Immigration, ACC, 1970: 50, 51), echoing the attempts that one delegate had made in 1963 and again in 1968, unsuccessfully, to interest the Convention in this question (Aus., Department of Immigration, ACC, 1963: 49; 1968: 40).

Although the Commonwealth Department of Health was represented at the Conventions and a number of doctors were included among the delegates, the experience of the medical profession in dealing with migrant health care never penetrated the Convention deliberations, apart from an occasional isolated and token reference to industrial accidents (for example, Aus., Department of Immigration, ACC, 1963: 54).

The Task Forces set up in each State in 1973 by A.J. Grassby, the Minister for Immigration in the new Labor Government, give some indication of what were at that time viewed as the most serious 'migrant problems'. In the few months that the Task Forces had to prepare their first reports (which also turned out to be their last), there was little time to collect new information, and health questions did not fall in the category of matters that were already well documented.

The Victorian report paid a great deal of attention to the inadequacy of interpreter facilities in all areas of community services and recommended a system of interpreter pools. One pool, to be established by the Commonwealth Department of Immigration, was to serve general practitioners, private hospitals, pharmacists and baby health centres; another, to be the responsibility of the State Hospitals and Charities Commission, was to provide for public hospitals, where existing services were 'totally inadequate' (Aus., Migrant Task Force Committee, Victoria, 1973: 35). In Victoria mental health has attracted more attention than other aspects of migrant medical care, and this was the only health question that the Task Force dealt with in detail. Drawing heavily on two publications of the Australian Council of Social Service, the report examined the deficiencies of mental health services—from prevention, through to diagnosis, treatment and after-care—and made comprehensive recommendations to State and Commonwealth authorities: for the use of hostels as orientation centres, the development of community health centres, the training and employment of bilingual professionals, the development of appropriate interpreter pool services, the provision of information to patients in their own language and of English classes for patients and staff in hospitals, and for a review of after-care services. Health forms and publications were also included in the general recommendation for the printing of multilingual forms and publications (1973: 53–7, 71).

The New South Wales Task Force reviewed attempts made in the early sixties by the Good Neighbour Council and the New South Wales Association for Mental Health to draw attention to the need for interpreters in hospitals and went on to make its own inquiries about the situation in 1973. It appears to have relied on the experience and help of social workers in hospitals and in the Commonwealth Department of Immigration to establish that existing interpreter services were seriously deficient. Lack of services undermined patient care: language barriers meant that a migrant patient was discharged 'little or no better off for his stay in hospital' or kept longer than was necessary (Aus., Migrant Task Force Committee, NSW, 1973: 10). The Task Force directed its recommendations to State and Commonwealth authorities: trained interpreters should be appointed to service hospitals and the use of voluntary, but trained, interpreters should be explored; the Commonwealth should consider subsidising State interpreting, counselling and migrant health services; and, as an emergency measure, a 'hot line' between major hospitals and the Emergency Telephone Interpreter Service (as TIS was then known) should be established. The approach of the New South Wales Task Force to migrant health was consistent with its overall view that 'lack of communication and the implications of this' is 'one of the major problems' (1973: 4).

The South Australian Task Force limited itself to brief comments on interpreter problems in one public hospital and the ambulance service, and the satisfactory situation reported in the mental health services, where non-English-speaking migrants were 'usually accompanied by a friend/relative or minister of religion who acts as interpreter' or other patients or staff were used if necessary (Aus., Migrant Task Force, S.A., 1973: 5). Communication problems of migrants in hospitals and other health services were to be the subject of a later report. The Tasmanian report also recommended that services, including health, should have access to interpreters. The Queensland and Western Australian Task Forces did not refer to health.

The Task Forces tapped a range of experience and opinion from professionals directly involved in providing health care. Health professionals have always played the greatest part in defining the health situation of migrants. Until recently the only audible voice among them—though itself not much above a whisper—came from the medical profession. In the last few years non-medicos in health care institutions have become more numerous and more articulate, and have made their own contribution to public knowledge about migrant health. Apart from the few but growing number of doctors and other professionals of ethnic origin, ethnics themselves have made no similar contribution. Such accounts as they have given—as patients or interpreters—are in the non-English press. Their experience enters into social knowledge only insofar as it is mediated by others.

Very little literature on migrant health comes from State health authorities or parliaments, apart from the occasional writings of government-employed doctors and social workers. A survey of the annual reports of the State health departments shows only one recurring theme of interest in migrant health, and that theme is common to all States: the comparatively high rate of notifiable disease among the non-Australian born. Reports on the incidence of diptheria, typhoid fever, hydatid disease, leprosy and poliomyelitis usually single out migrant cases for special comment, but it is tuberculosis in migrants that attracts the most attention and often leads to comments on screening procedures. The heart of the problem is not migrant health, but the danger migrants present to the Australian community: it is the 'significant pool of latent infection' among migrants (WA, Commissioner of Public Health, 1973: 35) that is the cause for concern. Although Queensland is not the only State to have received numbers of Asian refugees since 1975, it has expressed the most anxiety over the health condition of refugees. Since the early seventies, New South Wales has paid attention in each annual report to the health education of migrants, and Queensland to the low use of health services among migrants—both matters that I will return to in the next chapter.

Because the medical profession is organised into a national association which provides a major forum for the communication of medical knowledge and opinion through its weekly publication, the *Medical Journal of Australia* (*MJA*), it is possible to trace doctors' public accounts of migrant health care systematically over the whole period with which we are concerned. The *MJA*, plus a few other sources (mainly medical and other professional journals), has therefore provided the bulk of the material for answering the questions to be taken up in the following pages: who have been the definers of the health situation of migrants, what problems have they identified, what do they present as the causes of these problems and what as the solutions?

In reviewing this literature, I attempted to cover all items about the health of migrants in Australia, written in English and published since 1945 (although the first relevant item located was dated 1956). I did not, however, survey newspapers or news magazines. The contributions of the ACCs, Task Forces and government health authorities have already been discussed; they do not constitute items in any substantive sense and are not included in the literature survey.[2]

The survey located 118 items in all. Few are longer than article length; there are no books, nor does the literature contain any comprehensive overview of research on migrant health. Most items (57 per cent) appeared as articles in the *MJA* and most were accordingly written by doctors. Over a third of the items reported original research findings. A quarter reported the authors' personal observations, but were not presented as research findings: an influential article published by S. Minc in 1963, 'Of New Australian patients, their medical lore and major anxieties', is an example. The rest were reviews of work on particular problems (such as mental illness), general discussions of issues (most of these were editorials in the *MJA*) or information-giving notices (about arrangements for bilingual labelling of medicines, for example).

The definers

Of the 118 items, 103 had one or more individuals as authors; the rest were editorials or unsigned articles, most of them in the *MJA*. The 103 items were written by 116 different individuals, of whom 36 per cent lived in Melbourne, 32 per cent in Sydney, 11 per cent in Adelaide, 8 per cent in Perth–Fremantle and 6 per cent in Canberra. The country of their first degree was known for only 85 of the 116 authors (but for nearly all the doctors): 78 per cent of these took their first degree in Australia, 13 per cent in Britain and 8 per cent in Europe. The qualifications of the 105 for whom the information was available were: medical (excluding psychiatric), 58 per cent; psychiatric, 11 per cent; social work, 15 per cent; other, 15 per cent.

For our purposes, the most useful way of analysing authorship involves treating each item as if it had a unique author or set of authors. This procedure involves double-counting authors who wrote or contributed to more than one item, but clarifies changes in authorship over time. We shall call this set of double-counted authors, 'item-authors'. There were 154 of these altogether. Table 5.1 compares the item-authors of material published in 1956–1968 and 1969–1977. Only the dominant themes require further comment. More than half the item-authors lived in Melbourne during the earlier period, but in the later period the proportion of Melbourne residents had dropped to 40 per cent and Sydney's proportion had almost doubled to bring it to a third of the total. For those item-authors for whom country of first degree is known, the proportion with Australian degrees nearly doubled while those with European first degrees went down from 41 to 4 per cent. This change reflects the fact that a small number of immigrant and refugee doctors made a major contribution in the earlier period, but subsequently declined in absolute numbers, while contributions from authors with Australian first degrees have increased nearly seven-fold.

Substantial changes in the qualifications of item-authors from the first to the second period provide clear evidence of increasing diversity. Of item-authors in the first period, 90 per cent were doctors, but this decreased to 63 per cent in 1969–1977, when a variety of non-medical professionals and research workers trained in sociology, psychology and science began to make a contribution. The importance of psychiatrists in the earlier period comes largely from the work of the Mental Health Authority of Victoria on mental illness, particularly among Displaced Persons: nearly a third of all item-authors of 1956–1968 publications were employed by the Mental Health Authority, but by the later period their numbers were negligible. Place of employment shows the same diversification in recent years as does

Table 5.1 *Characteristics of 154 item-authors of publications on migrant health 1956–1977, in percentages**

	Year of publication		
	1956–1968 n = 29	1969–1977 n = 125	1956–1977 n = 154
Country of first degree			
Australia	38.0	58.4	54.6
Britain	17.2	12.0	13.0
Other English-speaking country	0.0	1.6	1.3
Europe	38.0	3.2	9.7
Unknown	6.8	24.8	21.4
	100.0	100.0	100.0
Place of residence			
Melbourne	51.7	40.0	42.2
Sydney	17.2	32.8	29.9
Adelaide	13.8	8.0	9.1
Perth/Fremantle	13.8	8.0	9.1
Brisbane	0.0	2.4	1.9
Hobart	0.0	0.8	0.7
Canberra	3.5	4.8	4.5
Outside Australia	0.0	0.8	0.7
Unknown	0.0	2.4	1.9
	100.0	100.0	100.0
Qualifications			
Medical, excluding psychiatric	62.1	52.0	53.9
Psychiatric	27.6	11.2	14.3
Dietetics	0.0	1.6	1.3
Science, pharmacy	0.0	0.8	0.7
Nursing	0.0	0.8	0.7
Social work	10.3	11.2	11.0
Other	0.0	12.8	10.4
Unknown	0.0	9.6	7.7
	100.0	100.0	100.0
Employer			
Hospital, clinic	41.4	18.4	22.7
University	10.4	35.2	30.5
Mental Health Authority Victoria	31.0	4.0	9.1
Government department	6.8	9.6	9.1
Welfare, church agency	0.0	4.0	3.3
Private professional	10.4	13.6	13.0
Other	0.0	8.0	6.5
Unknown	0.0	7.2	5.8
	100.0	100.0	100.0

* An 'item-author' is the author of an item with a named person as author. In the case of items with more than one author, each author is counted as an item-author. Because some persons were authors of more than one item, the number of item-authors is more than the number of authors.

occupation, with universities (mainly university medical schools) emerging as the main employer, and about half the item-authors coming from a wide range of private welfare and medical agencies as well as government departments and research institutes and professional associations. The issue of migrant health has undoubtedly permeated into more, and more varied, groups in the past ten years.

The nature of migrant health problems

Items were classified according to the nature of the original health problems or questions on which the research or discussion focussed. In most cases the title gave this information. Where, but only where, additional or subsidiary questions were raised in their own right— that is, not as causes, outcomes or modes of dealing with the original problem—they too were classified as original problems. Analysis of the nature of the original problem is thus limited to the stimulus or occasion for the discussion. For a full overview of problems dealt with, the reader must also take into account what are described here as causes, outcomes and solutions to problems.

The original question was defined as an Australian question only where the main issue was the experience of health personnel in dealing with non-English-speaking patients or clients, or concerned some aspect of the structure or operation of health services. However, most writers unequivocally focussed on what they defined as a migrant health problem: for example, 'Psychiatric disorders in East European refugees now in Australia' (Krupinski *et al.*, 1973). Exhibiting a diffidence—rare in the literature—about who in fact has the problems, a Sydney psychiatrist, John Ellard, began an address he gave in 1969 to the Medico-Legal Society of New South Wales by referring to Bartholomew's discussion of the legal position of immigrants in Australia (which he attributed to Dr A.A. Batholomew, rather than to G.W. Bartholomew, Professor of Law at the University of Singapore). This paper, he said, had made him realise that he did not know what a migrant was. Therefore, although his talk was called 'The problems of the migrant', he decided after 'due reflection'

> that the only person whose problems I can talk about with any validity and insight is myself: as a result, a more apt title for what I am about to say would be 'The Problems of Ellard, when asked to make a psychiatric assessment of a migrant'. (1969: 1039)

Unlike Ellard, the great majority of writers settled on something that they had no hesitation in defining as a migrant health problem. Of the 118 items reviewed, 6 gave background information relevant to migrant health, but were not classified in terms of an original health-related problem, 8 focussed on both migrant and Australian problems, 15 on Australian problems only, and 89 on migrant problems only. Altogether, the 112 items classified in this way yielded 139 problems. Of the 23 items concerned with an original Australian problem, all but 2 appeared after 1968. Table 5.2 shows that 16 of these dealt with the general inadequacy of health services and personnel in providing for migrant health care, or the lack of interpreters in hospitals.

Table 5.2 *Migrant health defined as an Australian problem, 23 items*

Nature of Australian problem	Mentions of migrant health as an Australian problem		
	1956–1968	1969–1977	1956–1977
Inadequate health services for migrants	0	10	10
Inadequacy of health personnel in dealing with migrants	0	3	3
Lack of interpreters in hospitals	0	3	3
Diagnostic problems	0	2	2
Other	2	3	5
Total, Australian problems	2	21	23
Items with original Australian problem	2	21	23
Items without original Australian problem	21	74	95
Total number of items	23	95	118

It can be seen from Table 5.3 that, over the whole period, 39 per cent of the original migrant problems were concerned with mental illness, alcoholism or suicide. The greater concentration on these questions in the earlier years is accounted for largely by the attention given the mental health of Displaced Persons in the fifties and sixties. No items were primarily concerned with physical illness in the earlier period,[3] but in 1969–1977 18 per cent of all items had physical illness as their focus. By this time, accidents, burns, and back and stomach conditions were attracting some interest, much of it stimulated by the fact that workers compensation claims are usually associated with disabilities of this kind and migrants have become a highly visible and controversial proportion of compensation cases.[4] The other important change is the appearance in the later period of items on migrants' experience in the use of health services: response to treatment, hospitalisation, inability to read directions on medicines, communication problems in general and overall poor access to health care.

Table 5.3 *Migrant health defined as a migrant problem, 97 items*

Nature of migrant problem	Mentions of migrant health as a migrant problem					
	1956–1968		1969–1977		1957–1977	
	n = 29 Mentions%	n = 23 Items%	n = 87 Mentions%	n = 95 Items%	n = 116 Mentions%	n = 118 Items%
Mental illness/stress	52	65	23	21	30	30
Alcoholism	17	22	2	2	6	6
Suicide/attempted suicide			3	3	3	3
Mental illness/suicide/alcoholism	3	4			1	1
Medico–social situation	21	26	14	13	16	15
Physical illness			20	18	15	14
Hospitalisation			10	10	8	8
Use of health services			9	8	7	7
Response to treatment			6	5	4	4
Communication problems			2	2	2	2
Inability to read directions on medicines			2	2	2	2
Attitudes, values, beliefs re medicine	3	4	1	1	2	2
Spread of disease to community	3	4	1	1	2	2
Other			6	5	4	4
Total, migrant problems	99	—	99	—	102	—
Items with original migrant problem		21		76		97
Items without original migrant problem		2		19		21
Total number of items		23		95		118

One main category of ethnic problems has to do with the medico-social situation of migrants, but is not concerned with specific illnesses or other aspects of health care. Examples of this kind of publication are J.M. Last, 'The health of immigrants: some observations from general practice' (Last, 1960) and an *MJA* editorial on 'Some of the complexities of migration' (*MJA*, 1967: 661–662). Of all items,

15 per cent had this as a central problem—26 per cent in the earlier period, 13 per cent in the later.

Causes and solutions

So far I have been dealing with what authors define as the central theme of their writings. Most items describe some disease or condition and suggest causes for its occurrence; some also propose measures of prevention or treatment. Writers commonly identify causes or sources of primary problems and then explain these, in their turn, by yet other factors. Causes and effects are confounded and combined. Nevertheless the search for causes permeates the literature and makes it possible to identify those factors that are seen to have a causal role, either on the primary health problem, on some subsidiary health problem or on some non-health factor which, through an extended causal chain, affects health.

As Table 5.4 shows, over three-quarters of the items attributed migrant health problems partly or wholly to migrants themselves. Half saw the Australian community or health institutions as in some way responsible. Over five times as many items placed the whole responsibility on migrants as on Australians: 37 per cent as compared with 7 per cent. Perceptions of the source of problems changed somewhat between the earlier and later periods. The increase in the proportion of items that did not propose any sources of migrant health problems —from 4 per cent to 17 per cent—reflects the appearance in recent years of a number of articles devoted to description of ethnic culture: an example is David Cox's paper on the social and cultural background of Greeks, presented in a seminar on 'Medico–social problems in the Greek population in Melbourne' in 1972. There is also a trend for the proportion of items that hold migrants solely responsible for their

Table 5.4 *Sources of migrant health problems: summary of Australian and migrant sources, 118 items, in percentages*

Sources	1956–1968 n = 23 %	1969–1977 n = 95 %	1956–1977 n = 118 %
Australian only	4	7	7
Migrant only	44	36	37
Australian and migrant	48	40	42
None	4	17	14
Total	100	100	100

own problems to decline, but the proportion attributing some or all of the cause to Australians also declines slightly.

The main sources of migrant health problems are set out schematically in Table 5.5. Two general trends are immediately apparent: there is much more refinement and elaboration of ideas about migrant sources than about Australian sources; and—whether located in migrants or Australians—the source of problems is presented in terms of personal characteristics and experience (for example, lack of ability to communicate, pre-migration ill-health, changes in role, ignorance, economic stress), rather than in terms of structural factors.

Table 5.5 *Main source of migrant health problems, 118 items*

Source	Number of items mentioning
1. Australian health personnel, communication	
(1) general poor communication on part of health personnel	19
(2) need to use interpreters; lack of, incompetent use of, interpreters; incompetent interpreters	14
(3) lack of bilingual health personnel	7
2. Australian health personnel, knowledge	
(1) lack of understanding, prejudice, stereotyping, on part of health personnel	16
(2) lack of knowledge of migrant culture, situation, experiences, on part of health personnel	9
3. Australian health services	
(1) fragmentation of health services, lack of comprehensive health policy, understaffing of health services	5
(2) defective selection of migrants	4
4. Migrants' pre-migration and migration experience	
(1) pre-migration ill-health, mental instability, low living standards	16
(2) war, post-war experience of Displaced Person refugees	14
(3) material and physical conditions of migration: travel by jet, change of diet, change from one kind of traffic system to another	7
(4) stresses inherent in the migration process	5
(5) social structure	
(i) change in roles, difficulties of acculturation and assimilation	18
(ii) loss of family, former way of life	10

Table 5.5 *Continued*

Source	Number of items mentioning
5. Migrants' demographic, health and physical characteristics	
(1) age on arrival, duration of residence	10
(2) physical, mental health	8
(3) diet	7
(4) heredity, racial temperament	4
6. Migrants' communication: lack of knowledge of English; inability, refusal to learn English	18
7. Migrants' knowledge	
(1) ignorance; illiteracy; limited education, intellect, horizons	17
(2) distinctive content of life-style, culture, values	13
(3) suspicion of hospitals, medical services	13
(4) value attached to sick role, anxiety about illness	7
(5) independent attitude to medical opinion	6
(6) ignorance of Australian health organisations and practice	5
(7) belief in folk medicine, superstition	4
8. Migrants' economic situation	
(1) economic stress, poverty, insecurity	25
(2) occupational frustration of skilled and professional; status drop	13
(3) both parents working; women working	7
(4) lack of occupational skills; capable of physical labour only	6
9. Migrants' social situation	
(1) loneliness, isolation	9
(2) sexual deprivation	2
10. Social structure of migrant community	
(1) nuclear family: marital discord, parent-child conflict, neglect of children and mentally ill, disruption	24
(2) community: isolation, lack of community support and cohesion	19
(3) nuclear family: isolation of women, women's loss of role	12
(4) extended family: lack of, no support from	6
11. Migrant–Australian interaction in the community	
(1) barriers of communication	15
(2) cultural distance, conflict of values	10
(3) Australian demands for conformity; migrants' inability to assimilate, gain approval; lack of mutual trust	6

Of the 118 items, 66 nominate the parties who should act to solve migrant health problems. The list of proposed actors appears in Table 5.6 (with two actors that were nominated only once omitted). Although writers present migrants as the main cause of their own health problems, they rarely entertain the idea that migrants are the ones to act in solving these problems. Instead, government authorities, official bodies (such as hospitals), doctors and other professionals are seen as the effective actors. As Table 5.7 shows, however, much of the advocated action involves getting migrants to change in some way: educating them about health, diet, the dangers of burning accidents in the home and the use of health services; encouraging them to learn English; preventing the potentially ill from migrating or repatriating the newly arrived who become sick. Improvement in communication between migrants and health personnel, and increased knowledge, understanding and tolerance of migrant characteristics, situations and cultures, and the organisation of research account for most of the proposals.

Although not always put in these terms, many recommendations about interpreters and multilingual workers have implications for structural change. If these—Table 5.7, rows 1(1) and 1(2)—are added to proposals of a structural kind, then over a quarter of the mentions of action to be taken by health services and personnel refer to the

Table 5.6 *Solutions to migrant health problems: who is to act, 118 items*

Who is to act	Number of items mentioning
1. Australians	
(1) government	38
(2) doctors	22
(3) hospitals	13
(4) non-medical professionals: social workers, dieticians, counsellors, psychologists, infant welfare sisters, health educators	11
(5) community in general	6
(6) professional medical associations	5
(7) welfare, community associations	4
(8) industry, employers, trade unions, insurance companies	3
(9) legal authorities, courts	2
(10) universities	2
(11) individuals	2
2. Migrants	
(1) migrant communities, associations, churches	6
(2) migrants as individuals	3

development of new functions or roles: to provide for a wide range of intermediaries between medical staff and patients, and for additional social-psychological support staff, such as social workers and multilingual counsellors. However, except in a very few recent publications,

Table 5.7 *Solutions to migrant health problems: action to be taken by Australian health services and professionals, 118 items*

Action	Number of items mentioning
1. Directly effecting change in health area: communication	
(1) train, appoint, use interpreters	21
(2) train, appoint, use bilingual doctors, social workers, counsellors, advisers, friends	9
(3) translate health insurance information and labels on medicines into migrant languages	4
2. Directly effecting change in health area: knowledge	
(1) increase health personnel's knowledge, understanding, acceptance of migrant cultures and situations	24
(2) research, monitor migrant health	21
(3) educate migrants re health, diet, burns, use of services	15
3. Directly effecting change in health area: structure and operation of services	
(1) screen out potentially ill among prospective and newly arrived migrants	8
(2) improve relations between doctors and patients	8
(3) carry out programmes for prevention and rehabilitation re mentally ill	6
(4) use social workers, accessible health personnel	4
(5) re-train migrants after accidents	2
(6) develop health teams, community health services	2
(7) bring out psychiatrists from Greece	1
4. Effecting change in non-health area: communication, develop English teaching for migrants	8
5. Effecting change in non-health area: knowledge, reduce community prejudice	3
6. Effecting change in non-health area: social structure	
(1) provide better and more accessible welfare services	2
(2) recognise migrant qualifications and employ according to skill	2

to be discussed later, the relevance to migrant health care of radical structural change in health services has attracted no attention. Indeed, most references to structural response are couched in such general terms that no one is likely to dispute them; they are laid down as no more than faint trails that some unnamed actor might care to pursue at some unspecified time. Thus, for example, a 1965 article on the incidence of mental disorder according to country of birth concluded that such epidemiological studies make it possible to plan 'social and clinical action . . . to prevent and rehabilitate those groups of migrants who have been shown . . . to be specially vulnerable to mental breakdown' (Krupinski and Stoller, 1965: 268).

Suggestions for action on the part of the community in general or migrants themselves have still less content and focus. The community's main role is to encourage tolerance and understanding of migrants. The migrants' contribution is to help themselves by adopting Australian values, adjusting to their new situation and learning to understand Australian ways and institutions.

Stereotyping and sacred texts

The literature review makes it possible to describe in general terms the process by which a body of knowledge about migrant health has emerged in the past thirty years. Although some writing excluded from the present survey contains the results of a series of inquiries on specific diseases, there has in general been a notable lack of cumulative research. The only body of work that is in any sense cumulative is the series of studies on mental illness and suicide, most published in the sixties or analysing sixties data and most emanating from the Mental Health Authority of Victoria. Even these, however, have tended to use more refined methods and different samples to re-examine the same problems, rather than moving from established to new insights.

From the standpoint of the present inquiry, however, the most striking thing about the literature reviewed is the disjunction between assertions of the importance of socio-cultural and economic sources of health-related problems, on the one hand, and indifference to systematic research on the effects of these sources on health, on the other hand. Research, most of it on the scientific model approved by the *MJA* and similar legitimating agents, concentrates on familiar 'hard' facts like age, sex, education, birthplace, duration of residence, family status, employment and knowledge of English. The meaning to be attached to these 'hard' facts has almost always to be sought *outside* the research data. It is found in the general experience of the researchers, in overseas literature and in the reported observations of colleagues. A study of female psychotics, published by F. Schaechter in 1962, provides an example. Schaechter gives a limited amount of 'hard' as well as 'soft' data about the sample of patients and describes the success that attended their being cared for in national groups by a nurse who could speak their own language. The reader assumes that clinical evidence led to the conclusion that pressure to assimilate was a major factor contributing to breakdown among these women. But this conclusion is offered against a background of social knowledge that clearly does not derive from this particular research context. This knowledge covers a number of areas. Concerning motivation: a Greek or Italian aims 'to make enough money in as short a time as possible and return as a rich man to his homeland', while the refugee Ukrainian or Pole 'has to assimilate, knowing that he will end his days in this country' and the Dutch and Germans, 'with empire-building traditional to their culture, usually come out here to seek wider economic horizons' (a different process, apparently, from making money). In general: 'any migrant on his own in a strange country regards his bank account as his only trustworthy friend', and 'coherent foreign communities' develop as a defence against the pressure to assimilate and a sense of inferiority. The children of migrants 'become assimilated most rapidly in our schools', but may come into conflict with their parents; eventually they build a bridge between the generations of their parents and their own children, who alone 'will be indistinguishable from the indigenous population' (Schaechter, 1962).

Throughout the period a number of writers drew on stereotypes of this kind, and selected and combined them in various ways as they seemed to elucidate some observed aspect of migrant health. The connection between observation and explanation was so indirect—and often presented, it should be acknowledged, as no more than speculation—that inconsistencies aroused little interest.

At times, however, the knowledge about migrants presented in the medical literature goes beyond stereotyping and takes on something of the character of myth, legitimated in 'sacred'—that is, unquestioned—texts. The major texts consist of two articles by I.A. Listwan, one published in 1956, the other in 1959, two by J.M. Last, 1960 and 1961, and one each by E.G. Saint and S. Minc in 1963. Listwan was a Polish psychiatrist. Last was a graduate of Adelaide University and in general practice in Adelaide. Saint (now Dean of Medicine at the University of Queensland) had come from England to Perth and was Professor of Medicine at the University of Western Australia. Minc had a medical degree from Rome, had 'lived in Russia, Poland and Italy' before coming to Australia twenty-two years earlier and was assistant physician at the Fremantle Hospital. All except Last brought to their work with immigrant patients in Australia a wide international experience.

From this rich background, these four men wrote with great perception as pioneers in the study of migrant health, but what they had to say about the individual characteristics of certain categories of migrants became received wisdom, while neither their observations on structures—migrant or Australian—nor the doubts they occasionally expressed about the competence of the medical profession to deal with migrant patients attracted attention, at least until the same 'truths' were rediscovered by others ten years or more later. For example, in focussing on group aspects of migrant health and Australian prejudice, Listwan's second paper foreshadowed a sociological approach that medical research has never in fact followed up. The role that Last and Minc saw for the medical profession in becoming part of the immigrant's 'supporting group' was not taken seriously by subsequent writers. Neither was Saint's gentle admonition: 'for ignorance of European languages and lack of interest in non-Anglo-Saxon culture we ourselves must accept some responsibility' (1963: 338).

What these writers said about migrant characteristics, however, has continued to be treated as authoritative into the seventies, if reference to their writings in current work is a guide (for an example outside the medical literature, see Bostock, 1977: 54–60). There are other kinds of evidence too. An obstetrician from Finland, visiting the Royal Brisbane Hospital, wrote a brief note on 'Migrants in hospital' (Laakso, 1973). He had three references, one to Last's 1961 article and one to Minc (the third was to Pasquarelli, 1966), and cited Minc's comments on the isolation of migrant women and Last's on the disparagement by nurses and doctors of the low pain threshold among migrants, as if these were timeless generalisations that could be applied to the situation he encountered—by implication among Finns—in his work in Brisbane in 1973. The continuing importance of Minc's article was also attested to—and promoted—by its republication in 1972 in a general book on *Australia's Immigration Policy*, edited by H. Roberts. The content remained unchanged, but the title was brought up to date: 'Of New Australian patients, their medical lore and major anxieties' became 'Medical and health problems of immigrants' (Minc, 1972).

Bizarre confirmation of the significance of Minc's article also comes from another source. In 1969 a Melbourne psychiatrist and medical student published an article called 'Mediterranean guts ache' (Portelli and Jones, 1969). It was little more than a plagiarisation of Minc's 1963 paper, applied specifically to one syndrome and one group, the Italians (see Ammon, 1969). The authors' only original contribution was the suggestion that social workers had a role to play in the treatment of Italian patients.

New definers

Perspectives on migrant health have changed somewhat in the last three to four years. We can briefly summarise the position before then. There was some accretion of knowledge about the incidence and nature of specific diseases, but none on the socio-psychological and cultural sources and context of illness. Instead, knowledge about the social aspects of migrant health became consolidated by selective repetition of the insights of a few early writers whose work had a potential for generating testable hypotheses but was never exploited in that way. Scarcely any of the writers on migrant health appeared to be acquainted with the sociological and psychological literature on migrants in Australia that accumulated during the sixties; neither did this literature address itself to the question of migrant health.

The most obvious change in the past few years is that individuals and groups other than doctors have begun to stimulate interest in migrant health. One example is a workshop on 'The Rehabilitation of the Psychiatrically Ill Amongst the Migrant Population', organised by the joint Migrant Welfare Committee of the Australian Council of Social Service and the Australian Council for Overseas Aid in 1970. The chairman was a social psychologist; the speakers were a psychiatrist and surgeon, and the participants included medicos, social workers and other workers in private welfare agencies. A searching general discussion of mental health problems also appears in an ACOSS paper, *Immigrants and Mental Health*, published in 1976.

Social workers and other non-medical health and welfare personnel have extended knowledge of the migrant health situation by drawing on their own experience, very different in many ways from the experience gained by doctors in their dealings with patients. In 1976, for example, an anonymous Greek interpreter published his account of the doctor-patient relationship in three cases in which he had been involved. He described stereotyped prejudice, uninformed diagnoses and authoritarianism on the part of the doctors concerned, and inconsistency in expectations between doctors and patients. He also described his own strategic role: in one case he disagreed with the doctor's diagnosis (revealed when he opened the referral letter from doctor to psychiatrist), disapproved of the psychiatrist taking that diagnosis at face value, and then intervened himself: 'As her interpreter I was able to make her aware of what was happening, and was able to get her to seek a second opinion about her headaches' (*Dissent*, 1976).

Giving concrete expression to a much-applauded ideal, several recent conferences and publications have focussed on informing medical personnel about migrant cultures and situations, and in so doing have brought the experience of social science research workers to bear on migrant health problems, virtually for the first time. At a symposium on 'Medico–social problems in the Greek population in Melbourne', held at the Royal Children's Hospital in 1971, a Greek-speaking sociologist and social worker, David Cox, gave a paper on the social and cultural background of Greek migrants. Cox's paper, along with the contributions of Spiro Moraitis, a general practitioner of Greek origin, and F. Retchford, a medical social worker, were published in the *MJA* in the following year, with the editor's warm endorsement: they presented, the editor said, 'facets of these [social and health] problems which are of considerable importance to all professional people concerned with the health of the Greek community' (*MJA*, 1972: 855). A special article, published in the *MJA* in 1976, had the same information-giving aim as Cox's paper. It was by Gillian Bottomley and contained 'an anthropologist's viewpoint' on rural Greeks and illness (Bottomley, 1976). A series of *MJA* editorials and comments on 'The plight of the migrant' in 1976 confirmed the journal's commitment to educating the medical profession about migrants and the medical implications of migrant situations. Two of these articles reported on migrants in industry (*MJA*, 1976*a* and 1976*b*). Another gave details about the Emergency Telephone Interpreter Service (*MJA*, 1976*c*), which produced varied reactions. Two Croation spokesmen objected to the listing of 'Yugoslav' as one of the languages available through TIS; there is no Yugoslav language, they insisted, only Croatian, Serbian, Slovenian or Macedonian (Rac and Tomasovic, 1977). A Sydney surgeon reacted to one *MJA* editorial by deploring the failure of migrants to learn English: 'Just how many native-born Australians could be helped to a life in their own country with the money spent on migration?', he asked (McKellar, 1976). A gynaecologist, also from Sydney, equally deplored the· lack of interpreters in hospitals (Molloy, 1976) and elicited information about the health education programme of the Health Commission of New South Wales and an offer from the Chairman of the Commission to try to assist hospitals that made their interpreter needs known (McEwin, 1977).

Dialogue of any kind has been rare enough in the past for even this kind of exchange to be noteworthy. Indeed, the pre-1970 period produced only one incipient debate. This occurred in 1969 when the relation between psychiatric admission rates and the size of immigrant groups was the subject of communications to the *MJA* from Alan Stoller and J. Krupinski, of the Melbourne Institute for Mental

Health, and J. Kraus, a psychologist research worker in the Department of Child Welfare and Social Welfare, Sydney. But the exchange did not develop around the differing perspectives of different disciplines, as it might have done, and debate was still-born (Kraus, 1969*a* and 1969*b*; Stoller and Krupinski, 1969).

Cultural and class explanations of migrant health

What is now beginning to appear in the literature is controversy on more basic questions.[5] Of these, the most fruitful appears to be the issue of cultural stereotyping.

It is becoming increasingly pertinent to appraise social knowledge about migrant cultures because the current visibility of ethnic issues in Australia encourages the definers to tap this knowledge for explanations of why migrants have certain health problems and use medical services in certain ways. Mann's comment on the reception of the Portelli and Jones article—it 'has met with wide approval from almost everyone in the medical profession with whom I have discussed it' (Mann, 1969: 932)—illustrates how ready medical personnel often are to accept cultural explanations of migrant behaviour. Although Mann questioned the bias and patronising tone of Portelli and Jones, he nevertheless complimented them on having 'made a genuine attempt to collect generalized data concerning the Italian community' (Mann, 1969: 932).

The more energetic questioning of cultural explanations of migrant health and use of health services that has appeared in the past few years can be illustrated from two examples. Bottomley's article on rural Greeks and the associated *MJA* editorial comment brought a reaction from a Sydney psychiatrist, Anthony Dinnen. The 'individual psychopathology of the migrant', said Dinnen, was being overlooked: 'familiar stories of family and personal problems' appear no less in 'rural Greece' than in 'urban St Ives'. 'The myth that all Greek migrants come from a secure, happy, cosy village where everybody loves one another continues to be propagated by those who prefer to overlook psychiatric truths' (Dinnen, 1976).

In a second case, a Greek social worker, Loula Rodopoulos, criticised the authors of an article on infantile autism for using 'a stereotype of the Greek family as presented in other literature instead of presenting case histories of the immigrant families studied' (Harper and Williams, 1976*a*; Rodopoulos, 1976). In their answer, the authors side-stepped the main issue raised by Rodopoulos, but in fact provided some of the kind of situational information she was asking for (Harper and Williams, 1976*b*).

With the politicisation of migrant issues that has occurred in the past four years or so, some critics of the disadvantaged position of immigrants in Australian society have telescoped class and cultural explanations of the migrant health situation. Greek spokesmen have been prominent in presenting non-English-speaking immigrants as an exploited class in Australian society, and contributions to the class-cultural interpretation of migrant health have also come mainly from Greeks. Spiro Moraitis has been particularly important in translating radical Greek views into the medical context. An article that he and a Melbourne lawyer, J.N. Zigouras, also of Greek origin, published in 1971, 'Impressions on Greek immigrants', was vigorously challenged by three Sydney doctors, also of Greek origin. The Sydney critics rejected the Moraitis-Zigouras article on the grounds that it gave a biassed, over-generalised and inaccurate picture of Greeks in Australia; Greek migrants, they said, are not as ill-educated, materialistic, poor, backward or ignorant as the article suggested (Papapetros *et al.*, 1971).

In a recent paper given at a seminar on 'The Injured Ethnic', Moraitis reiterated his earlier picture of the deprivations of rural Greeks: over 90 per cent, he said, of all Greek migrants in Australia. The Greek family 'disembarks in Australia destitute, in debt, with no home, no job, no language. They are thrust into a strange, hostile environment'. Being 'relatively illiterate' and unskilled, new arrivals have access only to the most menial, hardest and lowest paid jobs. Poverty makes both husband and wife work. Parent-child relations suffer and 'Greek youth have the conflict of two cultures'. Moraitis uses starker terms in the 1977 conference paper than he did in the 1971 *MJA* article: now, in a different context, there is no mention of the good health described in the earlier paper; instead 'intractable medico-social problems' are emphasised. The onus has also shifted from Greek characteristics and culture to Australian rejection and exploitation. Poverty is no longer due more to 'a desire . . . to pay off their homes speedily' than lack of money. The indifference and materialism of parents have disappeared as causes in the breakdown of relations between parents and children. Greeks are now described as visiting their homeland 'to see sick relatives, their aged parents, or for reasons of nostalgia'; references to the importance of the high cost of living and high unemployment rate, 'as well as the parasitic nature of relatives', forcing them to re-emigrate are gone. Condemnation of the impoverishment of Greek culture is replaced by praise for the 'thriving and organised subculture' created by the migrants: Greeks are at once isolated, disadvantaged and ridden with problems, and rich in community life and resources of all kinds—sport, newspapers, churches, ethnic schools, 'theatres, films, plays, and licensed night-clubs' (Moraitis and Zigouras, 1971; Moraitis, 1977).

As the 1971 article and the reactions to it from Papapetros *et al.* illustrate, most attempts to bring knowledge about ethnic cultures to bear on migrant health problems have been concerned with the rural cultures of southern Europe and the lack of fit between peasant experience and the demands and opportunities of Australian society. Nearly all the writers involved have been of the same ethnic origin as the cultures they describe (Cox and Bottomley are the exceptions), but, directly or by implication, have unequivocally dissociated themselves from the traditions, values and interests represented in those cultures. Sympathetic as the tone of most of this writing is, much of it has the kind of patronising tone that Mann gently chided Portelli and Jones for: even their 'turn of phrase', he said, 'talks down to the migrant' (Mann, 1969; see also Pasquarelli, 1966; Tahmindjis, 1978).

At the same time as the cultural-class literature contributes to the image of migrants as poor in circumstances and peasant in origins and culture, it also unobtrusively extrapolates from Greeks and Italians to the rest of the non-English-speaking migrant population. However general the scope of discussion appears at the outset, close scrutiny repeatedly reveals that the data base consists solely of Greeks, or, less commonly, Italians. Whereas in the fifties and sixties one migrant group was not distinguished from another and the whole migrant population appeared as a homogeneous mass, today there is a common trend—not only in the literature we have just been discussing, but in education and other areas as well—to imply that migrant equals Greek/Italian.

NOTES

1. Apart from official publications, listed on pages 219–24, sources used in Chapters 5 and 6 are contained in a separate bibliography on pages 237–247.
2. After they had been scanned, a number of items were excluded from the analysis because: they were concerned solely with the physical aspects of diseases associated with migrants; they were relevant only in that birthplace was one of a number of individual characteristics taken into account, without any migrant health problem being identified; or they contained no original content of research findings or commentary. Some items, mainly letters in the *MJA*, were excluded because too slight.
3. This observation should be read in the light of Note 2.
4. 'Those involved with the law have tended to see the migrant as both accident prone and subject to psychosomatic illness. However, there is no

sound evidence to support this assumption' (Aus., Commission of Inquiry into Poverty, 1975*b*: 236. See also Jakubowicz and Buckley, 1975: 43–4; and Aus., Commission of Inquiry into Poverty, 1976: 186–7).

5. The only related questions that produced any debate in the earlier literature were the recognition of overseas medical qualifications and the admission of immigrants with infectious disease.

6   Health Care

As we have seen in the previous chapter, migrant health has been
defined primarily as a problem located *within migrants*, not a problem
deriving from health care institutions or the practice of doctors and
other professionals. This definition, which is congruent with the
residual model of welfare described in Chapter 2, is now coming into
question, but the questioning has so far made little impact on health
care structures or activities. Response and nonresponse can usefully
be examined within the framework of communication, knowledge and
structures.

Improving communication

Although problems of communication have predominated over all
others in the consideration of migrant health care, communication
responses have been niggardly and unco-ordinated, apart from some
very recent developments in New South Wales, to be discussed shortly,
and the benefits flowing to the health area from the Telephone
Interpreter Service. Response has been largely confined to the minimal
adjustment necessary to meet the most dramatic disruptions caused
by migrant patients—that is, the provision of interpreters in public
hospitals. The body that has pursued this matter most persistently
appears to be the New South Wales Association of Mental Health,
through its Standing Committee for the Mental Health of Migrants.
The Committee made fruitless approaches to State authorities in 1965
and 1967 (NSW, Association of Mental Health 1972: 145), and W.
Matsdorf raised the matter at the 1963 Citizenship Convention (which
he attended as a delegate of the Mental Health Association) and at
the 1968 Convention (when he was a delegate of the Good Neighbour
Council of New South Wales). The Committee continued to be
seriously concerned at what it saw as the failure of health services
to provide for non-English-speaking migrants, and in 1972 reported
the results of a survey it had carried out in twenty-eight public

hospitals in Sydney. Only one hospital had what might be called an organised interpreting service; it employed three clerk interpreters during the normal working day, but because it was a maternity hospital the need for interpreters commonly arose outside those hours. Two other hospitals employed an interpreter each, one of them in its maternity ward only. All hospitals used medical and paramedical staff as interpreters where possible and all except two relied heavily on domestic staff. Only four used voluntary services frequently. Twenty-four hospitals (including the two that employed one interpreter) 'declared their facilities seriously inadequate throughout all departments' (1972: 146). The Committee recommended that the large hospitals employ a professional interpreter with the responsibility to recruit and train volunteers, and that peripatetic interpreters be used where appropriate. Professionals would have the responsibility to recruit and train volunteers, thus conforming to 'the well-tried, successful combination of institutional and voluntary effort, which has been and still is, a cornerstone in the building of social services in this country' (1972: 148). Inquiries conducted by the New South Wales Task Force a year later confirmed the findings of the Mental Health Association Committee. The Task Forces in the other States presented a similar picture and focussed their assessment of migrant health care on the lack of interpreters.

The paucity of services available in the health area is further documented in a number of recent inquiries on translating and interpreter services in general: by the Commonwealth Department of Immigration in 1973, ACOSS in 1974, the South Australian Government and an Interdepartmental Working Party of the Commonwealth Government in 1977. Overall, it is clear that the need for interpreters is met very largely by relatives or friends of patients, and by nurses and non-professional staff (mostly domestics) of hospitals and other institutions, who are untrained as interpreters and receive no extra pay for this service.

There is, however, little evidence of a sense of urgency about the need for interpreter services in health care. As the 1974 ACOSS report put it: 'the established *need* is not matched by the *demand*' (1974: 4). Those sections of the medical profession who in the past were probably most conscious of migrants as a problem for hospitals—doctors in maternity hospitals—are even likely to think that the reduction in immigration and the declining birth rate have removed whatever urgency there once was. Official expectations and standards remain simple and often mean, as is illustrated by a comment from the Victorian Health Minister on a campaign carried out during 1976 and 1977, to force the State Government to provide interpreters in Mental Health Authority (MHA) institutions. The Minister was reported as stating that there was 'nothing wrong' with relatives, children, domestic staff and other patients being used as interpreters, adding his own keen observation that

> All these things are aimed at the lack of interpreters in MHA institutions . . . There's nothing fresh about that. Various groups have been pushing for it for some time.
>
>   I think there is an urgent need for interpreters, but it isn't as if they have no interpreter services at all. (*Age*, 19 February 1977)

One hopes that the New South Wales authorities were less complacent about a 'radiation incident' described in the annual report of the Director General of Public Health for 1971:

> A total of 75 milligrams of radium . . . was apparently lost in the sewer of a city hospital by a patient undergoing gynaecological treatment. This woman, a migrant with a poor knowledge of English, used the toilet facilities instead of following the indicated procedures for such cases. (NSW, *Parliamentary Papers*, Vol. 4, 3rd Session, 1972–3: 407)

The Victorian campaign mentioned previously began in 1975 when the Social Work Sub-committee of the Mental Health Authority organised a small pilot study of the use of interpreters at Royal Park Psychiatric Hospital. The results showed that, of 280 occasions on which interpreters were used, formal outside interpreter services (other than nurses, domestic staff and relatives of patients) were used only in 6 per cent of occasions, and only 16 per cent were concerned with the patient's treatment (most occasions were assessment-oriented) (MHA, 1976). Such data are not readily available from other institutions, but it is certain that few hospital staff, in psychiatric hospitals or elsewhere, have had experience of working with trained interpreters and fewer still have used interpreters throughout the course of treatment for migrant patients (see ACOSS, 1976: 16–17, 28–35; see also ACOSS, 1974). In the absence of any accumulation of experience of this kind, the advantages of trained interpreters have been taken on trust. There has been no pressure from anywhere for serious examination of the limitations of interpreters (trained or untrained) and, for the moment, patients who find the assistance even of trained interpreters a poor substitute for direct communication remain inarticulate about their frustrations and helplessness. As we shall see shortly in considering the New South Wales Hospital Interpreter Program, the introduction of a comprehensive trained-interpreter service raises a range of problems about the use of interpreters that are unlikely to come up when no such service is available.

   With attention still concentrated on the shortage of interpreter facilities, thinking about alternative or additional ways in which migrant health needs might be met remains fragmentary and superficial, and institutional responses lack coherence and continuity. A brief review of other communication responses, and of knowledge and organisational responses, will illustrate the point.

During the many years of controversy over the registration of overseas-trained doctors, one aspect of the question attracted little attention from the established institutions. This concerned the fact that non-English-speaking migrants were being deprived of medical care by professionals of their own language and culture, and furthermore that there grew up a submerged system of illicit medical practice which allowed unqualified imposters to exploit fellow-countrymen desperate for medical advice they could understand.

The only significant group of doctors to come from non-English-speaking countries since the Second World War were the 370 who arrived as Displaced Persons. As E.F. Kunz's study shows, the implacable opposition of the AMA, coupled with government weakness and indifference, meant that more than a third of these doctors never legally resumed their profession and about a third of the working years remaining to those who were eventually registered 'were whittled away at unnecessary university courses and in menial occupations' (Kunz, 1975: 115). With the passage of time a number of doctors, nurses and medical social workers of ethnic origin, either born overseas or in Australia, have been trained in Australian institutions. No government policy has, however, at any time been directed at recruiting or giving special assistance to bilingual, bicultural professionals.

Table 2.4 presents the best available data on the ratio of ethnic professionals to ethnic populations. It shows a consistent trend for the older German, Dutch and Polish migrant groups to be much better-provided than Greeks, Italians, Maltese and Yugoslavs with doctors, nurses and social and welfare workers born in their respective countries. (The slightly better position of Yugoslavs in some categories probably reflects the fact that the Yugoslav population contains both 'old' and 'new' elements). If to these figures were added Australian-born persons of migrant origin, in the respective occupations, the advantage of the older groups would be more pronounced; indeed, the Germans would have higher rates of professionals in all three categories than the rates for the total population. Overall, the Greeks, Italians, Maltese and Yugoslavs clearly have available few health or welfare professionals of their own background and language: the number of doctors per 10 000 of population in each group ranges from 1 to 3, and the number of nurses from 1 to 8; no group has more than one social or welfare worker per 10 000. The comparable ratios of doctors, nurses and social and welfare workers for the total population are 13, 44 and 4 respectively.

Expanding knowledge

The literature on migrant health care is studded with advice to doctors and other health staff to become more knowledgeable and understanding about migrants, migrant cultures and health problems. The concluding paragraph to a 1967 *MJA* editorial on 'Some of the complexities of migration' provides an example.

> The successful existence within our community of parallel cultures, which are slowly advancing towards more complete integration, clearly depends on many factors, and the medical profession, if it has any genuine concern for the mental health of the community, needs to be aware of them. We conclude by listing two factors suggested by recent writings: constant vigilance by the appropriate governmental and non-governmental authorities, whose activities should be supported by continuing research studies of the progress of the various migrant groups; and increasing tolerance by individual non-migrants arising from a fuller understanding of the complexity of the problems facing the migrant and his children. Given these conditions, which are already apparent, Australia should be able to continue to welcome a constant stream of newcomers. (*MJA*, 1967: 662)

The punch-line comes of course in the last sentence: the editor of the *MJA* was giving notice that no passing qualms about professional or community attitudes to migrant well-being should interfere with the continuation of large-scale immigration.

Organised response on the part of the medical profession and health authorities to exhortations to change has consisted almost solely of a small number of information-giving papers written by interested individuals for the benefit of health care professionals. Minor optional components have been introduced into some professional courses (for example, the University of New South Wales, Department of General Studies course, 'Migrants in Australia', which is available to medical students). Discussions of migrant health problems occur from time to time in regular medical conferences, but the meeting on 'Medico-social problems of the Greek community' in 1971 appears to be the only conference specifically devoted to migrant health and organised under the sponsorship of the AMA. The meetings that have probably done most to stimulate medicos and others to think about migrant health have been the conferences organised by ACOSS (for example, the workshop on 'The Rehabilitation of the Psychiatrically Ill Amongst the Migrant Population', organised by ACOSS and the Australian Council for Overseas Aid, 1970), the seminar on 'The Injured Ethnic' organised by the Australian and New Zealand Society for Occupational Medicine and the Australian Greek Welfare Society in 1977, and the conference on 'Women's Health in a Changing Society' sponsored by the Commonwealth Department of Health and the

National Advisory Committee for International Women's Year in 1975.[1] It is worth noting that pressures from the women's movement for more knowledge about the situation of women in general have directed attention to *migrant* women in particular—their health and their employment, which will be discussed in the next chapter.

The other side of the knowledge response is the question of educating migrants in health matters, services and insurance. Again the literature contains little more than worthy sentiments and good advice (mostly directed at 'the government'), but there has been one sustained attempt to educate migrants in health matters. In 1971 the Division of Health Education in the New South Wales Department of Health initiated a programme of health education for non-English-speaking migrants by recruiting twenty individuals with the necessary language and cultural background and training them as health educators. Regular group discussions began in 1972 in eleven baby health centres in Sydney suburbs with large migrant populations—the educators and the health-centre sisters working as a team. In addition to giving information and reassurance about health and health services, the educators help mothers fill in forms, give advice on problems of welfare, arrange referrals to other agencies, assist with the organisation of English lessons and go on home visits. The programme has expanded from an attendance of less than 2000 in 1972 to an annual average of 5350 for the period 1975–1977. In the early stages, educators also attended meetings with parents and teachers in schools, but funds to develop this aspect of the work have not been available (Chesher and Moess, 1977).

The strength and continuity of the group discussions, which are the core of the programme, appear to come from several sources. Since the beginning, the group discussions have been seen as giving migrant women from those ethnic communities 'who do not generally avail themselves of health services' the opportunity 'to meet with others in a similar position' (Chesher and Moess, 1977: 2). They appeal because they can be accepted as a legitimate activity even where women are severely restricted in what they can do outside the family. As Terry Chesher and S. Moess have put it:

> In some ethnic groups wives are discouraged by their husbands from any non-essential outings, however, on many occasions when a husband has visited the Centre with his wife on the first visit, he has approved of the service and given his wife permission to attend regularly. (1977: 8)

Another important factor is that the programme has been incorporated into a health service—the baby health centres—that is well-established and highly respected and does not stigmatise its users as sick or inadequate. The involvement of migrants as educators has also been important. So has the flexibility, which has allowed educators to innovate and create their roles in response to the needs and interests that migrant parents express in situations of mutual trust and good communication. Continuing in-service training has been geared to providing the educators with the knowledge and skills that experience on the job has shown they need (Davies, 1972; Chesher and Moess, 1977).

Organisational change

An *MJA* editorial on the 1971 seminar on medico-social problems in the Greek community summed up the inadequacy of organisational response to migrant health care in an unusually direct statement:

> medical, social and educational departments and agencies are now confronted with problems of such magnitude that they do not have the organization or trained staff to cope. (*MJA*, 1972: 856)

In the absence of policies of organisational change to cope with the problems to which the editorial refers, informal responses have been necessary to enable hospitals and other medical services to operate with a non-English-speaking clientele, and informal responses have sometimes crystallised into convention or formal policy. The various arrangements evolved in numerous hospitals to make domestic staff available to act as unpaid interpreters are an obvious example.

The Hospital Interpreter Program of the New South Wales Health Commission is the most substantial and carefully developed plan for organisational change to meet migrant health needs (see Wintle, 1977). The team of twenty-seven interpreters trained in 1977 as a mobile force to serve seventeen Sydney hospitals is intended to fulfil a significant new role that goes far beyond the limited functions usually assigned to interpreters. The training programme, organised by a social worker in the Bureau of Personal Health Services, provides an introduction to the understanding of the hospital as a bureaucracy, interviewing skills, strategies for coping with conflict and approaches to welfare problem-solving. Training of this kind is justified on the grounds of a particular definition of the hospital situation: hospital interpreters cannot function simply as technologists or language specialists; to be effective as interpreters they must be skilled communicators in a wider sense and adept in handling interpersonal relations. The aim is to equip interpreters to make their own niche in the hospital structure and to establish a role for themselves that does not come into collision with the well-entrenched positions of other hospital staff. It is intended that future in-service training will develop the interpreters' counselling role and count towards promotion. Structural changes to provide greater opportunity for career advancement will also be necessary if the programme is to work as intended, for there is an incipient anomaly between, on the one hand, the high qualifications and extensive experience of a large number of the recruits and the professional role they are being trained for and, on the other hand, the comparatively low salary ceiling of the Public Service Board interpreters classification. The programme is too new for its impact to be assessed, but it is already clear that doctors and other hospital staff also need training to use an interpreter service effectively and that a formal service can be opposed as a disruptive influence on informal arrangements that have developed within, and in congruence with, the traditional hospital hierarchy of authority and status.

What once promised to be the most far-reaching organisational response to migrant health is not, however, occurring in hospitals or established medical institutions but in community health centres. The 'new sequence' of health care represented in community health centres involves, in Charles Kerr's words, 'a whole new professional approach embodied in the health team concept' (1973: 51). Because of this innovatory character, community health centres have been seen by some observers as potentially serving sections of the population ill-provided for by traditional institutions. The group that has most enthusiastically, and successfully, put forward this point of view is the women's movement, while the health centre literature largely ignores migrants and rarely mentions the value of bilingual professionals in the health team or the employment of interpreters (Kerr refers to neither in his list of team members, 1973: 58–60). However, in his report on the social-medical aspects of poverty in Australia, George S. Martin forecast that small community-based health facilities would serve migrants better than existing institutions. In addition, he favoured the comprehensive care centre based on a public hospital as proposed by Gross (1974), particularly on the grounds that such a development would acknowledge and build on the existing preferences of the large proportion of migrants who turn to the public hospital as their main source of primary health care (Aus., Commission of Inquiry into Poverty, 1976: 205–6). Like David Cox in his examination of the role of the ethnic group in welfare, Commissioner Martin also endorsed the use of the ethnic community in the delivery of health care. He envisaged a development of the present situation in which some migrant communities, through their welfare services, already act as a bridge between the migrant and medical services, and the further possibility that migrant communities might themselves become direct providers of services (1976: 206–8).

Because of widespread opposition or nonco-operation on the part of influential sections of the medical profession, however (Aus., Hospitals and Health Services Commission, 1976: 37–8), community

health centres have had a very uneven history: many have had to fight
for community acceptance, and a large proportion of them (particularly those in New South Wales) do not offer primary medical care—
that is, they have health teams but no doctors. Community health
centres, therefore, cannot be seen as a major source of response to
migrant health needs; even within the scope of the wider Community
Health Program, migrant health is one of the areas in which 'smaller
inroads' have been made (Aus., Hospitals and Health Services
Commission, 1976: 29). Through the Community Health Program the
Commonwealth does, however, contribute to four community health
centres designed specifically for migrants: the Cringila centre in
Wollongong, the Brunswick and North Richmond centres in Melbourne and the Western Region Migrant Health Education Program
in Sydney. Because of their location in areas of migrant concentration,
several other health centres, such as the Leichhardt Women's Health
Centre in Sydney, are also oriented to migrant needs.

In the final analysis, the structural change that has had most effect
on migrant health care is doubtless the introduction of Medibank.
Because of increasing concern in the early seventies that the voluntary
insurance scheme in operation at that time left somewhere between
a half and a quarter of southern European migrants uninsured
(Scotton, 1974: 197–198; see also Martin, 1975*b*), the Commonwealth
introduced measures to give migrants free health insurance cover for
two months after arrival. The benefits of this scheme were, however,
attenuated by the fact that newcomers had to make their own
arrangements with a private insurance company and then recover the
costs from the Commonwealth. The introduction of universal health
insurance under Medibank means that migrants are now automatically
covered, like everyone else (although the progressive dismantling of
Medibank by the Fraser Government also means that automatic cover
confers less benefits, particularly on low-income earners, then it did
under the original scheme).

Conclusion: the limits of response and responsibility

What the connection is between the social definition of the health
situation and problems of migrants, on the one hand, and practice
and policy, on the other, cannot be established within the parameters
of an inquiry such as this. The necessary information is not available
in public documents; a major research task would be involved in
examining the files of government departments, the AMA and other
bodies, even if they were available, or in trying to put the story together
through interviews. I can say, however, that the picture that was

shaped and reshaped over the years and the roles that various groups played in creating that picture are consistent with what has surfaced as policy and practice. Various actors undoubtedly influenced events behind the scenes, but action and inaction alike tally with public demeanour. If the arras sheltered no villains, neither did it conceal self-effacing thinkers or activists.

Until the last few years, social knowledge about the health situation and needs of migrants was almost solely the creation of the medical profession. The profession's interest in migrants has been sporadic and limited, but a common theme recurs: that migrants are medically vulnerable because of pre-migration experiences of deprivation and stress, and because of ignorance, low standards of education, and cultural beliefs and values alien to Australian ways. Except in the kind of rhetoric of social responsibility in which it is skilled, the profession has not defined migrant health as a problem of the medical profession or of health services. Migrant health is a migrant problem, to be solved by the established institutions, principally government authorities, doing things for migrants. Neither the AMA nor any of its State branches has produced a position or policy statement on migrant health care (AMA, 1977). The AMA's *Policy on Medical Services*, originally approved by the Federal Assembly in 1965, subsequently amended and published in 1971, contains no reference to the non-English-speaking population nor to interpreters or any similar roles in its reference to 'ancillary' medical services (AMA, 1971). Neither was there anything on the subject in a 1972 report by an AMA Study Group on Medical Planning, called 'Medical practice in Australia: an outline of desirable future developments in medical and allied services in Australia' (AMA Study Group, 1972). So far as I have been able to ascertain, neither the 1971 policy document nor the 1972 planning report has been superseded by more recent statements.

The role of the medical profession in defining migrant health is, of course, in keeping with its dominating position in the health services in general. R.B. Scotton has summarised the role of doctors in these words:

> The profession is at the heart of the system: although doctors comprise less than seven per cent of persons employed in the health care industry they are the elite to whom the remainder are subsidiary in function, and inferior in training, status and income. The economic power of the profession is based on a monopoloy of skills for which no close substitutes are recognized ... However, its dominant influence on the structure of the health service system rests not only on this economic base but also on its cohesiveness as a formal and informal interest group and the prestige and authority accorded to it by politicians, administrators and the community as a whole. (1974: 10)

Moreover, a long tradition of professional surveillance of members' public communications has established firm control over what is produced as social knowledge about medicos and medicine: what is not intended for public consumption is reserved 'for the use of members exclusively' (as the annual reports of the New South Wales AMA branch put it), while *The Medical Journal of Australia* provides a major channel through which the profession communicates to the world outside as well as among its own members. The prestige of doctors in Australian society ensures that, in relations between themselves and patients, other professionals and health personnel, and in their participation outside the field of health, what they define as good and what they propound as knowledge will be seriously attended to.[2]

The medical profession's definitions of reality have of course been challenged from time to time, but a significant element in the organised power of the profession lies in keeping criticism 'within the family'. It is only when events have passed into history, and sources of information outside the profession become available to throw light on the past, that an indignant Joan Clarke or E.F. Kunz can win enough credibility to set the record straight (Kunz, 1975; Clarke, 1976). Serious challenge from other established institutions has been rare and, although over the years the medical profession has made a number of concessions modifying its stance against public control of health services, it continues to exert a dominating influence over the nature, cost and accessibility of those services. Medibank and the national system of community health services, which the Labor Government introduced in 1972, produced a major confrontation between government and doctors, but the profession has emerged from this encounter with its power little impaired and its income levels much enhanced.[3]

There is no obvious way in which the interests of the profession would have been advanced had it assumed any active interest in migrant health care and, at least on the question of the registration of overseas-trained doctors, it is clear that doctors believed *their* interests would have actually been damaged by any concession to *migrant* interests. Neither has the professional identity of doctors been threatened by strains and tensions resulting from migrant use of medical services. Pressures arising out of migrant frustration and dissatisfaction have in any case been attenuated by migrants' under-use of health care institutions: quite simply, the system operates to keep them and their problems at arm's length. To the extent that they do necessarily get involved, the organisational structure of health services provides a buffer, in the form of cleaners, nurses, receptionists and a multiplicity of 'ancillary' staff, that protects doctors from the impact of patients' experiences. The inability of non-English-speaking patients to communicate the substance of their confusion and fears to an English-speaking medico—which even the presence of an interpreter often does little to mitigate—puts a further distance between doctor and patient. In short, the migrant presence has not led doctors to serious doubts about their capacity to fulfil their own medical functions properly. Such stresses and unmet needs as they perceive in migrants are not their problem. Operating with a medical-scientific model of health care, which defines psychological and social considerations as marginal and largely untreatable except when evident in the form of gross malfunctioning, they have continued to do their job to their own satisfaction with the minimum of insight into the experience of migrants or of other health personnel in contact with migrant patients.

The situation is very different with the group who have helped to achieve a modest re-definition of migrant health in the last few years. Most of them are employees in hospitals, clinics or research organisations, occupying positions as 'ancillaries', or what are now sometimes called 'associated health workers', well down the power hierarchy. The vocal ones among these associated workers are educated in the social sciences, mostly social workers, sociologists and psychologists. They have been trained to be sensitive to psychological and social issues and, even where language barriers intervene, their jobs give them direct access to migrants' personal experiences. In their work with migrants, they commonly face situations in which the lack of a common language, the inadequacy of organisational arrangements or the approach of other staff frustrates them in performing the tasks for which they have been trained, and from their vantage point it often seems that other health personnel are similarly handicapped. Working with migrants exacerbates the sense of their professional identity being under threat, a reaction that they are likely to have anyway as powerless representatives of 'unscientific' humanistic disciplines in an institutional atmosphere dominated by the 'science' of medicine. Although some of these associated workers belong to accredited professional associations such as the Australian Association of Scoial Workers and the Australian Psychological Society, no one group has an organisational structure or a channel of communication comparable with those of the medical profession, nor is there any regular publication through which, in combination, they can promulgate their definitions of health (or any other) services. The number of such workers in health institutions is also extremely small. It is from among these people—ranging from G.S. Martin, the member of the Commission of Inquiry into Poverty appointed to deal with the social-medical aspects of poverty, to social workers and interpreters employed in hospitals and sociologists carrying out research for welfare agencies

—that a new picture of migrant health is coming. It differs from the established picture in embodying a critique of the quality of health *care* received by migrants and in locating problems more in service institutions than in the individual and cultural characteristics of the migrants themselves.

I have said little about one major group of workers in the health field, the nursing profession. The reason is simply that nurses have contributed virtually nothing to the construction of public knowledge about migrant health. Mary Patten, Federal Secretary of the Royal Australian Nursing Federation, has summed up the situation in the words: 'Nurses working in community services have been aware of the problems of migrants and many have tried to learn more about their expectations but they have had a hard road and seldom write about it' (Letter, 7 April 1977). The nursing journals, which do not in any case circulate widely outside the profession, publish almost nothing about migrant health; on rare occasions when they do broach the subject, it turns out that they are presenting to nurses the views of one of the associated health workers described above (see, for example, the article by a social worker, Pamela Rutledge, on 'The Italian migrant and his problems', *Australasian Nurses Journal*, April 1972), or of some overseas writer (for example, the reprint in three parts of a long essay which won a British nursing prize: B. Alexandra, 'Meeting the needs of the immigrant in sickness and health', *Australasian Nurses Journal*, April, May, July, 1974). The only nursing contribution of any significance relevant to migrant health is Marie-Madeleine Dodds' *From Whence They Came*. In 1970 Sister Dodds travelled to five migrant source countries, plus Switzerland and the United States, to study family life, the care of the child 'in his natural environment' and family health services. Her report gives a brief sketch of what she found in each country, designed to help nurses 'in their daily contacts with our newcomers who speak little or no English for there is more to communication than just the spoken or written word' (Dodds, 1970: Acknowledgements). But she herself draws no conclusions; she leaves it to the reader to judge how far her inquiries provide a basis for understanding migrant health care problems in Australia or assessing how relevant Australian services are to migrants' needs.

The question of why nurses have contributed so little of their abundant experience to the definition of migrant health—or indeed of other health matters—goes beyond the scope of this study. It is possible that the traditional medical-scientific orientation of their training has left them without a sense that they have their own contribution to make, distinctive from that of the medical profession. Certainly they have been trained to *do* rather than to reflect or communicate their reflections outside the immediate work situation. It is also possible that, being deeply embedded in the rigid structure of health institutions, they have been able to maintain fairly inflexible and routine patterns of relating to migrant patients and that these patterns have protected them from the full awareness of migrant experience. In this connection it is significant that Mary Patten refers to nurses working in community services, not to hospital nurses, as the group aware of migrant problems.

Jane Shoebridge, one of the few nurses who is also qualified as a sociologist and has carried out research involving migrant patients in hospital (1977), sees nurses as victims of a kind of role conflict that inhibits their contribution to any kind of social knowledge on health care. In a private communication occasioned by her reading of a draft of the previous paragraphs, she wrote:

> I suggest nurses are blackmailed into silence by a socialisation process which leaves loyalty to profession (including, of course, medical profession) and bureaucracy stronger than loyalty to patient, or to service. The nurse tends to identify both as medico and as nurse. She must act for the doctor when he is absent, yet present merely a supportive face to patients when the doctor is present. This 'saving of the doctor's face' has origins, I believe, only vaguely connected with F. Nightingale in the Crimea or with female accommodation consonant with a dependent occupation. It seems much more attuned to the conscious ideology of encouraging the patient to have faith in the doctor, in medical science and in the hospital itself, for the sake of compliance, organisational order and the achievement of curative goals. Some nurses, I maintain, are not unaware of the migrant experience; but *communicating* views formally which may be construed as undermining patient faith in health professionals and their services is understandably felt to be firstly, disloyal, secondly, potentially disruptive to order and finally, hazardous with respect to their own employment.

Perhaps nurses can be expected to take a part in the construction of social knowledge about health as their education expands to include a behavioural sciences content, which should equip them better to perceive what migrant patients are actually experiencing and so give them something to say that adds to what doctors, social workers and other associated health staff can contribute.

There has been little to report, either, about the contribution of migrants to the definition of their health situation. Like other patients, migrants have been unorganised and inarticulate about their own interests. It is possible that, in the future, active broker organisations like CURA and the Ethnic Communities Councils in Sydney, Melbourne and Adelaide will contribute a migrant perspective on migrant health, but so far the efforts of such groups have been directed mostly to education and employment.

Although there has been no organised migrant voice, health personnel of ethnic origin have been important as mediators of the migrant health situation since Listwan's contributions of the mid-fifties. However, virtually every one of these people, both in the past and at present, speak from a position within the established institutional structure: as staff of hospitals, research institutes or welfare organisations, or members of voluntary associations like the Good Neighbour Council or the New South Wales Association of Mental Health. Most of them are involved more as observers of migrant health than as spokesmen on behalf of the migrant population. What they say carries weight just because they say it in legitimate, well-modulated voices, the overtones of migrant identification decently subdued.[4]

The high degree of institutionalisation, rigidity and lack of public accountability of the health services have allowed them to stave off change in a number of areas, while at the same time exercising an unquestioned autonomy in making the minimal informal arrangements necessary to allow them to cope with migrant clients and patients. The small number of migrants who have been co-opted into the system as unpaid, untrained interpreters have often benefited to the extent that they command a negotiable resource that enhances the value of their—usually limited—occupational skills, but their doubtful gains have been won at the expense of migrant professionals—linguists, interpreters, doctors and others—whose qualifications have remained unrecognised or unusable.

NOTES

1. The papers of the 'Women's Health in a Changing Society' Conference were published after this book went to press: Aus., Department of Health (1978): *Women's Health in a Changing Society*, 5 vols, AGPS, Canberra.
2. In the 17-point scale of status for occupational categories developed by Broom *et al.*, 'salaried', 'independent' and 'all medical practioners' rate 1. 'Independent medical practitioners' have the highest status score of any occupation and 'all medical practioners' the third highest: 915 and 880 in a range of scores whose lowest value is 331 for 'labourers food, beverages, tobacco' (1977: 103–111).
3. See Scotton (1974) for a detailed examination of the economics of the medical profession. Scotton shows that doctors have the highest income of any profession and that doctors' incomes were about five times the basic wage in 1938 and 6.7 times the minimum weekly wage in 1968–1969 (1974: 145–6). In the most recently available analysis of medical services and incomes, Deeble and Scotton (1977) attribute the estimated increase in

private services (from 3.80 use per head of population in 1962–63 to 4.21 in 1967–68, 5.48 in 1974–75 and 5.65 in 1975–76) to 'factors on the supply side' rather than patient demand. These factors are the proliferation of items within the fee schedule and the doctor-generated increase in specialised consultations and in prescription of diagnostic procedures, such a pathology and radiology. Doctors' incomes have risen not only because of this increase in services (partly real, partly an artifact of the fee schedule) but also because of the rate of fees charged and the decline in bad debts. Fees rose at a slightly lower rate than average weekly earnings in the period 1963 to 1973, but since 1973 there have been substantial fee increases: average weekly earnings increased from $155 in 1973–4 to $222 in 1975–6 (43 per cent), while the index of medical fees for all services increased from 136 to 223 in the same period (64 per cent). In the words of Deeble and Scotton: 'The benefits of increased medical productivity have thus accrued entirely to doctors' (1977: 345).

4. The issue of the registration of overseas-trained doctors has not been taken up in the present discussion, apart from the matter of health care raised on page 173, but it is important to note the battle which migrant doctors had to make their voices heard above the pronouncements of the AMA, and in the face of government indifference and powerlessness, during the fifties and sixties. Kunz shows that the support which in time they won from established Australian doctors and journalists was vital in producing the redefinition which finally culminated in changes in registration policy (see Kunz, 1975, especially ch. 4).

7   Trade Unions

Unlike the institutions of education and health, trade unions already had an established, public set of definitions about migrants long before the post-war migration movement began.

Opposition by organised labour to assisted migration was a recurring theme in the last half of the nineteenth century:

> Whenever the colony experienced economic distress, Government assistance to immigration was either reduced or stopped. It was during these periods . . . that the 'working class' raised its voice loudest in objection to the system. (Hayden, 1962: 25)

Racial prejudice added to the fear of competition from migrant labour to produce a consistent anti-migrant attitude, which in time was consolidated in union and Labor Party policies. Nevertheless, the migration programme initiated in 1946 was the work of a Labor Government. It had official trade union support, which remained firm until the seventies.

From time to time, however, there were rumblings that echoed traditional apprehensions. In 1952, for example, the *Decisions of the Australian Congress of Trade Unions* recorded that, because full employment did not exist, 'the intake of migrants should be immediately stopped', except for family reunions (Australian Council of Trade Unions, 1952: 5). A more strongly worded statement from the 1967 Congress 'demanded' that the Australian Council of Trade Unions (ACTU) be consulted before migrant labour was recruited to do work 'capable of being performed by labor domiciled in Australia' (ACTU, 1967: 15).

The outcome of this traditional stance of unions against migrants, combined with the general paucity of reflective, doctrinal and research literature produced by the union movement in Australia, is that unions have contributed almost nothing to social knowledge about their own response to the migrant presence in the past thirty years. A handful of academics, academic-activists, extra-union pressure groups and government authorities have recently begun to compose a public picture of this response, but most of the canvas is still blank. By contrast to the discussions of education and health, then, this chapter deals with a subject on which traditional ideas—formulated long before the period we are concerned with—far outweigh current interpretations.

In the light of these ideas, it was not to be expected that unions would go out of their way to incorporate post-war migrants as union members or promote migrant interests. Nor is it surprising that, as Ross Martin puts it, 'there has been a strong note of "assimilation–or–else" in official union attitudes' (1975: 65). Nevertheless—although unions may have acted as though migrant workers and *their* problems 'do not exist' (Zangalis, n.d. [1975]: 26)—the presence of migrant workers has been highly relevant to *union* problems at various times over the past thirty years. This has led to a series of advances and retreats which can be examined in four phases, according to the time when particular themes emerged into prominence:

1948–1954 Wooing migrant support: migrants as political resource.
1954–   Affirming assimilability: migrants as numbers.
1964–   Precarious institutionalisation: migrants as legitimate or disruptive minority within the union movement.
1973–   Being called to account: unionists and migrant workers as subjects of extra-union interest and research.

In the terms in which it developed in 1948–54, the theme of 'migrants as political resource' belonged specifically to that period. The other three themes continue as elements in the more differentiated union response that has developed since the mid-sixties.

Wooing migrant support

The first phase involved marshalling migrant support against communist power in the unions and produced the most dramatic events in the history of union response to migrants. The Grouper versus Communist conflict is well documented. Only those aspects of immediate concern need be summarised here (Gollan, 1975; R.M. Martin, 1975; Murray, 1970; Ormonde, 1972; Rawson, 1971). The arrival of 170 000 Displaced Persons in Australia between 1947 and 1952 coincided with the emergence of an organised attack by moderate and right-wing unionists against the communists, whose influence had strengthened, and in some unions become dominant, during the war. Displaced Persons were outspoken and often vehement in their anti-communism, and formed numerous groups—within the Catholic Church or based on former political, military or other affiliations—

to combat communism in Australia and to work for the liberation of their home countries from communist control. Many saw themselves as peculiarly qualified to inform Australians about the dangers of communism. They expected Australians to acknowledge their unique experience and grasp the opportunity to work with them in a vigorous anti-communist campaign on all fronts, national and international. They soon became deeply disillusioned: Australians, blind to the communist threat, rejected their overtures to pursue a common enemy (see Martin, 1965, 1972a; Richards, 1978).

However, the Industrial Groups, inspired by the Catholic Social Studies Movement (the Movement) and officially sponsored by the Australian Labor Party (ALP) in 1946 and the following years, did give the refugees from eastern Europe one chance to join with Australians in a vigorous and dramatic anti-communist battle. As Lyn Richards notes, the involvement of migrants in the Movement's bid to counteract communist influence in the union movement, and in the party split that followed, has gone largely unnoticed. Her own study of the origins of the New Australian Council subsequently formed by the break-away Democratic Labor Party (DLP) does much to fill the gap (Richards, 1978).

In contrast to the political arena, where the significance of migrant numbers was dampened by the fact that there was a five-year waiting period before an immigrant could be naturalised and so be eligible to vote, the migrants' vote was to be reckoned with in the unions immediately they entered the workforce (Richards, 1978: 12). The Movement needed migrant recruits in order to exploit the potential support of the newly arrived refugees from eastern Europe. It found them in a variety of ways: through the leader of the Movement, B.A. Santamaria; through their own priests; or more often through Australian organisers on the job. Some took the initiative themselves.

> Piecemeal, a very large number of migrants were drawn into the organization. Nobody ever counted them, and none of the organizers could even estimate numbers; indeed none seemed to have regarded them as a group. They were scattered throughout the different unions, never a team, not even an identifiable part of the Movement. (Richards, 1978: 7)

Apart from two organisers whom everyone knew, migrant workers in the Movement remained strangers to one another. Unconscious of being directed or organised, they nevertheless worked hard, translating, stencilling and distributing propaganda, recruiting new helpers and door-knocking.

By 1953 the Industrial Groups had succeeded in overturning communist control of some major unions and had gained positions for their own candidates in a number of union elections. But reaction in the ALP against the influence and tactics of the Industrial Groups accumulated, and at the end of 1954 the Federal Leader of the ALP, H.V. Evatt, denounced the Movement and the executive withdrew its support of the Groups. A right-wing faction subsequently split off from the ALP to form the DLP, and the phase in which migrants represented a resource to be cultivated in internecine union conflicts was over. Eastern Europeans faded from the union scene and the DLP made no attempt to absorb the industrial migrant organisation. Although the split had made union leaders realise the value of migrant support, the involvement of eastern Europeans in what came to be seen as a fanatical and dangerous incursion of politics into union affairs discouraged any other kind of interest in migrant workers. For their part, a number of migrants had made a contribution to the defeat of communist control in the unions, but in the process they had learnt how little they had in common with what one of the most active among them later called the 'sterile', 'negative' and 'primitive' anti-communism of the DLP (Richards, 1978: 27, 29). Some felt they had been used (Richards, 1978: 11). None had any reason to think that migrants, as migrants, had gained anything from the experience.

Involving migrants in the campaign against communist influence did not exhaust the interest of unions in migrants in the immediate post-war period, but attention to migrant concerns seems to have occurred more during the height of the conflict than later. In a study of 'The impact of immigration upon Australian labour', published in 1959, B. Luckham reported that the Federated Ironworkers' Association, with a large migrant membership, was the only union 'to have made a careful study of the effects and implications of immigration upon which to base its policies', but a New Australian section in the union journal, with German, Polish and Italian texts, lasted only from 1952 to 1954, 'when it was felt there was no continuing need in consequence of other means of contact being developed'. Items on migration in the union journal reached a peak in 1949–1952 and declined rapidly up to 1957, the year Luckham's survey ended (Luckham, 1959*a*: 40–41). Although Luckham interpreted the low level of interest in migrants as a sign of their assimilation and of a decline in hostility on the part of Australian workers, the scene that he reported in the mid-fifties is consistent with the somewhat different view that migrants attracted less attention from unions once the anti-communist fight was over.

Migrants as numbers

The second phase of union response to migrants coincided with a major shift in the composition of the migrant population. 'The migrants' of the late fifties and sixties were no longer 'the migrants' of the period of the Grouper-Communist conflict. In 1954, eastern Europeans were 28 per cent of the non-British overseas-born. By 1966, they were down to 20 per cent. Northern Europeans decreased from 24 per cent to 22 per cent in the same period, while southern Europeans increased from 28 per cent in 1954 to 40 per cent in 1966 (Aus., ABS, *Censuses,* 1954, 1966; Price ed., 1971: Table 1, A79; Price and Martin eds, 1976*a*: Table 1, A18–19).

Moreover, the size of the non-English-speaking labour force was increasing at a rate that outstripped comprehension of their situation or problems. As Table 7.1 shows, foreign-born workers increased by an average of 49 000 per year, double the per cent increase for the Australian-born labour force. Non-English-speakers comprised more than half the foreign-born increase. They in particular showed the 'relative lack of enthusiasm which many migrants have for organised unionism' (Jupp, 1966: 62). From the unions they neither demanded attention nor elicited it, except as a source of new members: the main interest unions took in migrants was getting them to join up.

Table 7.1 *Increase in the labour force, Australian-born and foreign-born compared, Australia, 1961–1966*

	Size of the labour force ('000)		Average yearly increase ('000)	Per cent increase
	1961	1966	1961–1966	1961–1966
Australian-born	3242.4	3628.7	77.3	11.9
Foreign-born	982.7	1227.7	49.0	24.9
Total labour force	4225.1	4856.4	126.3	14.9

Source: Calculated from Aus., National Population Inquiry, *Population and Australia,* 1975: Table VIII.6.

Precarious institutionalisation

A third phase can be dated from the General Motors Holden (GMH) and Mt Isa strikes of 1964. In the Australia-wide strike against GMH, Greek and Italian militants defied union officials. 'The mass meetings', says Jupp, 'were riotous, the conduct of the strike ballot a farce, and the breakdown in union leadership embarrassingly public' (1966: 59). Migrants from Europe accounted for nearly half the population of the Queensland mining town of Mt Isa and in the long drawn-out and bitter strike of 1964–1965, migrant workers were prominent among the rank and file who supported the militant rebels in persisting with strike action in opposition to the moderate, but weak and remote, Australian Workers Union hierarchy. When the Queensland Government sent police to the town with the aim of breaking the strike and getting the miners back to work, it was the Europeans, especially the Finns, who reacted most violently against this intimidation from a 'police state': 'the Finnish community in particular was regarded as the key to a return to work' (Sheldon, 1965: 11).

Migrants were again prominent in the 1973 strike at Ford's large car assembly plant at Broadmeadows in Melbourne, when Greeks played a decisive role in uniting the rank and file—80 per cent of them migrants from non-English-speaking countries—against union leadership. Two days after union officials had been attacked following a vote in favour of returning to work, some men went back, hundreds refused to and a riot followed. Smashed windows, damaged buildings and confrontations with police thrust the dispute on public attention and testified to a degree of hostility and resentment that no one had previously suspected. Union officials confessed their misunderstanding of the workers' attitudes, backed down on their recommendation that the men accept the company's terms and called an indefinite strike which continued for another two months. Observers agreed that the riot expressed the frustration of men working under severe assembly-line pressure and feeling that they were being treated like dirt by union officials as well as by foremen and management, while isolated from both sides by barriers of language (Hawkins, 1973; Game, 1973; Hills and Mitchell, 1973; see also Connell, 1977: 1–3).

The public attention given to these three strikes dramatised one continuing theme in this third phase: the demand by migrant workers that unions recognise their existence. As a Greek put it in the *Australian Left Review* in 1967: 'One signpost of thought should guide the labor movement—that there is a migrants' point of view' (Tsounis, 1967: 37).

Insistence that unions acknowledge migrants and their point of view comes mainly from left-wing migrants and is founded on the communist orthodoxy that the importation of migrant labour to fill the lowest status jobs is one crucial means by which the capitalist ruling class divides and weakens labour, 'a regulator to enervate the trade union movement' as I. Ivanoff said in the *Marxist Review* (1972: 36). The task of the activist is to defeat capitalist designs and secure the working-class unity without which the class struggle is doomed (see Zangalis, 1967, n.d. [1975]; Tsounis, 1967). Class unity is the primary aim; migrant welfare will be promoted to the extent that migrants are integrated into the union movement; migrant disaffection and ignorance have to be overcome because they threaten unity.

In the one serious attempt that has been made at a coherent marxist interpretation of the role of migrant workers in Australia, however, an academic observer, J.H. Collins, offers only a faint ray of hope that migrants will indeed unite 'to become an effective force within (not separate from) the Australian working class' and undermine the stability of Australian capitalism. Immigration has already provided a readily manipulated industrial reserve army. This army has made possible the emergence of an Australian labour aristocracy, who 'see themselves as benefiting from migrant exploitation' and are upwardly mobile at the expense of migrant workers.

> An artificial split in the working class emerges, is reinforced by, and manifested in the political neglect of migrants both at the ballot boxes and on the factory floors. The result is a decline in the political weight of the Australian working class. (Collins, 1976: 189)

Migrant militancy on the shop-floor and marxist interpretations in the world of ideas alike confirm migrants as an integral but identifiable section of the union movement. Even the threat that migrants will form their own unions because 'they are furious that the unions don't take proper care of them and that their complaints are not dealt with satisfactorily' (Ethnic Affairs Reporter, *SMH*, 1977) carries weight only because migrants are in fact firmly embraced within the system. A similar trend towards the acknowledgement of migrants as a legitimate minority within the movement is apparent in a number of organisational changes that have occurred in the past ten years or so. The accumulation of these changes represents a gradual process of institutionalisation and the spread of a definition of 'the migrant problem' as above all a problem of welfare and participation, not a problem for working class unity. These processes form the main themes of the third phase of union responses to migrants.

The emergence of new official positions within the union structure is the most important manifestation of such changes. Structural differentiation of this kind was not involved in the recruitment of migrants as shop-stewards and collectors, necessitated because, as Jupp put it, 'without them it would be impossible [for unions with numbers of migrants] to communicate with most of their members at all' (1966: 61). This long-standing and widespread practice may have represented a more significant response on the part of unions to the migrant presence than it is possible to gauge in the absence of field studies of union–migrant interaction on the shop floor. However, it is more likely that the use of migrant intermediaries between English-speaking foremen and union officials, on the one hand, and the non-English-speaking workers, on the other, tended to confirm the segregation of migrants from the rest of the workforce. A Yugoslav shop-steward's remark, quoted by June Hearn, makes this point: 'How could I be an organizer? My English is not good enough . . . No, I'm all right with the blokes on the job but that's as far as it goes' (Hearn, 1976*b*: 116).

In her study of migrants in Victorian unions June Hearn provides the most detailed available information on this trend towards the institutionalisation of the migrant official role. From her material it appears that there was only one full-time official organiser among the six non-British migrants holding administrative positions in the mid-sixties. He, along with one of the interpreters, belonged to the period of the split and both had become active in the DLP (Hearn, 1974: 111). The other four were a part-time organiser, two interpreters and an unofficial interpreter. By 1972, six of the nine non-British workers in official positions were organisers. The other three were 'officials "without portfolio" ', employed—like previous interpreters—as compensation officers and general advisers as well as interpreters (Hearn, 1976*b*: 114). Only the three organisers elected after 1970 began their official work in the unions in this role. The other three who were organisers in 1972 had previously been interpreters and/or unpaid organisers, filling jobs created in a more or less *ad hoc* manner by union leaders who saw a need to make special provision for non-British workers in particular industries.

Hearn's case studies show that the six of the nine men who were in administrative positions *before* 1970 (more obviously than the later-arrivals) worked for the most part independently and in ignorance of each other's existence to evolve their own roles in various marginal situations—the acknowledgement of their fellow-officials being always somewhat precarious and their fellow-countrymen figuring in their minds as obstacles to the proper performance of this role, rather than as supporters.

Some (probably nearly all the earlier incumbents) saw the unions as having been forced reluctantly—or at best pragmatically, without ideological commitment—to use officials of non-British origin. As one man put it: 'For the organization to exist, they have to do something about it (i.e. getting the migrant worker organised)' (Hearn, 1974: 168). Another said:

> 'these roots of bureaucracy are very deeply ingrained into the organiza-
> tions and they feel like it is their own little stronghold and now and
> then they decide who to let come in and who not. I think this is the
> reason why not many migrants have been encouraged to become officials
> except where sheer necessity pushes some of the secretaries who happen
> to be more pragmatic-minded to give some positions to migrants . . .
> Here again I believe that they encourage migrants more from op-
> portunistic reasons than from political conviction. After all, if the
> organization collapses, the leader is out of a job and this is, unfortunately,
> the only way some leaders see their role.' (Hearn, 1974: 186–7)

The great range of activities undertaken by these nine men overall demonstrates how they evolved their roles to meet the pressures and demands of the particular situations they were in. They negotiated with employers, acted as interpreters and public relations officers, handled compensation claims and edited foreign-language newspapers. With varying degrees of commitment, they saw it as their job to expose discrimination inside and outside the unions and workplace, to educate migrants about unionism and Australian unionists about migrants, and to influence union policy in support of migrant interests.

In considering factors that have affected the incorporation of migrants into trade union affairs, Hearn cites 'survival of the organization' as the only factor that has elicited an active, positive response from trade unions to the presence of migrants:

> The sheer necessity to keep the organization afloat has been one of the most compelling factors persuading union leaders to deliberately encourage migrant participation in leadership, especially in industries with large concentrations of migrant workers only partially unionized. (Hearn, 1976*b*: 118)

But migrants are more salient to the survival of some unions than others. The 'small and weak' unions (in industries with large numbers of non-unionised workers, many of them part-time) and a multitude of employers (the clothing and liquor trades are the main examples) have been forced to involve migrants in administration, but closed shops have not felt the same need. 'The bigger and stronger the organization, the easier it seems for the leadership to "safely" ignore the migrant section of its membership or potential membership' (Hearn, 1976*b*: 120).

Once in, the migrants in Hearn's study themselves became conscious of their own survival problems. Only one of the nine was patently co-opted: after years as an agitator in the motor industry, fighting both management and the union leadership, he was eventually elected as an organiser, being 'obviously regarded as a "trouble shooter"' . . . less dangerous within the fold under close surveillance' (Hearn, 1974: 264). But his contempt for the union hierarchy did not diminish, and Hearn envisaged that the leadership might remove him, thus foreshadowing the 'clean sweep' he believed could become necessary (Hearn, 1974: 271). The other eight all seemed to have accommodated themselves one way or another to the fact that they had little impact on union policy or practice concerning migrants. The more recently elected, career-oriented organisers were closely identified with the established view that there really was no 'migrant problem' in the unions. Others expressed varying degrees of disillusionment, despair and hostility, but clearly none could afford to step too far out of line in pressing migrants' interests. Several saw the force for change outside the unions, in the ethnic communities, and found in their community activities an alternative and more promising arena in which to pursue their personal commitments.

It is not possible to document in detail a number of small changes that are further confirming the institutionalisation of union response to migrants. They range from an increase in the number of migrant officials (Hearn reports that the number of non-British migrants in Victorian unions increased from 9 in 1973 to 16 in 1975 [Hearn, 1976b: 114]) to the publication of union materials in migrant languages, the translation of resolutions to be put to the vote and the use of languages other than English at union meetings. The Australian Congress of Trade Unions of September 1977 formally acknowledged a particular, if modest, responsibility towards migrant workers: Congress approved a 'Charter for Working Women', which included the provision of English classes for migrant workers and multilingual information; under 'Social Welfare Policy' it adopted the principle of 'Recognition that Australia is a multi-cultural society' and nominated migrants as one of ten groups whose disadvantaged members should be given special allowances (ACTU, 1977: 10, 28).

With even fairly minimal responses of this kind, some unionists are gaining experience that leads them to a more differentiated perceptive view of 'solutions to migrant workers' problems'—a process that parallels, on a simpler level, experience in education and health institutions. At a 'Migrants in Industry' seminar in 1975, for example, J.S. Thompson spoke somewhat ruefully about interpreters:

Unions encounter major problems of migrants at mass meetings. Some people say that to overcome this, interpreters should be provided—but this answer is not entirely satisfactory. It is a fact of life that when interpreters are used at a meeting the only people interested in listening to the interpreter are those who understand the language he is speaking in . . . The usual practice is for the first speaker to speak in English and then the various other languages to follow. After the English translation has been provided and the other interpreters commence interpreting in the other languages, within a very short space of time much of the meeting has left the meeting area . . . in many ways it is impractical to communicate at the level which is really necessary for every person present to understand the true situation. The usual practice is to distribute at the commencement of the meeting printed sheets in the major languages of the Plant explaining the reason for the meeting and the recommendations of the combined stewards in the Plant or of the Executive of the Union itself. It is often found however that even when a particular language is used some migrants find difficulty in understanding the translation of their own language. There is no doubt that understanding the English language is a tremendous asset to any migrant. It allows him to communicate with the whole of the meeting instead of his own particular nationality. (Thompson, 1975)

Unions called to account

With the institutionalisation of migrant interests both within and outside the union movement, there now exist several structures through which migrant workers can express and promote their particular concerns, and it seems likely that this process of institutionalisation is damping down illegitimate migrant militancy. In the fourth phase of union responses to migrants, non-union structures have become sources of pressure—or at least irritants—goading unions into acknowledging that they are accountable for their migrant members. The nature of this pressure can be indicated by reference to the involvement of two non-government and three government bodies. In 1973, CURA (Fitzroy, Melbourne) organised a series of seminars given by speakers of non-Anglo-Saxon backgrounds. The seminars took as their starting point a view expressed at an Australian Frontier Conference called 'The Migrant and the Community' a year before. This view was that migrant rights had to be claimed by migrants, on their own behalf, instead of depending on the paternalism of the Australian community. The two seminar papers on migrants and unions, both by Greeks, were polemical, rallying cries for action to bring migrants to a proper appreciation of unions and to convince the union movement of the urgency of migrant workers' needs and the necessity of 'transfusing this universal vitality of the migrants to all the arteries of its organisation from foot to head' (George, n.d. [1975]: 25). They are probably the first extended public statements in English claiming to portray migrant conceptions of unions. Since the publication of the seminar papers in 1975, they have become something of a landmark in the emergence of an 'ethnic rights' position (Storer ed., n.d. [1975]).

CURA is now the sponsor of a many-pronged approach to research on migrant questions. Its most ambitious project so far as migrant workers are concerned is a study of migrant women in thirty factories in Melbourne, reported by Storer and Hargreaves. The research began from the assumption that women of non-English-speaking background 'were among the most discriminated women in our society'. The aim of the project was to demonstrate this discrimination and 'develop strategies which would enable these women to organise and come together so that they themselves could articulate their situation, their grievances, their needs and requirements' (Storer and Hargreaves, 1976: 41). The research documents the perceptions of migrant women, union officials and employers—as well as the observations of the researchers themselves—about working conditions, relations between workers, relations of women with unions and with management, and problems associated with child care and lack of knowledge of English.

The picture that emerges is that migrant women workers are to a large extent invisible to union officials and the unions invisible to the women. Although the report acknowledges the claims of some union officials that employers restrict their access to workers and in subtle ways intimidate employees from taking an active part in union affairs —or even joining unions (1976: 84–5)—nevertheless it summarises the union position in these words:

> Most comments made by union officials were similar to those made by employers. They had surprisingly little to say about the actual conditions in factories . . . The general approach . . . was to attempt to police awards rather than to take up the issues about which the workers seemed most concerned. However most made regular attempts to change the awards, with the aim of improving working conditions. (1976: 59)

Migrant women find a 'lack of active unionism around them':

> Union officials, nearly always Australian-born men, are remote, making infrequent visits to factories in which the majority of workers are migrant women. Communication is minimal. (1976: 75)

In answer to a question about what in general they knew about their unions, three-fifths of the two-fifths of women who answered said that they 'knew nothing about the union, or were prevented from gaining such knowledge because of language difficulties' (1976: 66). Many women said they would take action over social as compared with economic aspects of their work, but they

> are not at present using their unions to take action, whether strike or other forms, over these issues, and nor are the unions presenting themselves to workers in a way that is either accessible or relevant to the majority of workers, especially migrant women. (1976: 71)

The CURA research was explicitly a lever for social change. Not only were its findings intended to have wide application, but in the process of the inquiry the researchers supported 'initiatives of migrant workers to organise and come together, to articulate their situation and put forward their requirements'. The researchers themselves were instrumental in forging links between unions and workers, and in providing information to all parties. The report concludes with a coherent, focussed set of recommendations (1976: 99–103).

The Ethnic Communities Councils (ECCs) represent the institutionalisation of the ethnic rights movement foreshadowed in the 1973 Fitzroy seminar series. A working party paper on 'Immigrants in the Workforce', presented at a meeting of the New South Wales ECC in April 1976, gave notice that the Council's efforts on behalf of disadvantaged migrant workers were to be directed at the trade unions 'since fundamentally the unions are the organisations which are especially established to represent the needs and interests of the workforce'. The paper went on:

Even if the unions have been unresponsive to migrant issues in the past, it is they who are in a position to bring about fundamental changes, because union interests can be expected to reflect those of their members.

It is felt that the focus of the Ethnic Communities Council's activity in this area should be towards establishing links with the trade union movement in order to raise their awareness of the issues, to make constructive suggestions, and to increase the participation of migrants in union affairs. (Buckley and Richter, 1976: 29)

That the union movement might not altogether welcome such attention from the New South Wales ECC is indicated in the recent public airing of the ECC's criticism of the State Labor Council for failing to take up a grant of $15 000 made by the New South Wales State Government to study migrants in the workforce and the trade union movement. The chairman of the New South Wales ECC was reported to have expressed disappointment 'at the general lack of response from the Labor Council concerning migrants in the work-force. "We . . . sent our position paper nearly a year ago but all we have received so far is a letter of acknowledgement", he said' (*SMH,* 14 April 1977).

The New South Wales ECC is not, however, an isolated body. Its membership includes nearly 400 ethnic organisations. It is financially subsidised by the State Labor Government and has close links with the Ethnic Affairs Division in the Premier's Department: a number of senior employees in the Division are on the ECC, which in its turn provides an extra-governmental source of support for the Division's policies.

One government inquiry that has addressed the issue of union responses to migrants is the Jackson Committee's inquiry into manufacturing industry. In a 'study of human resources and industrial relations at the plant level in seven selected industries', carried out for this Committee, G.W. Ford and his co-workers found that migrant workers were differentially distributed through the seven industries, being 'concentrated in those sectors of manufacturing with the worst physical working conditions, the worst pay and the jobs which are physically hard and contain the most menial tasks' (Aus., Committee to Advise on Policies for Manufacturing Industry, Vol. 4, 1976: 20). There was, however, no commensurate variation in union attitudes or activities: 'The unions they must join do not recognise that they require any special consideration' (1976: 10). Ford's conclusions about the meat industry, with migrants forming between 30 and 70 per cent of the workforce in the plants studied, are worth quoting in detail: migrants

were spread throughout the works, occupying the skilled jobs as well as the unskilled, and they exercised considerable influence on the policy of the union and on the attitudes of the management. However, this influence was of a negative nature; that is, they are regarded as problems. They do not conform to the standard image of a worker and do not react as managers have come to expect workers to react. Their motivation is not the same as traditional Australian workers, and they do not view the strike weapon in the same way as does the union or their Australian workmates. In short they do not hold the same values, or share the same experiences as their bosses or their union officials. . . Unfortunately, unions often have no clear policy or understanding of the dimensions of the issue. (1976: 20)

Ford and his co-workers concluded that the 'plight of newly-arrived migrants was one of the key issues identified in the study' (1976: 62), and advocated several programmes to overcome the particular disabilities of newly arrived workers. They recommended that the resolution of industrial conflict should be decentralised, but that will not automatically help migrant workers because:

In many Australian factories there is no delegate. More often than not, migrants and women in manufacturing industry are never represented at any level within their union. (1976: 70)

In his capacity as Commissioner for Community Relations, A.J. Grassby, former Minister for Immigration, has also attempted to use his powers under the *Racial Discrimination Act 1975* to sheet home to trade unions their responsibility for the disabilities experienced by migrant workers, particularly migrant women, who are 'the largest single group of workers in the community which has claimed it suffers general pervasive and widespread discrimination' (Aus., Commissioner for Community Relations, 1976: 23). A serious communication gap exists within the unions as well as between workers and management. The unions 'have not kept up with the times in terms of change in the Australian workforce' (1976: 23).

CURA, the ECCs, the New South Wales Government's Ethnic Affairs Division, the Jackson Committee and the offices of the Commissioner for Community Relations are examples of the new structures that are beginning to bring pressure to bear on trade unions to take cognisance of their migrant members. Bodies of this kind in turn seek to mobilise support for their position through influencing the deliberations of government inquiries and committees. Des Storer, of CURA, for example, submitted to the Committee on Community Relations a paper originally prepared for a Migrant Workers' Conference in 1973, and in its final report the Committee drew heavily on Storer's submission and the seminar papers to sustain the conclusion that unions 'are not attuned to the needs of large sections of their union membership', and to support the recommendation that unions should take urgent action to involve migrants in union affairs and leadership (Aus., Committee on Community Relations, 1975: 22).

These extra-union influences all come from comparatively new sources. The fact that they are institutionalised means that they can be drawn on to legitimate pressure exerted by migrants from within the union movement. Some of these pressures were crystallised in the two Migrant Workers' Conferences held in Melbourne in 1973 and 1975, and the one in Sydney in 1973. The inspiration for the first conference came from George Zangalis, a Greek who was one of the speakers on unions at the Fitzroy seminar early in 1973. The organising committee was firmly identified as 'representing unions, job organisations and individual workers' and the appeal was to the unity of the trade union movement as a whole. As the handout announcing the conference said, 'The problems of migrant workers, as of all lower paid, are the problems of the Australian Labour Movement, and should be at the centre of the working class struggle.' However, the tone of most contributions was as critical of the unions as of the capitalist system. According to Hearn, the conference became a battleground for the spokesmen of opposing political factions, while the rest of the migrant delegates showed their hostility to the disruption of discussion and their 'resentment that they were being used as a political football' by staying away in large numbers after the first day (Hearn, 1974: 445).

The outcome, nevertheless, was agreement that the trade union movement had 'the major responsibility to change' the exploited and disadvantaged position of migrant workers. The conference promulgated a series of proposals for union action and support, covering: wages and conditions (including recognition of overseas trade qualifications, retraining, leave to visit home countries), trade union involvement (including establishment of a Trade Union Advisory Centre for migrant workers, employment of multilingual personnel in union offices, logs of claims to contain the demands that English be taught on the job and employer and government-established child care centres), social needs and rights (including documents to be available in migrants' languages, overseas remittances to dependants to be tax deductible), and education, culture and language (a strong statement on the right to learn English and retain migrant languages and cultures).

The second Migrant Workers' Conference, held in Melbourne in November 1975, followed the same lines as the first, although the 'right to work' loomed larger. There was some progress to report since 1973, and it was noted with satisfaction that three months earlier an ACTU Congress had for the first time passed a resolution on migrant workers' problems. But there was still much to be done 'to challenge the Australian society and particularly the Trade Union movement, our movement, to stop and take notice of a new reality'—the numerical strength of migrant workers, their exploitation, alienation and isolation from union affairs (Zangalis, n.d. [1975]).

Although legitimate in the formal sense, the Migrant Workers' Conferences represented a not very thinly veiled threat by activist migrants against the union establishment. It is little wonder that they received no attention in the regular union press. Closer to accepted ways of operating inside the movement was the contest for leadership in the Port Kembla-Wollongong branch of the Federated Ironworkers' Association (FIA) in 1970 and 1974. In 1970, an Italian, F. Lelli, became Assistant Secretary when the Rank-and-File list of candidates won a majority over the right-wing leadership which had been in power since the early fifties. In 1972 Lelli was elected Secretary in a by-election, and in 1974 he headed the Rank-and-File Ticket to win all leadership positions in the branch. Lelli gave the first address at the first Migrant Workers' Conference. He spoke as a union official and expressed none of the biting antagonism to union leadership that came from other participants. Migrants' problems, he said, did not receive the attention they deserved at the recent ACTU Congress, 'not because of unawareness or unwillingness to have them dealt with, but because there was not enough representation to put these problems forward by the migrants themselves'. Some of his audience may have wondered if they were hearing aright when, speaking of the language barrier, Lelli asserted that it was 'high time that positive action is taken to see that the migrant is given the opportunity to assimilate in the quickest possible way' (Brennan ed., 1974: 2).[1]

The 1974 win for the Rank-and-File put the Port Kembla-Wollongong branch out of favour with the national leadership, still headed by L.E. Short who led the Industrial Groups' fight against communists in the FIA in 1949–1950. The branch is, however, slowly winning acceptance again. With 60 per cent of its members overseas-born, it has, according to Lelli, 'the highest migrant membership of any union in Australia' (*Illawarra Mercury*, 14 November 1977). Lelli takes proper pride in its multilingual staff and the measures it has adopted to do 'something constructive towards solving the problems faced by newcomers to Australia', but there are few migrants of non-English-speaking origin among its officials or on the committee of management, and when in 1976 the Trade Union Training Authority (TUTA) organised a meeting in Wollongong to discuss migrant issues, no union officials attended. It seems that in this case the election of a migrant as Secretary has given the union the chance to respond to migrant needs without having to face a challenge from members of non-English-speaking origin to Anglo-Australian control of union affairs.

In this fourth phase the union movement is beginning to pay some attention to the education of migrant workers, and to research on the migrant workforce and the role of migrants in unions. This is of course part of a general trend towards an increasing, though far from unanimous, acceptance of the importance of education and research in the trade union movement as a whole (Ford, 1968: 204–7; R.M. Martin, 1975: 134–5). The notion of the need for converting migrants into good unionists has of course been around for a long time, but until recently it meant little more than the simple process typified in George Zangalis's statement: 'in the fifties I spent the best part of my time trying to sell the unions to migrant workers, now I have changed my priorities, I try to sell the problems of migrant workers to the unions. Then I am certain we will get somewhere' (n.d. [1975]: 28). The establishment of TUTA, with national and State arms, under the provisions of the *Trade Union Training Authority Act 1975*, has encouraged unions to think systematically about the education of unionists. One of TUTA's emerging functions is clearly to establish the definition of migrant workers and migrant unionists as problems demanding attention. The importance of this function has been brought home to the New South Wales Training Centre because of the failure of its first efforts in this direction: in 1976 a one-day school, 'designed for unions that have high migrant membership in the hope that the union movement will be better equipped to formulate strategies for assisting migrant trade-union members' (*SMH*, 27 February 1976), had to be cancelled because of lack of enrolments, and a meeting organised in Wollongong—referred to previously— attracted only disaffected migrants and no union officials. The ground was more carefully prepared for a residential course on 'Problems of the Migrant Unionist' organised for May 1977 and 'aimed at full time officials and shop stewards in large migrant based workshops . . . (as) a practical attempt to pose solutions to the problems faced by migrant unionists' (TUTA, NSW, *Programme 1977*: 21). But again the course was cancelled because of lack of interest. In both Victoria and New South Wales, efforts on a small scale directed at particular groups of *migrant* unionists meet with more success.[2]

The research function of Australian unions is largely confined to the preparation of material in support of unions' claims in cases of arbitration and negotiation with employers (see R.M. Martin, 1975: 60), and the impetus to develop research facilities has come mainly from what G.W. Ford described in 1968 as the need 'to match the growing research facilities which the employers have developed to present their cases before unions, industrial tribunals, governments and the public' (1968: 205). So far as migrant workers are concerned, the only significant research has been initiated outside the unions.[3] The fact that two notable studies, the CURA project already described and a Sydney survey also published in 1976 (Cox *et al.*, 1976), are about migrant women illustrates the way in which the process of re-defining the migrant situation gains strength and recognition from being associated with the re-definition of more comprehensive issues commanding support from a society-wide base. In the case of the CURA study, the support could in fact be said to have had an international base, because the project was funded by the Commonwealth Government as part of its International Women's Year (1975) programme. In general, the women's movement has been the main stimulus for research interest in migrant women in the workforce, and this has led to the position where there is more social knowledge about migrant women workers than about men.[4]

Research on migrant workers or migrant-union relations remains, however, minimal. G.W. Ford spreads the blame widely for what he sees as a dangerous state of ignorance:

Manufacturing industry in Australia is increasingly dependent on migrants, the majority of whom are from non-English-speaking countries. Yet the advisers, policy-makers and administrators in the public and private sector, the unions and the universities are almost all people with British heritage and traditions. The self-interest and even intellectual isolation of these groups is perhaps best illustrated by their failure to encourage any research into the problems of migrants at work over the last twenty years. The failure of our society to allocate appropriate resources to improving the migrant's understanding of the English language and Australian institutions has meant the creation of a class of industrial serfs who have little or no communication with policy-makers in Australia. The violence at the Ford strike at Broadmeadows in 1973 should have been an adequate warning of what can happen when frustrated people cannot communicate by language. But Australian history has shown that our moralising, isolated elites rarely learn anything from industrial conflict. (Aus., Committee to Advise on Policies for Manufacturing Industry, Vol. 4, 1976: 94)

One recent development brings into focus the ambivalent trends in union response to migrants at the present time. In 1974, with the support of the Labor Government, the ACTU established a Social Welfare Unit—and Commonwealth support has continued since that time. The original objectives of the Unit were to undertake surveys, identify the major disadvantaged groups in and outside the workforce, prepare research papers and publish reports 'to highlight and delineate industrial and social welfare policy issues' (Staats ed., n.d. [1976]: 9). In 1976, the Unit published a collection of papers on *Social Policy and Problems of the Work Force*. Apart from some general discussion of welfare policy, this volume is totally devoted to migrants. Disappointingly it has a Melbourne orientation, not a national one, and contains no new research material. However, the inclusion of two CURA studies—the one on migrant women and a survey of Italians in the Coburg-Brunswick area (Melbourne)—makes them more widely available than before.

Social Policy and Problems of the Work Force was called 'Volume 1' and the results of further surveys were promised in 'the successive volume', with the 'broad themes of this volume' to be followed up 'in a forthcoming series' (Staats ed., n.d. [1976]: 10, 25). However, the precarious status of the Unit, dependent on an annual grant from the Commonwealth Government, is indicated by the fact that its work has been in abeyance since the first editor, Steven Staats, resigned in early 1977—and nothing further has been published. The discrepancy between the original wide-ranging aims of the Unit, on the one hand, and, on the other, the meagreness of its achievements to date and the indifferent support it has elicited from the ACTU or the Government reflects the ambiguous place of social research and welfare issues, in general, and of migrant aspects, in particular, in current union thinking.

Conclusion

Four phases have been identified in the response of trade unions to the presence of migrants in the workforce in the past thirty years. In the first, right-wing sections of the union movement, in conflict with communist leadership, solicited the support of Displaced Persons and won considerable numbers as active allies. In the second, union leaders saw migrants primarily as a recruitment problem: they were numbers to be organised. This phase yielded little information on how officials related to migrants: they were a subject of nondecision-making. It is only through the eyes of the migrants themselves that we get an occasional glimpse of the recruiters' approach: ' "if they could have done without us, they would have . . . It's as simple as this: the union either recruits migrant workers or goes under" ' (Hearn, 1976*b*: 119).

The notion of migrants as a recruitment problem continues into the third phase, but a variety of perspectives on migrants and unionism now emerges, alongside some degree of consensus about crucial issues: the unions' responsibility for creating the conditions for migrant participation in union activities (which involves among other things the education of Australian unionists), and the employers' responsibility for responding to the special problems of communication, safety and welfare associated with a migrant workforce (which involves among other things providing opportunities for migrants to learn English). Underlying this degree of consensus is the recognition of migrants as a legitimate minority *within* the union movement. Militant left-wing definers use familiar rhetoric to dramatise the 'voracious exploitation' of migrants by the capitalist system and present migrant workers as 'a dormant industrial volcano' (George, n.d. [1975]: 23). A range of moderates adopts a more reasoned, welfare-oriented position, working for change without going out of their way to alienate either the established union leadership or the militants. Probably most migrant officials stand for this definition, as do most external observers. Some of these observers, like June Hearn, specifically reject the militants' claim about the threat of 'restive migrant masses' (Hearn, 1976*b*: 122).

Many definitions advanced in the last three phases share a common explanation of the source of migrant-union problems: the backwardness of migrants, their ignorance and lack of experience of unions, and their obsession with personal economic security. The fourth phase gives weight also to additional factors: ignorance and lack of understanding on the part of the entrenched union leadership and poor communication between migrants and union officials. There also appear serious attempts by more or less isolated pockets of definers, both in and outside the union movement, to probe these explanations and make concrete and articulate the reality of the migrant's situation as worker and unionist. The fourth phase publicly advances the notion that unions are accountable for this reality.

That the processes going on in the fourth phase have gathered some momentum is clearly associated with three important structural developments: the forging of links between different elements within the union movement and between unions and outside bodies, particularly the ethnic communities; the concomitant emergence of a pool of individuals with experience and contacts spanning a number of groups and events; and the emergence of new organisations, such as the ECCs, CURA, TUTA and the ACTU Social Welfare Unit, articulating, prodding and even at times threatening, from the vantage point of independence from executive responsibility. Migrants are now catalysts for change in the union movement, calling into question the 'essentially pragmatic' style of Australian trade unionism (R.M. Martin, 1975: 136) and the stance of trade union officials 'who disclaim any wider accountability than for short-term benefits to their members' (Aus., Committee to Advise on Policies for Manufacturing Industry, Vol. 1, 1975: 213).

NOTES

1. I am grateful to Mary Dickenson for giving me access to her unpublished material on the Port Kembla-Wollongong branch of the FIA. This material is part of the research data for her Ph.D. thesis, Department of Political Science, Research School of Social Sciences, Australian National University (see Dickenson, 1978). The interpretation and perspective given here are, however, mine.

2. The future of TUTA is itself in doubt, and its current activities are hampered by continued indecision as to the shape of the changes that the Fraser Government is planning. In an article describing TUTA as 'threatened with reduction to a Departmental satrapy', Canberra journalist Bruce Juddery documents how: 'On the one hand, the organisation has been crippled by the economic and government climate in which it has sought to establish itself. On the other, it has been the victim of unrelenting departmental [Department of Employment and Industrial Relations] hostility' (Juddery, April 7, 1978).

3. Since this book went to press, there has appeared a collection of papers, *The Worker in Australia*, edited by Allan Bordow, which contains three chapters that deal with migrant workers (Hurwitz, 1977; Johnston, 1977; Phillips, 1977). Hurwitz's excellent paper on 'Factory Women' is, to my knowledge, the only substantial published contribution to the study of migrant workers to have been the outcome of employer initiatives. Hurwitz was employed by Leyland Australia to co-ordinate the work of a Migrant Advisory Service established by the Company at its Waterloo (Sydney) plant and under the direction of social worker, Roy Richter. The service lasted only a year and was disbanded in 1975 when Leyland closed its Waterloo operations. It served primarily a welfare and referral function, but Hurwitz's account of the working lives of the migrant women employees represents an unusually insightful and informed addition to the research literature. The picture she paints grimly confirms the findings of the studies by Storer and Hargreaves and by Cox *et al.* These women, she says, were beset by 'life-shattering' concerns on all sides, but 'Unions have up to now not understood or responded to the special problems of women any more than managements have' (1977: 258). The women 'felt the union was not able to help them except in money matters', and the presence of a few women shop stewards in a predominantly male union did little for them (1977: 242). The language barrier locked them 'into a solitary cell of silence' and isolated them from learning about training, safety directions, or the union (1977: 238).

4. Another project funded by the International Women's Year Committee was the Migrant Handicraft Program, Melbourne. The report of this Program (1977) throws light on migrant women's craft skills, on their commonly held view that those skills are irrelevant to their lives in Australia, and their varied responses to the opportunity to exhibit their handicrafts in the community. Unfortunately there is no published account of this extremely interesting project.

8 Conclusion

During the first twenty years of post-war migration there was little variety in the meaning that the institutions of Australian society attached to the migrant presence. In unanimously defining migrants as assimilable, they were in effect confirming the wisdom, morality and non-threatening character of the migration programme. With one stroke of magic, as it were, Australia's economic interests would be served and the resourceful, the needy and the victims of war in Europe be given the chance for a new life, while the continuity of our cultural identity would still be guaranteed. To define migrants as assimilable implied that they were to become incorporated into Australian life *as individuals*. In a series of stages based on citizenship and duration of residence, the politico-legal status of the individual would be transformed from alien immigrant to Australian; his social position and understanding of his own interests and identity would change concurrently. The source of failure to assimilate lay within the individual migrant, even if he were the unhappy victim of circumstances outside his control, like war or political oppression.

To define migrants as assimilable was to assert that they would neither destroy the cultural identity of Australian society nor upset the existing structure of classes and status groups. Concern about equality revolved around this latter issue: migrants must not be granted concessions or considerations that would advantage them in comparison with Australians; the interests of Australians must not suffer as the result of the migrant presence. The abundance of opportunities for economic achievement would ensure that as they became Australians, migrants would be distributed throughout the class hierarchy according to their deserts, like everyone else. It was self-evident that settlers from Britain should receive preferred treatment, because by this means existing cultural attachments and structural links were confirmed.

The assimilability thesis had a predominating ideological aspect in terms of the meaning of ideological put forward in Chapter 1. Irrespective of the interests which, as time went by, it came to serve or negate, it was framed and perpetuated (without input from the major participants in the action it described) to legitimate a policy that the state had to sell to the community. To that end it was designed to keep Australians favourably disposed to large-scale immigration from countries traditionally regarded as foreign, and to encourage migrants to transform themselves into Australians without delay. It purported to be founded in migrant experience and to be aimed at furthering migrant interests, but was not informed by understanding of either; what passed as proven facts about migrants and migrant-Australian interaction consisted largely of stereotypes and clichés, or was so selective that only supporting evidence was adduced, though sometimes in the form of results from 'scientific' inquiries. It also purported to rest on a solid basis of evidence confirming the economic wisdom of the immigration programme, but, as the 1971 AIPS conference publicly established, no such basis existed. At that meeting, Maximilian Walsh quoted a former treasurer, who in 1969 acknowledged that 'As to the cost associated with migrants, I have never bothered to take out these figures. Against the general background of the welcome that we give to them, of the splendid contribution that they are making to this country . . . I think it unnecessary to take into consideration the money involved', and an MP expressed surprise that the Secretary of the Department of Immigration had questioned the figures given by a speaker who put up a strong economic argument against continued immigration 'because he himself [the Secretary] didn't know the right figures, or if he did know he didn't say' (Walsh, 1971: 177; Wilkes ed., 1971: 188).

Among the factors that brought about the challenge to the assimilability thesis at the end of the sixties was the growing and visible disjunction between public knowledge and experience, between 'theory' and 'practice'. Diverse groups of people working in established structures came to perceive this disjunction as a threat to their own interests and identities and tried to press for re-definitions: shop-stewards frustrated by migrant indifference or hostility to their unions; teachers unable to get through to migrant students and hampered in the rest of their work because of the presence of migrants in their classes; welfare and medical personnel who saw their inability to communicate with migrant clients and patients as undermining their professional role; and partisans of many colours, not necessarily directly associated with migrants but convinced that high migrant intakes were helping to destroy the city environment, making insupportable demands on resources and undermining the quality of life in general. While Labor opponents of Liberal dominance in Victoria and the Commonwealth Parliament produced the most coherent of a diffuse and diverse series of critiques of this kind, some observers on the other hand thought that immigration was taking the blame for the government's more fundamental 'failures in planning, for the wrong-headed priorities, and for the lack of imagination in tackling environmental problems' (Wilkes ed., 1971: 189). What was beginning to emerge was no clear-cut line-up of forces but a complex disposition of invaders and invaded, regulars and reserves, official battle units and illegal guerrillas.

Although this metaphor gives a misleading impression of powerful contenders joined in serious combat, there was nevertheless contention of a kind and from it there entered a new element into the public definition of migrants: they were problems. This view was less ideological than the assimilation thesis, because it could be adopted to legitimate a variety of practices and claims on resources from a range of groups—established and migrant—and because it developed out of the contributions of numerous actors who had previously never been heard. It also had a better claim to validity, but some of the new definers were as ready as the old to cite evidence selectively to establish their point. The emphases on migrants as 'factory fodder' and on migrant poverty are the obvious examples.

Most of the active 'response to the migrant presence' recounted in this book occurred within a context of meaning that portrayed migrants as problems—or, more acceptably, as people *with* problems. In the name of this concept, there have been substantial additions to the content of knowledge about migrants and some increases in the flow of resources directed specifically for the use of migrants. As we have seen, however, the nature of response varied greatly from one institution to another. Of the three institutions considered in detail, education has entertained by far the most diverse conceptions of migrant problems and, after a period of adjustments and re-arrangements aimed at neutralising the need for change in existing structures, has now embarked on a degree of re-organisation that is radical to the extent that it provides regular and legitimate means by which the experience of migrants and migrant-Australian interaction can feed into the system. There is no doubt that Commonwealth resources have provided a major stimulus to communication, interaction, innovation and the accumulation of public knowledge about education, and State resources are again—after some abortive beginnings in the fifties and Victoria's initiatives in the late sixties—beginning to make their mark also. The institutions of health care have paid less attention to defining migrant health problems and such re-structuring as has occurred (community health and hospital interpreter services, for example) has been at the margins of the health care institutions and has to some degree made it easier for hospitals and private medical practice *not* to change in any radical way. Largely isolated, at least until very recently, from the effect of change in public thinking about migrants, trade unions have to a considerable extent staved off the conception of migrants as problems and have added almost nothing to public knowledge about migrant workers, either in the form of making their own contribution or in challenging the ideological elements in received views. Concern for migrant problems and structural adjustments have scarcely impinged at all on the trade union movement as a whole. Of the major institutions, only industry—not dealt with in this book —appears to have responded less.

Those in authority in education, health and trade unions have not been the ones to take the initiative in responding to problems of migrants and problems created by migrants. Instead, the call for response has been associated with more or less discrete challenges to institutional authority. The success of these challenges has been influenced by the structural position of the challengers and their access to channels for contributing to social knowledge. By virtue of their professional training and the norms operating in educational institutions, teachers and other school professionals can claim to be heard on educational questions, even when administrative hierarchies are obstructive and refuse to listen. With an increase in school and teacher autonomy, their claims may extend to the control of what happens in schools and some teachers have taken advantage of their new freedom to develop their own response to the migrant problem; in communicating their experience through the readily available channels of education journals and conferences, some of them have helped crystallise and give substance to the challenge to established structures. Teachers have found support from academics outside the school system who are engaged with similar questions because of past experience (for example, as teachers themselves) or current functions (as, for instance, teacher trainers or researchers).

In medicine those most aware of migrants and migrant-created problems were domestic employees, subprofessional and so-called ancillary medical staff, and to a lesser extent nurses. By training, by sex (they are mostly women) and by virtue of their subordinate role in hierarchical and rigid health structures, these people have been ill-placed to transform their personal experience into social knowledge or to see themselves as influencing health care. The arrival on the health care scene of a small number of welfare and social workers, social science researchers and similar non-medical staff has led to some articulation of problems related to migrant health, but these outsiders have had little impact on established health care institutions.

The challenge to authoritative definitions of migrant questions in the trade unions is not, of course, the counterpart of the challenges we have been concerned with in health and education. With the minimal degree of professionalisation that has occurred in the staffing of trade union administration in Australia, there has been no intermediary group within the unions to articulate migrant viewpoints and experiences. Until migrant unionists began to promote their own interests, no one else did it for them, and they have found their support outside the main union movement: among academics, in catalyst bodies like CURA and in the new structure of TUTA centres, within, but still marginal to, the union movement. Significantly, the Sydney TUTA appears to have abandoned hope of re-educating Australian trade unionists and is concentrating on building up knowledge and experience among migrants themsleves, so that they can promote their own interests within the union movement.

In the past, the poverty of organisational response to migrants meant that there were few opportunities for migrants to capitalise on their unique skills and knowledge. No one had any use for their knowledge of non-Anglo-Saxon cultures and languages, for the competence as translators and interpreters that some of them possessed, nor for their experience as migrants and settlers. Furthermore, the fact that many individuals were unable to gain recognition of trade or professional qualifications gained overseas had the effect of reducing the number of migrants who could use their linguistic skills and unique knowledge in established roles as, for example, foremen, teachers or doctors. Lack of organisational response not only meant waste of talent and goodwill and denied migrants opportunities for individual mobility; it also meant that few migrants occupied vantage points from which, as migrants, they could contribute to the social definition of the migrant presence. When, in the late sixties and early seventies, a small number of individuals of post-war migrant origin began to make such a contribution, they did so as specially informed 'normal' participants in established structures, not as representatives of migrant or ethnic interests. In education and health, they spoke as teachers and doctors who happened also to be of migrant origin. The numbers of these people are greater today (though by no means in proportion to the number of people of migrant background in the population) and include many individuals ready to identify themselves as members of ethnic communities, or at least to take up the role of intermediaries between ethnic groups and other bodies. At the same time there are also emerging some career structures that give migrants scope—limited though it is—to build on their particular experience and competence; health educators and interpreters are examples.

Structural change in established institutions, the development of new structures—in the form of broker organisations, and migrant and inter-ethnic pressure groups—and the growing prominence of definers with acknowledged migrant affiliations are thus interdependent developments.

While new definers—migrants and others—have contributed to the perception of migrants as people with problems, they have also helped to forge a more differentiated and complex response to the migrant presence and they vigorously deny many entrenched convictions: that migrant individuals, rather than Australian institutions, are the source of problems; that migrants are the dependent beneficiaries of Australian paternalism (the view that much of the problem-oriented discussion fostered, if only implicitly); that migrants are 'factory fodder' (the definition that fits migrants into a simplistic 'marxist' concept of the Australian class structure); that migrants are a threat to good order (an interpretation that official sources scrupulously avoid, but that internal dissension among migrant communities in Australia or overt migrant involvement in international conflicts immediately sparks off in the media). By contrast, they insist on ethnic rights and ethnic dignity and on ethnic pluralism as a positive, creative force, not simply a defensive reaction against insecurity and rejection.

At the same time, differentiation in perspectives among migrants themselves is becoming salient for the construction of social knowledge. Some ethnic groups are extremely vocal, while some others are never heard. Inter-ethnic organisations try to contain differences and forge a 'migrant viewpoint' as part of a strategy to achieve a favourable bargaining position and public image. The process by which the more organised and powerful groups within the migrant population contribute to social knowledge has itself a strong ideological aspect, and yields an interpretation of the experience of large sectors of the migrant population that is still only marginally richer than the blurred stereotypes produced by others in the past.

Social and cultural pluralism

What I have attempted in this book is a case study in the construction of knowledge relevant to public policy, an examination of one form of 'knowledge/power', in Foucault's terms (Gordon, 1976: 31). I have argued that the construction of knowledge and the exercise of control over social relations and activities are fully interdependent processes. Differences in the participation of groups in access to knowledge and in its construction bear out differences in their structural positions: that is, differences among them not only in terms of their dominance or subordination within the same structures, but also in terms of their engagement in different structures. Thus, in a complex society like our own, classes and status groups (in Weber's terms) provide the contexts for different kinds of experience, but so also do other alternative contexts that are not (or not intrinsically) hierarchically ordered: regional, occupational, religious, ethnic and generational contexts are the important ones. The crucial question in relation to public knowledge and public policy is whether the ordered production of knowledge and the complementary participation in social structures enable these diverse experiences to become publicly relevant, or whether—on the contrary—the experiences of only the favoured few are acknowledged as legitimate sources of social knowledge. This latter situation is commonly justified and perpetuated by the fact that other groups and individuals lack command over an explanatory framework of sufficient power and relevance to permit them to interpret their experience in the general terms necessary for it to influence knowledge or policy.

Without developing the argument in any detail, I wish in these final pages to outline its implications for the structure of an ethnically diverse society like our own. This outline is presented against the background of an analysis of Australian society contained in the work of political scientist, Trevor Matthews (1976*a* and *b*). Although Matthews' paper for the Coombs Commission was geared to the Commission's task of inquiring into 'the administrative organization and services' of the Commonwealth Government, it expresses a comprehensive perspective on the socio-political structure as a whole:

> If we consider the potential power of interest groups in Australia there are clearly great differences among them. Political resources are spread very unevenly from group to group . . . [But] many important interests are in fact unorganised and inactive, and lack determination and persistence; e.g. the aged, the poor, the chronically ill, Aborigines, and certain migrant groups. These interests tend to be ruled out of, or are only marginally included in the pluralist balancing process . . . Many interests . . . are not articulated; and many demands are not recognised as issues by the decision-makers . . . Lastly there is the bias towards interest groups that are recognised by the government and consulted by it. These are mainly sectional associations. Official recognition thus favours sectional groups as opposed to promotional groups; and among sectional groups, favours legitimate and established associations at the expense of new groups, particularly breakaway and dissident groups. It is a bias towards the conservative. Among associations that are in the charmed circle of groups that are regularly consulted by the government, the most significant (in this context) are those whom the government cannot afford not to consult. These are the producer associations . . .

Matthews goes on to quote with approval the views of the American critic of pluralism, H.S. Kariel:

> It is essential . . . that the bureaucracy be encouraged to ferret out the interests of the disorganised and the inarticulate. 'The fact that such interests are not neatly spelled out, that they are unrealised ideals, should

not exclude them from consideration in the bureaucracy's effort to maintain a genuinely pluralistic society.' (1976a: 345-7)

In a society of this kind there can emerge—as has happened in Australia—ethnic communities that function with varying degrees of commitment, varying resources and so on, as multi-interest, identity-making and confirming groups. They may be more committed to interests or identity, but commonly perceive the two as inextricably interwoven. They may act as pressure groups in the sense of making claims 'either directly or indirectly, on the Government, so as to influence the making or administering of public policy without [themselves] being willing to exercise the formal powers of government' (Matthews, 1976b: 220). In this form or less overtly, ethnic groups try to take part in the development of community perspectives on their interests and identity: that is, to transform their unique experience into social knowledge.

But ethnic interests can also be articulated for them, and made manifest to them, by others. The state may claim that role (and may, as our earlier discussion of the residual model of welfare illustrated, conceive of the defined as unstructured categories, not groups, and hence negate the possibility of group definition or negotiation of interests). Or certain classes may claim ethnic interests as particular instances of class interests and speak therefore on behalf of the ethnic population (whether organised into groups or not); this is most likely to take the form of marxists attempting to absorb ethnics into the class struggle. Or diverse groups may similarly adopt ethnic interests to further their own causes and/or in fulfilment of their own moral identities as supporters or catalysts of the unorganised, inarticulate or oppressed.

The professionals, 'sub-professionals' or 'ancillary workers' who have emerged as strategically important in changing social knowledge about migrants may operate within any of these three contexts, or, as a series of unorganised, individual voices, may constitute a fourth structural context through which ethnic interests are explicated. They are akin to the 'specific intellectuals' whom Foucault sees as replacing the old 'universal intellectuals'. These specific intellectuals work

in specific sectors, at precise points where they are situated either by their professional conditions of work or their conditions of life (housing, the hospital, the asylum, the laboratory, the university, familial and sexual relations). (1977: 12)

It is the very concrete, situation-specific experience of these new intellectuals (who in this position encounter problems that are ' "non-universal", often different from those of the proletariat and the masses', 1977: 12) that involves them in a new kind of politicisation. In less dramatic form than the situation Foucault doubtless has in mind—indeed often muffled and defused—this process of politicisation 'on the basis of each individual's specific activity' can properly be applied to the activities of certain professionals and other workers described in previous chapters.

In order to explicate the relationship between the ideological aspects of knowledge and the context in which knowledge is produced, it is necessary to say something more about *participation* in constructing knowledge. Clearly there are diverse degrees and modes of participation: it is not a simple question of participating or not. This being so, ethnics may participate in varying degrees in the activities of others engaged in producing knowledge about them: at the one extreme they may have no share in those activities, at the other their experience may be mediated (which may involve nothing more than translation from one language to another and circulation in some documentary form) with fidelity through rigorous procedures of research. Thus, certain of the four contexts described above may yield more ideologically impregnated knowledge than others. There must be structures through which ethnic interests are made publicly relevant, and what those structures are and how they operate will affect the perception of ethnic interests that they produce, but they need not be ethnic community structures. Or, to put it differently, ethnics may participate in developing knowledge about their own interests without doing so through ethnic groups.

Cultural identity is, however, another matter. Taking cultural identity as that part of the web of meaning that a group attaches to its own self-image vis-à-vis other groups, I would argue that one group cannot in any lasting and non-ideological sense construct or carry cultural identity for another. Neither can the society as a whole, through its established institutions, support cultural identities that are unattached to specific, group-supported webs of meaning. If sectional groups or established institutions claim to be acting on behalf of ethnic peoples in this way, they are concocting something out of nothing that is immediately relevant to ethnics' identity (though it may become relevant to their economic interests, as, for example, when an alert businessman revives lost arts as his contribution to maintaining ethnic culture); or they are trivialising the cultural tradition by picking out catchy tunes and putting them together as if they represented the whole work; or, finally, they are forcing their own composition on the ethnic musicians.

Ethnic cultures, then, require ethnic groups. But established institutions can promote definitions of an ethnically diverse society that disjoin culture and structure. Highly coercive structures may promote purely symbolic forms of confirming identity: that is, forms of reward, recognition and group organisation that have no follow-through, no implications, for ethnic interests or for substantive participation in social structures. What is often called tokenism is part of response of this kind, but far more than overt tokenism is involved. In less coercive situations, established institutions may cultivate the idea that what is needed for ethnics to be successfully incorporated into the society is fundamentally a change of heart: understanding, sympathy and tolerance on the part of the host community, adaptability and optimism on the part of ethnics can effect what no social re-arrangements could do, and so render structural change redundant.

In Australia public endorsement of a safe cultural pluralism includes both elements: symbolic as a substitute for substantive response and an emphasis on the priority of individual attitudes over social forms. The proposition that we are, or are in process of becoming, a culturally pluralist society has a specifically ideological aspect. First, it has been created by established institutions looking for a way to accommodate ethnically diverse populations with the minimum of change on their own part. Second, ethnic minorities themselves have had little share in formulating the idea (despite the fact that individual ethnics and some ethnic associations have on occasion been involved), while the experience of ethnics in establishing a structural base for their own lives—through kin, informal networks and formal associations—does not surface as relevant public knowledge (and, so far as the vital political orientation of much ethnic group life is concerned, is actively suppressed). Third, the thesis of cultural pluralism rests on the unspoken assumptions that ethnic culture can be sustained without ethnic communities and that a culturally diverse society is something different from a structurally pluralist one, assumptions that defy the weight of historical experience.

Bibliography

Abbreviations

AAP	Australian Assistance Plan
ABS	Australian Bureau of Statistics (formerly Bureau of Census and Statistics)
ACC	Australian Citizenship Convention
ACOSS	Australian Council of Social Service
ACTU	Australian Council of Trade Unions
AEAC	Australian Ethnic Affairs Council
AGPS	Australian Government Publishing Service
AMA	Australian Medical Association
ANU	Australian National University
ANZAAS	Australian and New Zealand Association for the Advancement of Science
ANZJP	*Australian and New Zealand Journal of Psychiatry*
ANZJS	*Australian and New Zealand Journal of Sociology*
APIC	Australian Population and Immigration Council
CO.AS.IT	Italian Assistance Association
COPQ	Committee on Overseas Professional Qualifications
CURA	Centre for Urban Research and Action
ECC	Ethnic Communities Council
ERDC	Educational Research and Development Committee
House of Reps.	House of Representatives
IAC	Immigration Advisory Council
IPC	Immigration Planning Council
MEB	Migrant Education Branch
MJA	*Medical Journal of Australia*
NAATI	National Accreditation Authority for Translators and Interpreters
Parl. Debates	*Parliamentary Debates*
Parl. Papers	*Parliamentary Papers*
SMEC	State Multicultural Education Committee
SMH	*Sydney Morning Herald*
TUTA	Trade Union Training Authority
VTU	Victorian Teachers' Union

Unpublished files for selected periods 1947–1977

Australia, Department of Immigration. Canberra.

Catholic Education Offices. Canberra, Hobart, Melbourne, Sydney.

Inner City Education Alliance. Sydney.

New South Wales Teachers' Federation.

New South Wales, Queensland, South Australia, Tasmania, Victoria, Western Australia, Departments of Education.

Victorian Teachers' Union.

Official reports and statements; parliamentary papers

Australia, Australian Broadcasting Control Board, Advisory Committee on Program Standards (1976): *Report*, Chairperson Patricia Edgar, Australian Broadcasting Control Board, Melbourne.

Australia, Australian Bureau of Statistics, ABS (1947–1971): *Censuses*. Government Printer and AGPS, Canberra.

Australia, ABS (Annual): *Demography Bulletins*, Government Printer and AGPS, Canberra.

Australia, Australian Ethnic Affairs Council, AEAC (1977): *Australia as a Multicultural Society*, Chairman J. Zubrzycki, submission to the Australian Population and Immigration Council, AGPS, Canberra.

Australia, Australian Population and Immigration Council, APIC (1976): *A Decade of Migrant Settlement: Report on ahe 1973 Immigration Survey*, prepared by the Social Studies Committee, Chairman J.I. Martin, AGPS, Canberra.

Australia, APIC (1977): *Immigration Policies and Australia's Population: A Green Paper*, AGPS, Canberra.

Australia, Commission of Inquiry into Poverty (1975a): *First Main Report April 1975. Poverty in Australia*, Commissioner R.F. Henderson, AGPS, Canberra.

Australia, Commission of Inquiry into Poverty (1975b): *Second Main Report October 1975. Law and Poverty in Australia*, Commissioner Ronald Sackville, AGPS, Canberra.

Australia, Commission of Inquiry into Poverty (1976): *Third Main Report March 1976. Social/Medical Aspects of Poverty in Australia*, Commissioner George S. Martin, AGPS, Canberra.

Australia, Commissioner for Community Relations (1976): *First Annual Report*, Commissioner A.J. Grassby, AGPS, Canberra.

Australia, Committee on Community Relations (1975): *Final Report*, Chairman W.M. Lippmann, AGPS, Canberra.

Australia, Committee on Overseas Professional Qualifications, COPQ (1977): *The Language Barrier*, report to COPQ by its Working Party on Interpreting, August 1974, AGPS, Canberra.

Australia, Committee to Advise on Policies for Manufacturing Industry (1975–7): *Policies for Development of Manufacturing Industry: A Green Paper*, Chairman Gordon Jackson, vols 1 & 4, AGPS, Canberra.

Australia, Commonwealth Office of Education (1948–1965): *Annual Reports*, Commonwealth Office of Education, Sydney.

Australia, Commonwealth Office of Education (1966): *Annual Report*, Government Printer, Canberra.

Australia, COPQ, see Committee on Overseas Professional Qualifications.

Australia, Department of Education (1974*a*): 'Migrant Education', Conference of Migrant Task Forces, February, Canberra.

Australia, Department of Education (1974*b*): *The Multi-Cultural Society*, National Seminar for Teacher Educators, Macquarie University, August, Department of Education in co-operation with the Department of Labor and Immigration, Canberra.

Australia, Department of Education (1975): *Report of the Inquiry into Schools of High Migrant Density*, Department of Education, Canberra.

Australia, Department of Education (1976*a*): *Bulletin: Teaching English as a Second or Foreign Language*, Language Teaching Branch, Department of Education, Canberra.

Australia, Department of Education (1976*b*): 'The development of English language teaching for migrants in Australia—an overview', *English . . . A New Language*, vol. 14 (December), pp. 1–32.

Australia, Department of Education (1976*c*): *Report of the Committee on the Teaching of Migrant Languages in Schools*, Chairman J.W. Mather, AGPS, Canberra.

Australia, Department of Education (1977*a*): *Directory of Education Research and Researchers in Australia*, Research Branch Report 4, AGPS, Canberra.

Australia, Department of Education (1977*b*): *Migrant Education Program 1975–76*, AGPS, Canberra.

Australia, Department of Immigration (1971): *Migrant Education Programme 1970–71*, Government Printer, Canberra.

Australia, Department of Immigration (1973*a*): *Australian Immigration, Consolidated Statistics* AGPS, Canberra.

Australia, Department of Immigration (1973*b*): *Migrant Education Programme 1972–73*, AGPS, Canberra.

Australia, Department of Immigration (1973*c*): *Survey of Interpreting and Translating Needs in the Community*, Survey Section, Department of Immigration, Canberra.

Australia, Department of Immigration (1973*d*): *Survey of the Emergency Telephone Interpreter Service in Sydney and Melbourne—1973*, Department of Immigration, Canberra.

Australia, Department of Immigration (1974): *Survey of Views of Local Government Authorities relating to Immigrant Settlement and Integration*, Survey Section, Department of Immigration, Canberra.

Australia, Department of Immigration, Australian Citizenship Convention, ACC (1950–1970): *Digests* and Background Papers of the Australian Citizenship Conventions, Department of Immigration, Canberra.

Australia, Hospitals and Health Services Commission (1976): *Review of the Community Health Program*, AGPS, Canberra.

Australia, House of Representatives (1946): *Parl. Debates*, Vol. 189.

Australia, House of Representatives (1970): *Parl. Debates*, Vol. 67.

Australia, House of Representatives (1971): *Parl. Debates*, Vol. 71.

Australia, House of Representatives (1977): *Parl. Debates*, Weekly Hansard no. 8.

Australia, Immigration Advisory Council, IAC (1957): *Third Report of the Committee Established to Investigate Conduct of Migrants*, Chairman W.R. Dovey, Department of Immigration, Canberra.

Australia, Immigration Advisory Council, IAC (1960): *The Progress and Assimilation of Migrant Children in Australia*, Special Committee of the Immigration Advisory Council, Chairman W.R. Dovey, Department of Immigration, Canberra.

Australia, Immigration Advisory Council, IAC (1961): *The Incidence of Mental Illness among Migrants*, Department of Immigration, Canberra.

Australia, Immigration Advisory Council, IAC (1966): *Departure Movement of Migrants*, progress report of the Committee on Social Patterns, Chairman W.R. Dovey, Department of Immigration, Canberra.

Australia, Immigration Advisory Council, IAC (1967): *The Departure of Settlers from Australia*, final report of the Committee on Social Patterns, Chairman W.R. Dovey, Department of Immigration, Canberra.

Australia, Immigration Advisory Council, IAC (1969): *Immigration and the Balance of the Sexes in Australia*, Department of Immigration, Canberra.

Australia, Immigration Advisory Council, IAC (1972): *Inquiry into the Departure of Settlers from Australia*, progress report of the Committee on Social Patterns, Chairman J. Zubrzycki, Department of Immigration, Canberra.

Australia, Immigration Advisory Council, IAC (1973): *Inquiry into the Departure of Settlers from Australia*, final report of the Committee on Social Patterns, Chairman J. Zubrzycki, AGPS, Canberra.

Australia, Immigration Advisory Council, IAC (1974): 'Interim Report', Committee on Migrant Education, Department of Immigration, Canberra.

Australia, Immigration Planning Council, IPC (1968): *Australia's Immigration Programme for the Period 1968 to 1973*, report to the Minister for Immigration, AGPS, Canberra.

Australia, Interdepartmental Working Party on Interpreters and Translators, (1977): *Report*, Department of the Prime Minister and Cabinet, Canberra.

Australia, Migrant Task Force Committee, NSW (1973): 'First report of a task force established by the Minister for Immigration, into the immediate problems of migrants and recommendations for their resolution', Department of Immigration, Canberra.

Australia, Migrant Task Force, Qld (1973): 'Initial report to the Minister for Immigration', Department of Immigration, Canberra.

Australia, Migrant Task Force, SA (1973): 'First report to the Minister for Immigration', Department of Immigration, Canberra.

Australia, Migrant Task Force, Tas (1973): 'Report to the Minister for Immigration', Department of Immigration, Canberra.

Australia, Migrant Task Force Committee, Vic (1973): 'Recommendations to the Minister for Immigration', Department of Immigration, Canberra.

Australia, Migrant Task Force Committee, WA (1973): 'Report to the Minister for Immigration', Department of Immigration, Canberra.

Australia, Minister for Immigration and Ethnic Affairs (1977): 'New body will boost translating and interpreting', news release by M.J.R. Mackellar, Minister for Immigration and Ethnic Affairs, September 14.

Australia, Minister for Social Security (1976): 'The Migrant Telephone Interpreter Service', statement by Margaret Guilfoyle, Minister for Social Security.

Australia, National Accreditation Authority for Translators and Interpreters, NAATI (1978): 'Survey of interpreters and translators', news release by G. Cartland, Chairman of NAATI, March 19.

Australia, National Population Inquiry (1975): *Population and Australia: A Demographic Analysis and Projection*, first report, Chairman W.D. Borrie, AGPS, Canberra.

Australia, National Population Inquiry (1978): *Population and Australia: Recent Demographic Trends and their Implications*, supplementary report, AGPS, Canberra.

Australia, Parliament, Joint Committee on Foreign Affairs and Defence (1976): *The Lebanon Crisis*, AGPS, Canberra.

Australia, Review of the Commonwealth Employment Service (1977): *Report*, Chairman J.D. Norgard, AGPS, Canberra.

Australia, Review of Post Arrival Programs and Services to Migrants (1977): 'Scope of the Inquiry', Chairman F. Galbally, Prime Minister's Department, Canberra.

Australia, Review of Post Arrival Programs and Services to Migrants (1978): *Migrant Services and Programs*, Report and Appendixes, vols 1 & 2, AGPS, Canberra.

Australia, Royal Commission on Australian Government Administration (1976): *Report*; *Appendix* vol. 2, Chairman H.C. Coombs, AGPS, Canberra.

Australia, Royal Commission on Human Relationships (1977): *Final Report*, vols 1–5, Chairman E. Evatt, AGPS, Canberra.

Australia, Schools Commission (1975): *Report for the Triennium 1976–1978*, AGPS, Canberra.

Australia, Schools Commission (1976): *Report: Rolling Triennium 1977–1979*, AGPS, Canberra.

Australia, Schools Commission (1977a): *Rolling Triennium 1978–1980. Report for 1978*, AGPS, Canberra.

Australia, Schools Commission (1977b): Unpublished data on migrant education.

Australia, Schools Commission (1978): *Report for the Triennium 1979–81*, Schools Commission, Canberra.

Australia, Senate, Standing Committee on Foreign Affairs and Defence (1976): *Australia and the Refugee Problem*, AGPS, Canberra.

Australia, Social Welfare Commission (1973): *The Australian Assistance Plan*, Discussion Paper no. 1, AGPS, Canberra.

Australia, Task Force on Co-ordination in Welfare and Health (1977): *Proposals for Change in the Administration and Delivery of Programs and Services*, first report, Chairman P.H. Bailey, AGPS, Canberra.

New South Wales, Department of Education (1971): *Migrant Education in New South Wales*, Research Bulletin no. 34, Division of Research and Planning, Department of Education, Sydney.

New South Wales, Department of Education and Public Service Board (n.d. [1977]): *Report of the Enquiry into the Operations of the Adult Migrant Education Service . . . Undertaken . . . October to December, 1976*, Public Service Board, Sydney.

New South Wales, Director General of Public Health (1968–1971): *Reports*, Sydney.

New South Wales, Health Commission (1973–1975): *Reports*, Sydney.

New South Wales, Minister for Education (1978): 'Language programs for secondary schools', news release containing statement by E. Bedford, Minister for Education, February 10.

New South Wales, Parliament (1972–1973): *Parl. Papers*, vol. 4, 3rd Session.

Queensland, Department of Education (1961): 'A survey of migrant children and children of migrants in Queensland State Schools, 1959', *Bulletin*, no. 22, RR4.

Queensland, Health and Medical Services (1967–1976): *Annual Reports*, Brisbane.

South Australia, Department of Education (1956): 'Teaching of English to migrant children', report of Committee to Investigate the Teaching of English to Migrant Children in Primary Schools, Adelaide, Chairman N.L. Haines, Department of Education, Adelaide.

South Australia, Department of Public Health and the Central Board of Health (1968–1973): *Reports*, Adelaide.

South Australia, Working Committee on Interpreting and Translating Services (1977): *Report*, Chairman D. Faulkner, Public Service Board, Adelaide.

Tasmania, Director–General of Health Services (1967–1975): *Reports*, Hobart.

Victoria, Education Department (1977): Letter from Ian J.W. Adams, Special Services Division concerning migrant education, November 16.

Victoria, Education Department, Migrant Resources Section (1975): 'Multi-cultural Education Workshop for Primary School Teachers', report of workshop held at Sorrento, October 30–November 1.

Victoria, Legislative Council (1952): *Parl. Debates*, vol. 239.

Victoria, Commissioner of Public Health, (1962–1968): Annual *Reports*, Melbourne.

Victoria, Hospitals and Charities Commisson, (1949–1968 & 1972): Annual *Reports*, Melbourne.

Victoria, Mental Hygiene Authority, (1949, 1950, 1952–3): Annual *Reports*, Melbourne.

Victoria, Mental Health Authority (1953–1966): Annual *Reports*, Melbourne.

Western Australia, Commissioner of Public Health (1968–1974): *Reports*, Perth.

General references

Appleyard, R.T. (1962): 'Determinants of return migration—a socio-economic study of United Kingdom migrants who returned from Australia', *Economic Record*, vol. 38 (September), pp. 352–68.

Australian Academy of the Humanities (1975): 'Survey of foreign language teaching in the Australian universities (1965–1973)', First Report of the Committee on Foreign Languages, Australian Academy of the Humanities, Canberra.

Australian Assistance Plan, AAP (1976): *Migrants and the AAP*, Inner City Regional Council for Social Development, Sydney.

Australian Council of Social Service, ACOSS (1971): 'Workshop on the rehabilitation of the psychiatrically ill amongst the migrant population', Proceedings of a seminar organised by the Joint Migrant Welfare Committee, ACOSS, and the Australian Council for Overseas Aid, Melbourne, May 1970, ACOSS, Sydney.

ACOSS (1973): *Poverty: The ACOSS Evidence*, evidence prepared for Commonwealth Commission of Inquiry into Poverty, ACOSS, Sydney.

ACOSS (1974): 'Report of working party on national level interpreter needs', ACOSS, Sydney.

ACOSS (1976): *Immigrants and Mental Health: A Discussion Paper*, Standing Committee on Migration Issues, ACOSS, Sydney.

ACOSS (1977): Letter to the Prime Minister, December 22, Sydney.

Australian Council of Trade Unions, ACTU (1952, 1967, 1977): *Decisions of the Australian Congress of Trade Unions*, ACTU, Melbourne.

Bachrach, P. and Baratz, M.S. (1970): *Power and Poverty*, Oxford University Press, New York.

Bartholomew, G. (1966): 'The legal position of immigrants in Australia', in Stoller, A. (ed.): *New Faces*, Cheshire, Melbourne.

Berger, P.L. & Luckmann, T. (1971): *The Social Construction of Reality*, Penguin, London.

Bertelli, L. (ed.) (1977): 'Ethnic minorities and mental health: a bibliography', first draft, *Chomi Reprint* no. 15, Ecumenical Migration Centre, Richmond, Victoria.

Bini, L. (1977): 'Protecting ethnic minorities and the Australian Constitution', *Chomi Reprint* no. 119, Ecumenical Migration Centre, Richmond, Victoria.

Birrell, R. & Hay, C. (eds) (1978): *The Immigration Issue in Australia*, Department of Sociology, La Trobe University, Melbourne.

Bordow, A. (1977): *The Worker in Australia*, University of Queensland Press, St Lucia.

Bourke, S.F. & Keeves, J.P. (1977): *The Mastery of Literacy and Numeracy: Final Report*, Australian Studies in School Performance, vol. III, ERDC Report no. 13, AGPS, Canberra.

Brennan, N. (ed.) (1974): *The Migrant Worker*, proceedings and papers of the Migrant Workers' Conference October 1973, Trades Hall, Melbourne, the Migrant Worker Conference Committee and the Good Neighbour Council of Victoria, Melbourne.

Buckley, B. & Richter, R. (1976): 'Immigrants in the workforce', in ECC of New South Wales: *Proceedings of the Meeting Held in Sydney Town Hall, on 11th April, 1976*, Sydney.

Buckley, K. (1976): *All About Citizens' Rights*, Nelson, Melbourne.

Bullivant, B.M. (1977): 'Studying an ethnic school—towards a neo-ethnographic methodology', *Ethnic Studies*, vol. 1, no. 3, pp. 36–51.

Burnley, I.H. (1974): 'International migration and metropolitan growth in Australia', in Burnley, I.H. (ed.): *Urbanization in Australia*, Cambridge University Press, Cambridge.

Calwell, A. (1967): 'Immigrants', *Quadrant*, vol. 11, no. 4, pp. 92–5.

Campbell, E. & Whitmore, H. (1966): *Freedom in Australia*, Sydney University Press, Sydney.

Catley, R. & McFarlane, B. (1974): *From Tweedledum to Tweedledee*, ANZ Book Co., Sydney.

Claydon, L., Knight, T. & Rado, M. (1977): *Curriculum and Culture: Schooling in a Pluralist Society*, Allen and Unwin, Sydney.

Clyne, M. (1977): 'Bilingual education—present and past', paper presented at ANZAAS (August), Macquarie University, Sydney.

Coles, M.L. (1967): 'Some aspects of education in a migrant community', *The Leader* (New South Wales, Department of Education), vol. 4, no. 1, pp. 47–9.

Collins, J.H. (1976): 'Migrants: the political void', in Mayer, H. & Nelson, H. (eds): *Australian Politics: A Fourth Reader*, Cheshire, Melbourne.

Connell, R.W. (1977): *Ruling Class, Ruling Culture*, Cambridge University Press, Cambridge.

Coper, M. (1976): 'The reach of the Commonwealth's immigration power: judicial exegesis unbridled', *Australian Law Journal*, vol. 50 (July), pp. 351–58.

Cox, D. (1975): 'The role of ethnic groups in migrant welfare', in Cox, D. & Martin, J.I., *Welfare of Migrants*, Research report for the Commission of Inquiry into Poverty, AGPS, Canberra.

Cox, E., Jobson, S. & Martin, J. (1976): *We Can Not Talk our Rights— Migrant Women 1975*, New South Wales Council of Social Services and the School of Sociology, University of New South Wales, Sydney.

Cox, J.B. (1951): 'Helping migrant children to settle into school life', *New Era* (World Education Fellowship, Adelaide), vol. 32, no. 2, pp. 31–34.

Davies, A.J. (1971): 'Two Australian Public Bureaucracies', vols 1 & 2, Ph.D. thesis, University of New England.

De Lemos, M. M. (1974): *Study of the Educational Achievement of Migrant Children*, Australian Council for Educational Research, Hawthorn, Victoria.

Deliyannis, P. (1975): 'Submission to Committee on the Teaching of Migrant Languages in Schools', *Greek Action Bulletin* (August).

Dickenson, M. (1978): 'Political divisions in the Port Kembla Branch of the F.I.A.', unpublished paper, Department of Political Science, Research School of Social Sciences, ANU, Canberra.

di Nicola, M. (1975): 'The Migrant Resources Committee—a perspective', a note on the Migrant Resources Committee, established in Sydney, June 18.

di Nicola, M. (1976): 'Report on an experiment', in AAP: *Migrants and the AAP*, Inner City Regional Council for Social Development, Sydney.

ECC, see Ethnic Communities Council.

Economo, M.T. (1975): 'Social forces affecting language development and the concept of bilingualism in Australia', in *Bilingual Education in an Australian Context* (Workshop, Melbourne, 26–27 July, 1975), Prahran College of Advanced Education, Prahran, Victoria.

Elliott, M.J. (1977): 'Migrant Education in Fitzroy 1965–1975', M.Ed. thesis, University of Melbourne.

Ethnic Affairs Reporter (1977): 'Migrants angry at neglect by unions', *Sydney Morning Herald* April 11.

Ethnic Communities Council (ECC) of New South Wales (1977): *Newsletter,* no. 3 (June).

ECC of New South Wales, Organizing Committee (1975): 'Ethnic Communities Council of New South Wales', document produced for public meeting, Sydney, July 27.

Faulkner, A. (1977): 'The continuing crisis: Good Neighbour Council— Annual General Meeting 1977', *Ekstasis*, vol. 18 (June), pp. 30–33.

Ferber, H. (1977): 'Citizens' Advice Bureaux', in McCaughey, J. *et al.*: *Who Cares?* Macmillan, Melbourne.

Fitzgerald, R.T. (1973): 'Factors Affecting Change and Education: A Perspective on the Seventies from the Forties', Ph.D. thesis, La Trobe University.

Ford, G.W. (1968): 'Unions and the future', in Matthews, P.W.D. & Ford, G.W. (eds): *Australian Trade Unions*, Sun Books, Melbourne.

Ford, G.W. (1976): 'A study of human resources and industrial relations at the plant level in seven selected industries', in Australia, Committee to Advise on Policies for Manufacturing Industry: *Policies for Development of Manufacturing Industry: A Green Paper*, vol. 4, AGPS, Canberra.

Foucault, M. (1977): 'The political function of the intellectual', *Radical Philosophy*, vol. 17, pp. 12–14.

Galbally, F. (1975): 'Migrants and the law', *Polycom*, vol. 9, pp. 15–21.

Game, P. (1973): 'Behind the shouting . . . a language gap', *Herald* (Melbourne) June 22.

Geertz, C. (1973): *The Interpretation of Cultures: Selected Essays*, Basic Books, New York.

George, C. (n.d. [1975]): 'Migrants and Australian unions', in Storer, D. (ed.): *Ethnic Rights, Power and Participation*, Monograph no. 2, Clearing House on Migration Issues, Ecumenical Migration Centre and CURA, Melbourne.

Georgiov, P. (1969): 'Migrants, Unionism and Society', B.A.(Hons) thesis, Department of Political Science, University of Melbourne.

Gerth, H.H. & Mills, C.W. (eds) (1947): *From Max Weber: Essays in Sociology*, Paul, Trench, Trubner, London.

Giles, J.R. (n.d. [1977]): 'Policies and programmes', unpublished paper given at conferences in Perth and Brisbane, Education Department, South Australia, Adelaide.

Gilson, M. & Zubrzycki, J. (1967): *The Foreign-Language Press in Australia 1848–1964*, ANU Press, Canberra.

Glazer, N. (1977): 'Changing notions of cultural pluralism and educational practice in the United States', unpublished seminar paper, History of Ideas Unit, ANU, Canberra.

Goding, A. (1971): *The Problems of Migrant School Children*, Victoria, Psychology and Guidance Branch, Education Department, Melbourne.

Goding, A. (1973): 'The problems of migrant school children', in Parker, N. (ed.): *Focus on Migrants*, ACOSS, Sydney.

Goldsmith, O. [n.d.]: *The Works of Oliver Goldsmith*, Nimmo, Hay & Mitchell, Edinburgh.

Gollan, R. (1975): *Revolutionaries and Reformists*, ANU Press, Canberra.

Gordon, C. (1976): 'Nasty tales', *Radical Philosophy*, vol. 15, pp. 31–32.

Gordon, C. (1977): 'Birth of the subject', *Radical Philosophy*, vol. 17, pp. 15–25.

Grassby, A.J. (1973): *A Multi-Cultural Society for the Future*, Immigration Reference Paper, Australia, Department of Immigration, AGPS, Canberra.

Graycar, A. (1977): 'Federalism and social welfare', in Jaensch, D. (ed.): *The Politics of 'New Federalism'*, Australasian Political Studies Association, Adelaide.

Greek Orthodox Community of Melbourne and Victoria (1974): 'We accuse and demand', *Secondary Teacher*, vol. 194 (April), pp. 8–10.

Greek Orthodox Community of Melbourne and Victoria, Greek Professionals Association, Australian Greek Welfare Society (1973): 'Survey into the needs of migrant children: a Greek viewpoint', Melbourne.

Harris, C.P. (1977): 'Federalism, regionalism and local government 1972–3 to 1976–7', in Jaensch, D. (ed.): *The Politics of 'New Federalism'*, Australasian Political Studies Association, Adelaide.

Harris, C.P. & Grewal, B.S. (1977): 'Income security programs in Australia since 1954', *Social Security Quarterly*, vol. 5 (winter/spring), pp. 31–38.

Harris, R. (1973): 'Our changing attitude to migrants', *Dialogue*, vol. 7, no. 3, pp. 40–51.

Hawkins, T. (1973): 'Greek community backs strikers with words—and money', *National Times*, June 18–23.

Hayden, A.A. (1962): 'The anti-immigration movement, 1877–1893', *Royal Australian Historical Society Journal*, vol. 48, part I, pp. 25–43.

Hearn, J. M. (1974): 'Migrant Experiences in Trade Unions: A Study in Migrant Participation in Leadership in Victorian Trade Unions', Ph.D. thesis, University of Melbourne.

Hearn, J.M. (1976a): 'Migrants in the work force', in Staats, S. (ed.): *Social Policy and Problems of the Work Force*, vol. 1, ACTU, Melbourne.

Hearn, J.M. (1976b): 'Migrant participation in trade union leadership', *Journal of Industrial Relations*, vol. 18 (June), pp. 112–123.

Henderson, R.F. (1969): 'The dimensions of poverty in Australia', in Masterman, G.G. (ed.): *Poverty in Australia*, Australian Institute of Political Science, 35th Summer School, Angus & Robertson, Sydney.

Henderson, R.F., Harcourt, A. & Harper, R.J.A. (1970): *People in Poverty: A Melbourne Survey*, for the Institute of Applied Economic and Social Research, Cheshire, Melbourne.

Hill, B. (1977): *The Schools*, Penguin Books, Ringwood, Victoria.

Hills, B. & Mitchell, N. (1973): 'Anatomy of the Ford strike', parts 1 & 2, *Age*, July 12 & 13.

Holzner, B. (1968): *Reality Construction in Society*, Schenkman, Cambridge, Massachusetts.

Houbein, L. (1976): 'Survey of ethnic and migrant writings in Australia: work in progress', *Adelaide A.L.S. (Australian Literary Studies) Working Papers*, vol. 2, no. 1, pp. 45–64.

Houbein, L. (1978): 'Ethnic writings in English from Australia: a bibliography', *Adelaide A.L.S. (Australian Literary Studies) Working Papers*, special issue.

Hughson, G.J. (1962): 'Some problems in the education of New Australian children', *School Management*, Bulletin 5, pp. 20–26.

Hurwitz, H. (1977): 'Factory women', in Bordow, A. (ed.): *The Worker in Australia*, University of Queensland Press, St Lucia.

Isaacs, E. (1976): *Greek Children in Sydney*, ANU Press, Canberra.

Ivanoff, I. (1972): 'Migrants and class unity', *Marxist Review*, vol. 1 (July), pp. 35–36.

Jackson, M. (1977): 'Parallel classes in E.S.L. education', *Child Migrant Education Newsletter* (New South Wales Department of Education), vol. 6 (May), p. 15.

Jaensch, D. (ed.) (1977): *The Politics of 'New Federalism'*, Australasian Political Studies Association, Adelaide.

Jakubowicz, A. & Buckley, B. (1975): *Migrants and the Legal System*, Research report for the Commission Inquiry into Poverty, AGPS, Canberra.

Jegorow, W. (1977): 'The aims of the E.C.C.', *Newsletter* (ECC of New South Wales), vol. 1 (January), pp. 1–4.

Johnston, R. (1972): *Future Australians: Immigrant Children in Perth, Western Australia*, ANU Press, Canberra.

Johnston, R. (1977): 'The immigrant worker', in Bordow, A. (ed.): *The Worker in Australia*, University of Queensland Press, St Lucia.

Juddery, B. (1978): 'Innovative union body still under cloud of Damocletian uncertainty: Trade Union Training Authority threatened with reduction to a Departmental satrapy', *Canberra Times*, April 7.

Jupp, J. (1966): *Arrivals and Departures*, Cheshire-Lansdowne, Melbourne.

Kelly, B. (1977): 'The Ethnic Communities Council Education Sub-committee: A Migrant Action Group in a Multicultural Society', B.A. (Hons) thesis, Department of Sociology, University of New South Wales.

Kelly M.J. (1974): 'History of the Good Neighbour Movement', unpublished ms, Department of Sociology, La Trobe University, Melbourne.

Kelly, M.R. (1975): 'Differential cognitive development of children exposed to a bi-lingual and bi-cultural stiuation', in Pilowsky, I. (ed.): *Cultures in Collision*, Australian National Association for Mental Health, Adelaide.

Kiosoglous, J.A. (1974): 'Ethnic groups in a multicultural society', paper presented at the 20th Annual State Conference of the Good Neighbour Council of South Australia, Adelaide.

Knight, T. (1977): 'The migrant child and the remedial child: are they necessarily one and the same?', *Polycom*, vol. 15, pp. 18–28.

Krabbe, H. (1922): *The Modern Idea of the State*, translated and with an Introduction by G.H. Sabine & W.J. Shepard, Appleton & Co, New York.

Kunz, E.F. (1975): *The Intruders: Refugee Doctors in Australia*, ANU Press, Canberra.

Kunz, E.F. (1977): 'The genesis of the post war immigration programme and the evolution of the tied-labour Displaced Persons scheme', *Ethnic Studies*, vol. 1, no. 1, pp. 30–41.

Lane, P.H. (1972): *The Australian Federal System*, The Law Book Co., Sydney.

Lewins, F. (1977): 'Migrant policy and the Catholic Church in Australia', unpublished paper, Department of Sociology, Faculty of Arts, ANU, Canberra.

Liberal and National Country Parties (1975): 'Immigration and ethnic affairs policy', Liberal Party Federal Secretariat, Canberra.

Luckham, B. (1959a): *Immigration and the Australian Labor Movement*, Australia, Department of Labour and National Service, Canberra.

Luckham, B. (1959b): 'The impact of immigration upon Australian labour', *R.E.M.P. Bulletin*, vol. 7 (January/March), pp. 1–5.

Lukas, I. (1977): 'To this man, the law means justice', *Sydney Morning Herald* September 26.

Lumb, P. (1975): 'Educating migrant secondary students and their teachers', *Polycom*, vol. 8, pp. 3–5.

Lumb, R.D. & Ryan, K.W. (1974): *The Constitution of the Commonwealth of Australia Annotated*, Butterworths, Sydney.

McCaughey, J. & Chew, W. (1977): 'The family study', in McCaughey, J. *et al.*: *Who Cares?*, Macmillan, Melbourne.

McCaughey, J., Shaver S., Ferber, H. *et al.* (1977): *Who Cares?*, for the Institute of Applied Economic and Social Research, University of Melbourne, Macmillan, Melbourne.

McGrath, J.P. & Fegan, L. (1976–77): 'Overcoming language barriers: the work of the T.I.S.', *Social Security Quarterly*, vol. 4 (summer), pp. 5–7.

McKay, J. & Lewins, F. (1977): 'Ethnicity and the ethnic group: a conceptual analysis and reformulation', unpublished paper, Department of Sociology, Faculty of Arts, ANU, Canberra.

McKell, Sir W. (1952): 'We are pioneers of our future', in Australian Citizenship Convention: *Digest*, Australia, Department of Immigration, Canberra.

Manley, F.R. (1967): 'Migrant crash course experiment: report', Fitzroy High School, Victoria.

Martin, J.I. (1965): *Refugee Settlers*, ANU Press, Canberra.

Martin, J.I. (1971): 'Migration and social pluralism', in Wilkes, J. (ed.): *How Many Australians? Immigration and Growth*, Australian Institute of Political Science, 37th Summer School, Angus & Robertson, Sydney.

Martin, J.I. (1972a): *Community and Identity*, ANU Press, Canberra.

Martin, J.I. (1972b): *Migrants—Equality and Ideology*, Meredith Memorial Lecture, La Trobe University, Melbourne.

Martin, J.I. (1972c): 'Quests for Camelot', *ANZJS*, vol. 8, no. 1, pp. 3–18.

Martin, J.I. (1975a): 'The economic condition of migrants', in Cox, D. & Martin, J.I.: *Welfare of Migrants*, Research report for the Commission of Inquiry into Poverty, AGPS, Canberra.

Martin, J.I. (1975b): 'Family and bureaucracy', in Price, C.A. (ed.): *Greeks in Australia*, ANU Press, Canberra.

Martin, J.I. (1976): 'Ethnic pluralism and identity', in Murray-Smith, S. (ed.): *Melbourne Studies in Education 1976*, Melbourne University Press, Melbourne.

Martin, J.I. & Meade, P.H. (1978): 'Preliminary findings of a longitudinal investigation of the education experience of 3043 Sydney secondary students 1974–1977', unpublished paper, ANU, Canberra, and University of New South Wales, Sydney.

Martin, R.M. (1975): *Trade Unions in Australia*, Penguin Books, Ringwood, Victoria, in association with University of Queensland Press.

Matheson, A. (1974): 'A welfare rights program for ethnic groups', *Social Security Quarterly*, vol. 1 (autumn), pp. 10–14.

Matheson, A. (1975): 'Lest we forget . . . observations and memories of the Annual General Meeting of the G.N.C.—Victoria 1975', *Ekstasis*, vol. 12 (June), pp. 2–9.

Matheson, A. (1977): 'Good Neighbour Council of Victoria: yet another crisis', *Ekstasis*, vol. 18 (June), pp. 24–29.

Mathews, R. (1977): 'Revenue sharing and Australian Federalism', in Jaensch, D. (ed.): *The Politics of 'New Federalism'*, Australasian Political Studies Association, Adelaide.

Matthews, P.W. (1977): 'Multicultural education in Australia: an historical overview, 1970–1976', *Child Migrant Education Newsletter* (New South Wales Department of Education), vol. 6 (September), pp. 3–7.

Matthews, T.V. (1976a): 'Interest group access to the Australian Government bureaucracy', in Australia, Royal Commission on Australian Government Administration: *Appendix*, vol. 2, AGPS, Canberra.

Matthews, T.V. (1976b): 'Australian pressure groups', in Mayer, H. & Nelson, H. (eds): *Australian Politics: a Fourth Reader*, Cheshire, Melbourne.

Medding, P.Y. (1968): *From Assimilation to Group Survival*, Cheshire, Melbourne.

Medding, P.Y. (ed.) (1973): *Jews in Australian Society*, Macmillan and Monash University, Melbourne.

Menart, V. (1977): 'Organisational basis of representation', *Newsletter* (ECC of New South Wales), vol. 2 (March) pp. 2–3.

Migrant Handicraft Program (1977): 'The Migrant Women's Handicraft Program: a project funded by the International Women's Year Committee', report to the Office of Women's Affairs, Department of the Prime Minister and Cabinet, Melbourne.

Migration Action (1976): 'Adult migrant education in N.S.W.: who gets what?', *Migration Action*, vol. 2 (autumn), pp. 12–14.

Millbank, A.J. (1977): 'Directions for the development of 10+ materials', discussion paper, Language Teaching Branch, Australia, Department of Education, Canberra.

Mitchell, M. (1976): 'Report and evaluation of interpreter service provided by the Springvale Community Aid and Advice Bureau for the 1976 Census', Community Aid and Advice Bureau, Springvale, Victoria.

Moraitis, S. (1974): 'Community involvement in schools', *Greek Action Bulletin*, vol. 1 (December), pp. 17–18.

Murray, R. (1970): *The Split*, Cheshire, Melbourne.

Needham, E. (1966): 'Refugee and migrant welfare problems in Australia', in Australian Council for Overseas Aid: *Refugee and Migrant Service Conference, Canberra, February 22–23, 1966*, Australian Council for Overseas Aid, Canberra.

New South Wales Teachers' Federation (1977): 'Education in a multicultural society', proceedings of conference held in Sydney, November 26–27, 1976.

Nichols, O. (1970): 'The language problems of migrant children', background paper for the Australian Citizenship Convention 1970, Australia, Department of Immigration, Canberra.

Nicoll, P. (1975): 'Response in N.S.W. to the Interim Committee for the Australian Schools Commission's Proposals for Disadvantaged Schools and "Needy" Non-government Schools', M.Ed. essay, University of New England.

Nicoll, P. (1977): *Directions for Research in Migrant Education*, Australia, Department of Education, Canberra.

Ormonde, P. (1972): *The Movement*, Nelson, Melbourne.

Overberg, H. (1975): 'The training of teachers for an Ethnic Studies Programme', *Migration Action*, vol. 2, no. 1, pp. 7–10.

Parsons, L. A. (1977): 'The Social World of the Classroom: Teacher and Pupil Interactions as the Construction of Teaching and Learning—An Interpretive Approach', Master of Educational Studies thesis, University of Queensland.

Phillips, C. R. (1977): 'The disadvantaged worker', in Bordow, A. (ed.): *The Worker in Australia*, University of Queensland Press, St Lucia.

Price, C.A. (1957): 'The effects of post-war immigration', *Australian Quarterly*, vol. XXIX (December), pp. 28–40.

Price, C.A. (1962*a*): 'Overseas migration to Australia 1947–61', *Migration*, vol. 2 (April/June), pp. 21–34.

Price, C.A. (1962*b*): 'Overseas migration to and from Australia 1947–1961', *Australian Outlook*, vol. 16 (August), pp. 160–174.

Price, C.A. (1967): Review of J. Jupp, *Arrivals and Departures, ANZJS*, vol. 3 (October), pp. 157–159.

Price, C.A. (ed.) (1960): *The Study of Immigrants in Australia*, Proceedings of Conference on Immigration Research, Canberra, 1960, Department of Demography, ANU, Canberra.

Price, C.A. (ed.) (1966): *Australian Immigration: A Bibliography and Digest*, Department of Demography, ANU, Canberra.

Price, C.A. (ed.) (1971): *Australian Immigration: A Bibliography and Digest, No. 2, 1970*, Department of Demography, ANU, Canberra.

Price, C.A. & Martin, J.I. (eds) (1976*a*): *Australian Immigration: A Bibliography and Digest, No. 3, 1975*, Part 1, Price, C.A. (ed.): 'The demography of post-war immigration', Department of Demography, ANU, Canberra.

Price, C.A. & Martin, J.I. (eds) (1976*b*): *Australian Immigration: A Bibliography and Digest, No. 3, 1975*, Part 2, Martin, J.I. & Willcock, H.F. (eds): 'The education of migrant children in Australia', Department of Demography, ANU, Canberra.

Price, C.A. & Pyne, P. (1976): 'Australian immigration. A: The foreign-born population and their children born in Australia, B: Some characteristics of settler loss', Working Papers in Demography no. 3, Department of Demography, ANU, Canberra.

Rabinowitz, D. (1977): *New Lives: Survivors of the Holocaust Living in America*, 2nd printing, Alfred A. Knopf, New York.

Rado, M. (1976): 'Bilingual education in Australia', *Folia Linguistica*, vol. IX–1–4, pp. 45–57.

Rawson, D.W. (1971): 'The ALP industrial groups', in Isaac, J.E. & Ford, G.W. (eds): *Australian Labour Relations: Readings*, 2nd edn, Sun Books, Melbourne.

Richards, L. (1978): *Displaced Politics: Refugee Migrants in the Australian Political Context*, La Trobe Sociology Papers 45, Department of Sociology, La Trobe University, Melbourne.

Richmond, K. (1973): *Women in the Workforce*, La Trobe Sociology Papers 2, Department of Sociology, La Trobe University, Melbourne.

Robbins, J. (1977): 'Local government and the new Federalism: present trends and future prospects', in Jaensch, D. (ed.): *The Politics of 'New Federalism'*, Australasian Political Studies Association, Adelaide.

Roberts, M. (1976): 'A possible relationship between migrants and the AAP structure', in Australian Assistance Plan: *Migrants and the AAP*, Inner City Regional Council for Social Development, Sydney.

Rodopolous, L. (1975): 'Social work with Greek migrants: a personal experience of the issues and dilemmas', *Australian Social Work*, vol. 28, no. 1, pp. 45–50.

Rodopolous, L. (ed.) (1977): *Aspects of Social Service Delivery to Immigrants: A Selection of Readings and a Guide to Further Study*, Clearing House on Migration Issues, Richmond, Victoria.

Ronan, M.J. (1975): 'Speaking in two tongues, *Polycom*, vol. 8, pp. 17–20.

Roper, T.W. (1972): *Bibliography on Migration to Australia from Non-English Speaking Countries with Special Reference to Education*, Centre for the Study of Urban Education, La Trobe University, Melbourne.

Ryan, K.W. (n.d. [1966]): 'Immigration, aliens and naturalization in Australian law', in O'Connell, D.P. (ed.): *International Law in Australia*, The Law Book Co., Sydney.

Ryan, W. (1971): *Blaming the Victim*, Orbach & Chambers, London.

Sawer, G. (1977): 'New Federalism', in Jaensch, D. (ed.): *The Politics of 'New Federalism'*, Australasian Political Studies Association, Adelaide.

Shaver, S. (1977): 'The care-taker network', in McCaughey, J. *et al.*: *Who Cares?*, Macmillan, Melbourne.

Sheldon, G. (1965): *Industrial Siege: The Mount Isa Dispute*, Cheshire, Melbourne.

Smart, D. (1975): 'Federal Aid to Australian Schools', Ph.D. thesis, Australian National University.

Smart, W.H. (1967): 'A plea for New Australians', *Activity Bulletin* (New South Wales Department of Education), vol. 24, pp. 25–26.

SMEC, see State Multicultural Education Committee, New South Wales.

Smolicz, J.J. & Secombe, M.J. (1977): 'A study of attitudes to the introduction of ethnic languages and cultures in Australian schools', *The Australian Journal of Education*, vol. 21 (March), pp. 1–24.

Staats, S. (ed.) (1976): *Social Policy and Problems of the Work Force*, vol. 1, ACTU, Melbourne.

State Multicultural Education Committee, New South Wales, SMEC (1977): 'Submission to Senator J.L. Carrick, Minister for Education, on a pilot programme for the teaching of community languages and cultures', Sydney.

Steinle, J.R. (1976): 'New course to help in migrant teaching', *Teachers Journal* (South Australian Institute of Teachers), vol. 8, no. 3.

Storer, D. (ed.) (n.d. [1975]): *Ethnic Rights, Power and Participation: Toward a Multi-Cultural Australia*, Monograph no. 2, Clearing House on Migration Issues, Ecumenical Migration Centre, and CURA, Melbourne.

Storer, D. & Hargreaves, K. (1976): 'Migrant women in industry', in Staats, S. (ed.): *Social Policy and Problems of the Work Force*, vol. 1., ACTU, Melbourne.

Strauss, G. (1962): 'Catering for the migrant pupil', *Educational Magazine* (Victoria, Education Department), vol. 19 (April), pp. 97–102.

Taft, R. (1972): 'Ethnic groups', in Hunt, F.J. (ed.): *Socialisation in Australia*, Angus & Robertson, Sydney.

Tenezakis, M.D. (1977): 'Later development of English with and without another language. Evidence from testing English monoglot and Greek-speaking children in Sydney', Research Report, School of Education, Macquarie University, Sydney.

Thompson, J.S. (1975): 'Migrants in industry: the union's point of view', paper presented at Migrants in Industry Seminar (November), Division of Occupational Health and Radiation Control, Health Commission of New South Wales, Sydney.

Thornton, E. (1967): 'Migrants and unions', *Australian Left Review*, vol. 6, pp. 37–38.

Trade Union Training Authority, TUTA, New South Wales (1977): *Programme 1977, January–July*, TUTA, Surry Hills.

Tsounis, M.P. (1967): 'Migrants and the work force', *Australian Left Review*, vol. 6, pp. 35–37.

Tsounis, M.P. (1974): *Greek Ethnic Schools in Australia*, Australian Immigration: Monograph no. 1, Department of Demography, ANU, Canberra.

TUTA, see Trade Union Training Authority.

Victorian Migrant Education Branch (MEB), Staff Association (1976): 'Adult Migrant Education in Victoria', *Migration Action*, vol. 3 (winter), pp. 10–14.

Wallace, A.F.C. & Fogelson, R.D. (1965): 'The identity struggle', in Boszormenyi-Nagy, I. & Framo, J.L. (eds): *Intensive Family Therapy*, Harper & Row, New York.

Walsh, M. (1971): 'The politics of it all', in Wilkes, J. (ed.): *How Many Australians? Immigration and Growth*, Australian Institute of Political Science, 37th Summer School, Angus & Robertson, Sydney.

Wilkes, J. (ed.) (1971): *How Many Australians? Immigration and Growth*, Australian Institute of Political Science, 37th Summer School, Angus & Robertson, Sydney.

Bibliography 237

Wilkinson, P.J. (1978): *Migrant Education Program: Full-time English Courses for Adult Migrants*, submission to the Minister for Immigration and Ethnic Affairs by the Good Neighbour Council of Victoria, Paper 2, Multicultural Australia Papers, Good Neighbour Council of Victoria in conjunction with the Clearing House on Migration Issues of the Ecumenical Migration Centre, Richmond, Victoria.

Willcock, H.F. (1976): 'Bibliography of the education of migrant children 1945–1975', in Price, C.A. & Martin, J.I. (eds): *Australian Immigration: A Bibliography and Digest, No. 3, 1975*, Part 2, Department of Demography, ANU, Canberra.

Wiltshire, K. (1977): ' "New Federalisms"—the State perspective', in Jaensch, D. (ed.): *The Politics of 'New Federalism'*, Australasian Political Studies Association, Adelaide.

Wood, M. (1977): 'The "new federalisms" of Whitlam and Fraser and their impact on local government', in Jaensch, D. (ed.). *The Politics of 'New Federalism'*, Australasian Political Studies Association, Adelaide.

Wyndham, H. (1958): 'How non-English-speaking migrant children fare in schools', *Education* (New South Wales Teachers' Federation), vol. 39, no. 3, p. 6.

Young, R. (1977): 'Multicultural education in New South Wales', paper presented at ANZAAS (August), Macquarie University, Sydney.

Zangalis, G. (1967): 'Immigration and the Labor movement', *Australian Left Review*, vol. 5, pp. 46–52.

Zangalis, G. (n.d. [1975]) 'Our unions or theirs', in Storer, D. (ed.): *Ethnic Rights, Power and Participation*, Monograph no. 2, Clearing House in Migration Issues, Ecumenical Migration Centre and CURA, Melbourne.

Zubrzycki, J. (1968): 'The questing years', in Australian Citizenship Convention: *Digest*, Australia, Department of Immigration, Canberra.

Migrants and health: sources used for Chapters 5 and 6 (other than official reports, cited pages 219–24)

ACOSS, see Australian Council of Social Service.

Adams, A.I., Chancellor, A. & Kerr, C. (1971): 'Medical care in western Sydney: a report on the utilization of health services by a defined population', *MJA*, March 6, pp. 507–516.

Alexandra, B. (1974): 'Meeting the needs of the immigrant in sickness and health', *Australasian Nurses Journal*, vol. 2, no. 33, p. 15; vol. 2, no. 34, p. 7; vol. 2, no. 36, p. 9.

AMA, see Australian Medical Association.

Ammon, R. (1969): 'Mediterranean guts ache', Letter, *MJA*, November 15, p. 1031.

Australian Council of Social Service, ACOSS (1971): *Workshop on the Rehabilitation of the Psychiatrically Ill Amongst the Migrant Population*, Proceedings of a seminar organised by the Joint Migrant Welfare Commission, ACOSS, and the Australian Council for Overseas Aid, ACOSS, Sydney.

Australian Council of Social Service, ACOSS (1974): 'Report of working party on national level interpreter needs', ACOSS, Sydney.

Australian Council of Social Service, ACOSS (1976): *Immigrants and Mental Health: A Discussion Paper*, Standing Committee on Migration Issues, ACOSS, Sydney.

Australian Medical Association, AMA (1971): *Policy on Medical Services*, AMA, Sydney.

Australian Medical Association, AMA (1977): Correspondence with AMA and State branches in Perth, Adelaide, Melbourne, Hobart, Brisbane and Sydney, August–September.

Australian Medical Association, AMA, New South Wales Branch (1973): 'Flaws in migrant health tests', *Monthly Bulletin* (December), p. 4.

Australian Medical Association, AMA, Study Group on Medical Planning (1972): 'Medical practice in Australia: an outline of desirable future developments in medical and allied services in Australia', Report no. 2 of Study Group, *MJA* (Supplement), August 19, pp. 73–80.

Balla, J.I. & Moraitis, S. (1970): 'Knights in armour—a follow-up study of injuries after legal settlement', *MJA*, August 22, pp. 355–361.

Benjamin, M. (1970): 'Mental health of migrants', in Australian Council of Social Service: *Workshop on the Rehabilitation of the Psychiatrically Ill Amongst the Migrant Population*, ACOSS, Sydney.

Bostock, W.W. (1977): *Alternatives of Ethnicity*, Cat & Fiddle Press, Hobart.

Bottomley, G. (1976): 'Rural Greeks and illness: an anthropologist's viewpoint', *MJA*, May 22, pp. 798–800.

Boyer, R.J.F. (1952): 'Paying a debt to the future', in Australian Citizenship Convention: *Digest*, Australia, Department of Immigration, Canberra.

Bridges-Webb, C. (1976): '4. Patients: Migrants', *MJA* (Special Supplement), October 2, pp. 11–12.

Broom, L., Duncan-Jones, P., Lancaster Jones, F. & McDonnell, P. (1977): *Investigating Social Mobility*, Departmental Monograph no. 1, Department of Sociology, Research School of Social Sciences, ANU, Canberra.

Buckland, D. (1978): 'Isolation of immigrant women in Australian society', in Australia, Department of Health: *Women's Health in a Changing Society: Problems of Isolation*, vol. 5, Proceedings of a conference sponsored by the Commonwealth Department of Health and the National Advisory Committee for International Women's Year, University of Queensland, 25–29 August 1975, AGPS, Canberra.

Burvill, P.W. (1973): 'Immigration and mental disease', *ANZJP*, vol. 7, no. 3 (September), pp. 155–162.

Burvill, P.W. (1975): 'Attempted suicide in the Perth Statistical Division 1971–1972', *ANZJP*, vol. 9, no. 4, pp. 273–279.

Burvill, P.W., McCall, M.G., Stenhouse, N.S. & Reid, A. (1973): 'Deaths from suicide, motor vehicle accidents and all forms of violent deaths among migrants in Australia, 1962–66', *Acta Psychiatrica Scandinavica*, vol. 49, pp. 28–50.

Cade, J.F.J. & Krupinski, J. (1962): 'Incidence of psychiatric disorders in Victoria in relation to country of birth', *MJA*, March 17, p. 400.

Chesher, T. & Moess, S. (1977): 'Health education program for migrants', unpublished paper written for the Health Commission of New South Wales.

Clarke, J. (1976): *Dr Max Herz, Surgeon, The Human Price of Civil and Medical Bigotry in Australia*, Alternative Publishing Co-operative, Sydney.

Cole, E.S. (1970): 'Psychiatric aspects of compensable injury', *MJA*, January 17, pp. 93–100.

Congalton, A.A. & Najman, J.M. (1972): 'Migrant mortality: Parts 1 and 2', *Hospital and Health Administration*, vol. 7 (July), pp. 2–4; vol. 8 (August), pp. 9–11, 15 & 17.

Constantinou, C. (1971): 'Immigrants and medical certificates', Letter, *MJA*, December 4, p. 1206.

Cox, D. (1972): 'Medico-social problems in the Greek population in Melbourne: Part 1. Social and cultural background', *MJA*, October 14, pp. 879–881.

Cox, D. (1975): 'The role of ethnic groups in migrant welfare', in Cox, D. & Martin, J.I.: *Welfare of Migrants*, Research report for the Commission of Inquiry into Poverty, AGPS, Canberra.

Crock, H.V. (1970): 'The current status of the roles of psychiatry and orthopaedics in the management of injured migrants—a surgeon's view', in Australian Council of Social Service: *Workshop on the Rehabilitation of the Psychiatrically Ill Amongst the Migrant Population*, ACOSS, Sydney.

Cumming, R.W. (1970): 'The Greek approach to ill-health', project report, Department of Preventive and Social Medicine, University of Sydney, Sydney.

Davies, W. & Finlayson, J. (1972): 'Towards better health for our migrants', *Health in NSW*, vol. 13, no. 3, pp. 5–6.

Davis, E. (1974): 'Treating a Chinese girl suffering from tuberculosis', *Bulletin —International Union Against Tuberculosis*, vol. 49 (Supplement 1, August), pp. 47–50.

Deeble, J.S. & Scotton, R.B. (1977): 'Health services and the medical profession', in Tucker, K.A. (ed.): *Economics of the Australian Service Sector*, Croom Helm, London.

Dinnen, A. (1976): 'Rural Greeks and illness', Letter, *MJA*, July 24, p. 149.

Dissent (1976): 'Stories from a Greek interpreter', *Dissent*, vol. 33 (Autumn).

Dodds, M.-M. (1970): *From Whence They Came*, J.H. Heinz Co. Aust. Ltd.

Ducrou, W. & Kimber, R.J. (1969): 'Stomatocytes, haemolytic anaemia and abdominal pain in Mediterranean migrants: some examples of a new syndrome?', *MJA*, November 29, pp. 1087–1091.

Duff, G. (1974): 'Turkish children, immunization and ascorbic acid', Letter, *MJA*, May 4, p. 722.

Dunt, D.R. & Le Moine Parker, M. (1973): 'A computer data processing system for hospital obstetric records, obstetric complications in non-English speaking migrants', *MJA*, October 6, pp. 693–698.

Dunt, D.R. & Le Moine Parker, M. (1977a): 'A comparative study of obstetric care in Greek Migrant and Australian-born women: I. Use of obstetric services', *MJA*, July 9, pp. 45–48.

Dunt, D.R. & Le Moine Parker, M. (1977b): 'A comparative study of obstetric care in Greek migrant and Australian-born women: II. Determinants of satisfaction', *MJA*, July 16, pp. 80–84.

Ellard, J. (1969): 'The problems of the migrant', *MJA*, November 22, pp. 1039–1043.

Field, L.K., Nicoll, D.M. & Elphick, H.R. (1974): 'Tuberculosis in migrants', 7th Australian Tuberculosis Conference, Adelaide, 2–6 April 1973, *MJA*, July 13, p. 68.

Gross, P.F. (1974): 'Options for the future development of community health services in Australia', *Australian Family Physician*, vol. 3 (June), pp. 229–235.

Hammett, J. (1965): 'Marginality and mental health: the price of failure to adjust', *Australian Journal of Social Issues*, vol. 2 (autumn), pp. 18–26.

Harper, J. & Williams, S. (1976a): 'Infantile autism: the incidence of national groups in a New South Wales survey', *MJA*, March 6, pp. 299–301.

Harper, J. & Williams, S. (1976b): 'Infantile autism—national groups', Letter, *MJA*, May 8, pp. 721–722.

Harper, J. & Langmore, R. (1976): *The Social Context of Depression in Italian Migrant Housewives*, CO.AS.IT (Italian Assistance Association), Melbourne.

Health (1966): 'T.B. screening of migrants tightened', *Health*, vol. 16, no. 2, pp. 23–24.

Hendry, R., Hunter, R. & Harvie, N. (1974): 'Social problems with tuberculosis in migrants', 7th Australian Tuberculosis Conference, Adelaide, 2–6 April 1973, *MJA*, July 13, p. 68.

Hetzel, B.S. (1976): 'Migrants' in *Health and Australian Society*, rev. edn, Penguin, Ringwood, Victoria.

Hills, L.L. (1971): 'Cholelithiasis and immigration', *MJA*, July 10, pp. 94–5.

Hobbs, M.S.T., Carney, A., Field, B., Simpson, D., & Kerr, C.B. (1974): 'Incidence of anencephalus and spina bifida and variation in risks according to parental birthplaces in three Australian States', *British Journal of Preventive and Social Medicine*, vol. 28 (February), p. 166.

Holt, H.E. (1956): 'Building for a better Australia', Addresses to the Australian Citizenship Convention, Australia, Department of Immigration, Canberra.

Jakubowicz, A. & Buckley, B. (1975): *Migrants and the Legal System*, Research report for the Commission of Inquiry into Poverty, AGPS, Canberra.

Kerr, C.B. (1971): 'Health problems of immigrants as evidence of prejudice', in Stevens, F.S. (ed.): *Racism: The Australian Experience*, vol. 1, ANZ Book Co., Sydney.

Kerr, C.B. (1973): 'Self help via community health centres', *Bulletin of the Post-Graduate Committee in Medicine* (University of Sydney), vol. 29 (June), pp. 50–61.

Kraus, J. (1969*a*): 'The relationship of psychiatric diagnosis, hospital admission rates, and size and age structure of immigrant groups', *MJA*, July 12, pp. 91–95.

Kraus, J. (1969*b*): 'Some social factors and rates of psychiatric hospital admissions of immigrants in New South Wales', *MJA*, July 5, pp. 17–19.

Krupinski, J. (1967): 'Sociological aspects of mental ill health in migrants', *Social Science and Medicine*, vol. 1, pp. 267–281.

Krupinski, J., Schaechter, F. & Cade, J.F.J. (1965): 'Factors influencing the incidence of mental disorders among migrants', *MJA*, August 14, pp. 269–277.

Krupinski, J. & Stoller A. (1965): 'Incidence of mental disorders in Victoria, Australia, according to country of birth', *MJA*, August 14, pp. 265–268.

Krupinski, J. & Stoller, A. (1966): 'Family life and mental ill-health in migrants', in Stoller, A. (ed.): *New Faces*, Cheshire, Melbourne.

Krupinski, J., Stoller A. & Wallace, L. (1973): 'Psychiatric disorders in east European refugees now in Australia', *Social Science and Medicine*, vol. 7, p. 31.

Krupinski, J., Stoller, A. & Meredith, E. (1971): 'Sociopsychiatric study of schizophrenia: the follow-up', *ANZJP*, vol. 5, no. 3, pp. 146–155.

Kunz, E.F. (1975): *The Intruders: Refugee Doctors in Australia*, ANU Press, Canberra.

Laakso, L. (1973): 'Migrants in hospital', *Australian and New Zealand Journal of Obstetrics and Gynaecology*, vol. 13, no. 4, p. 231.

Lander, H. (1971): 'More maladies in Mediterranean migrants: stomatocytosis and macrothrombocytopenia', *MJA*, February 20, pp. 438–440.

Last, J.M. (1960): 'The health of immigrants: some observations from general practice', *MJA*, January 30, pp. 158–162.

Last, J.M. (1961): 'Culture, society and the migrant', *MJA*, March 18, pp. 420–425.

Legh, K.A. (1968): 'Study of Yugoslav migrants in the major psychiatric hospitals in the Sydney metropolitan area', *Australian Journal of Social Work*, vol. 21, no. 1, pp. 2–7.

Le Sueur, E.J. (1977): *The Australian Government Rehabilitation Service*, Research report for the Commission of Inquiry into Poverty, AGPS, Canberra.

Lipson, A. (1972): 'Rickets in Melbourne', Letter, *MJA*, December 23, p. 1468.

Listwan, I.A. (1956): 'Paranoid states: social and cultural aspects', *MJA*, May 12, pp. 776–778.

Listwan, I.A. (1959): 'Mental disorders in immigrants: further study', *MJA*, August 25, pp. 566–568.

Lovell, R.R. & Prineas, R.J. (1974a): 'Differences in blood pressure measurements and prevalence of hypertension between Australian-born and Italian-born middle-aged men and women in Melbourne', *MJA*, December 21, pp. 893–898.

Lovell, R.R. & Prineas, R.J. (1974b): 'The identification and treatment of hypertensives in two Australian urban communities', *International Journal of Epidemiology*, vol. 3, no. 1, pp. 25–29.

Lyons, K.M. (1976): 'Problems of Vietnamese orphans', Letter, *MJA*, January 3, p. 36.

McCall, M.G. & Stenhouse, N.S. (1971): 'Deaths from lung cancer in Australia', *MJA*, March 6, pp. 524–525.

McEwin, R. (1977): 'The plight of the migrant: communication in emergency', Letter, *MJA*, January 1/8, pp. 38–39.

McKellar, C.C. (1976): 'The plight of the migrant: communication in emergency', *MJA*, November 13, p. 772.

Mann, Arnold 1969 'Mediterranean Guts Ache.' Letter. *MJA* November 1: 932.

Martin, Jean I. 1975 'Family and Bureaucracy.' Pp. 188–222 in C.A. Price (ed.), *Greeks in Australia*. Canberra: Australian National University Press.

Mayne, V. and D. McCredie 1972 'Rickets in Melbourne.' *MJA*, October 14: 873–875.

Medical Journal of Australia (MJA) 1967 'Some of the Complexities of Migration.' Editorial. *MJA* April 1: 661–662.

MJA 1969 'A committee on overseas professional qualifications.' Editorial. *MJA* April 26: 863–864.

MJA 1970 'Bilingual Prescribing and Dispensing.' *MJA* September 26: 566.

MJA 1972 'Medico-social Problems in the Greek Community.' Editorial. *MJA* October 14: 855–856.

MJA 1975 'Migration, Stress and Disease.' Editorial. *MJA* June 21: 765–767.

MJA 1976a 'The Plight of the Migrant: Basic Considerations.' Editorial. *MJA* June 26: 983–984.

MJA 1976b 'The Plight of the Migrant: In Industry.' Editorial. *MJA* July 31: 155–156.

MJA 1976c 'The Plight of the Migrant: Communication in Emergency.' Editorial. *MJA* September 18: 433–434.

MJA 1976d 'Migrant Women in Melbourne Industry.' Editorial. *MJA* September 11: 399–400.

Mental Health Authority, Victoria, Mental Health Social Workers' Group 1976 'Facilities for Migrant Patients within the Mental Health Authority', unpublished report, Melbourne.

Minc, S. (1963): 'Of new Australian patients, their medical lore and major anxieties', *MJA*, May 11, pp. 681–687.

Minc, S. (1972): 'Medical and health problems of immigrants', in Roberts, H. (ed): *Australia's Immigration Policy*, University of Western Australia Press, Nedlands.

MJA, see Medical Journal of Australia.

Mok, C.H. (1972): 'A study of a children's casualty department in a general hospital', *MJA*, May 27, pp. 1147–1149.

Molloy, W.B. (1976): 'The plight of the migrant: communication in emergency', Letter, *MJA*, October 23, p. 664.

Moraitis, S. (1972): 'Medico-social problems in the Greek population in Melbourne. Part 2. Paediatric problems as seen by the medical practitioner', *MJA*, October 14, pp. 881–883.

Moraitis, S. (1977): 'Greek ethnic attitudes in Australia', paper presented to 'Injured Ethnic' Seminar, Australian and New Zealand Society of Occupational Medicine and Australian Greek Welfare Society, March 5, Melbourne.

Moraitis, S. & Zigouras J.N. (1971): 'Impressions on Greek immigrants', *MJA*, March 13, pp. 598–600.

Najman, J.M. & Congalton, A.A. (1972): 'Migrant mortality: a research report. Part 2', *Hospital and Health Administration*, vol. 8 (August), pp. 9–11, 15 & 17.

New South Wales Association for Mental Health, Standing Committee for the Mental Health of Migrants (1972): 'A survey of professional interpreter services in hospitals', *Mental Health in Australia*, vol. 4, no. 4, pp. 144–148.

Owles, E.N. (1975): 'A comparative study of nutrient intakes of migrant and Australian children in Western Australia', *MJA*, July 26, pp. 130–133.

Packer, R. (1974): 'Greeks and mental illness', *Greek Action Bulletin*, vol. 1, no. 4, p. 5A.

Papapetros, P., Tziniolis, J. & Constantine, G. (1971): 'Impressions on Greek migrants', *MJA*, April 10, pp. 824–825.

Parker, N. (1972): 'Malingering', *MJA*, December 2, pp. 1308–1311.

Pasquarelli, G. (1966): 'The general medical and associated problems of the Italian migrant family', *MJA*, January 8, pp. 65–70.

Portelli, A.J. & Jones, I. (1969): 'Mediterranean guts ache', *MJA*, October 4, pp. 717–720.

Porteous, N. (1977): 'The health care professional and the migrant', *MJA*, June 11, pp. 891–896.

Porter, K.S. & Burke, D.T. (1971): 'Bilingual dispensing labels', Letter, *MJA*, August 21, p. 448.

Proust, A.J. (1974): 'The Australian screening programme in regard to tuberculosis in prospective migrants', *MJA*, July 13, pp. 35–37.

Rac, R. & Tomasovic, A.A. (1977): 'The plight of the migrant: communication in emergency', Letter, *MJA*, February 12, p. 232.

Redshaw, G.M. (1956): 'Psychiatric problems amongst migrants', *MJA*, December 8, pp. 852–853.

Retchford, F. (1972): 'Medico-social problems in the Greek population in Melbourne. Part 3. Social work experience in public hospitals', *MJA*, October 14, pp. 883–885.

Rodopoulos, L. (1976): 'Infantile autism—national groups', *MJA*, April 17, pp. 594–595.

Rutledge, P. (1972): 'The Italian migrant and his problems', *Australasian Nurses Journal*, vol. 1 (April), p. 7.

Saint, E.G. (1963): 'The medical problems of migrants', *MJA*, March 9, pp. 335–338.

Salter, W., Selwood, T. & Leeton, J. (1977): 'Non-attendance among post-natal women at a hospital family planning clinic', in Australia, Commission of Inquiry into Poverty: *Family Planning and Health Care of Infants and Mothers*, Social/Medical Aspects of Poverty Series, AGPS, Canberra.

Savage, J.P. & Leitch, I.O. (1972): 'Childhood burns. A sociological survey and inquiry into causation', *MJA*, June 24, pp. 1337–1342.

Schaechter, F. (1962): 'A study of psychoses in female migrants', *MJA*, September 22, pp. 458–461.

Schaechter, F. (1965): 'Previous history of mental illness in female migrant patients admitted to the psychiatric hospital, Royal Park', *MJA*, August 14, pp. 277–279.

Scotton, R.B. (1974): *Medical Care in Australia: An Economic Diagnosis*, for the Institute of Applied Economic and Social Research, University of Melbourne, Sun Books, Melbourne.

Selecki, B.R., Ness, T.D., Limbers, P., Blum, P.W. & Stening, W.A. (1975): 'The surgical management of low back and sciatic syndrome in disc disease or injury: results of a joint neurosurgical and orthopaedic project', *Australian and New Zealand Journal of Surgery*, vol. 45, no. 2, pp. 183–191.

Shoebridge, J. (1977): 'Ethnicity and Institutional Dominance', B.A.(Hons) thesis, Department of Sociology, Faculty of Arts, Australian National University.

Southby, R.F. (1971): 'Health care in Australia: an impending crisis', *MJA*, May 22, pp. 1127–1132.

Stenhouse, N.S. & McCall, M.G. (1970): 'Differential mortality from cardiovascular disease in migrants from England and Wales, Scotland and Italy, and native-born Australians', *Journal of Chronic Diseases*, vol. 23, no. 5, pp. 423–431.

Stoller, A. (1966): 'Migration and mental health in Australia', *British Journal of Social Psychiatry*, vol. 1, pp. 70–77.

Stoller, A. & Krupinski, J. (1969): 'Mental health of immigrants', Letter, *MJA*, August 16, p. 365.

Stoller, A. & Krupinski, J. (1973): 'Immigration to Australia: mental health aspects', in Zwingman, C. & Pfister-Ammende, M. (eds): *Uprooting and After*, Springer-Verlag, New York.

Tahmindjis, A. (1975): 'Medical problems of migrant women', *Health*, vol. 25, no. 4, p. 32.

Tahmindjis, A. (1976): 'The unemployed partially disabled migrant', *MJA*, December 4, p. 884.

Tahmindjis, A. (1978): 'Medical problems of migrant women', in Australia, Department of Health: *Women's Health in a Changing Society: Problems of Isolation*, vol. 5, Proceedings of a conference sponsored by the Commonwealth Department of Health and the National Advisory Committee for International Women's Year, University of Queensland, 25–29 August 1975, AGPS, Canberra.

Thodey, A. (1973): 'Migrant unmarried mothers', in Parker, N. (ed.): *Focus on Migrants*, ACOSS, Sydney.

Trinker, F., Gunter, S., Ewing, M., Best, J.B. & Yeatman, J.S. (1975): 'A study of patients who come by choice to the casualty department of the Royal Melbourne Hospital', *MJA*, April 26, pp. 528–533.

Turnley, B. (1973): 'Migrants and the public hospital', *Navigator*, vol. 60 (June), pp. 3–7.

Ulman, R. & Abernethy, J.D. (1975): 'Blood pressure and length of stay in Australia of Italian immigrants in the Australian National Blood Pressure Study', *International Journal of Epidemiology*, vol. 4, no. 3, pp. 213–215.

Wall, S. (1978): 'Greek migrant women: medical care or negligence?', in Australia, Department of Health: *Women's Health in a Changing Society: Problems of Isolation*, vol. 5, Proceedings of a conference sponsored by the Commonwealth Department of Health and the National Advisory Committee for International Women's Year, University of Queensland, 25–29 August 1975, AGPS, Canberra.

Ward, E. (1965): 'The migrant in a hospital setting—some obstacles to communication', in Australian Association of Social Workers: *People are Different*, Proceedings of the 9th National Conference, Adelaide (August), Australian Association of Social Workers, Adelaide.

Watkins, G. (1971): 'The meaning of a pregnancy to a single Greek migrant girl', *Australian Journal of Social Work*, vol. 24 (March), pp. 23–27.

Wensing, P. (1978): 'Social and ethnic isolation', in Australia, Department of Health: *Women's Health in a Changing Society: Problems of Isolation*, vol. 5, Proceedings of a conference sponsored by the Commonwealth Department of Health and the National Advisory Committee for International Women's Year, University of Queensland, 25–29 August 1975, AGPS, Canberra.

Whitlock, F.A. (1971): 'Migration and suicide', *MJA*, October 23, pp. 840–848.

Wintle, M. (1977): 'Happiness is . . . understanding and being understood', *Health in N.S.W.*, vol. 17 (Spring), pp. 1–4.

Index